Random House
Dictionary of
Abbreviations

Random House
Dictionary of
Abbreviations

RANDOM HOUSE
NEW YORK

ISBN: 0-679-76434-8

Typeset and Printed in the United States of America

First Edition

9 8 7 6 5 4 3 2 1

New York   Toronto   London   Sydney   Auckland

Acknowledgments

The *Random House Dictionary of Abbreviations* is derived from the large computerized database that is part of the Random House Living Dictionary Project. This abbreviations dictionary was compiled and edited by the staff of the Random House Reference Department. The staff gratefully acknowledges the valuable contributions made by Archie Hobson, Julia Penelope, Lenka Sosic, and Roger M. Stern.

Pronunciation Key

The symbol (′), as in **moth′er,** is used to mark primary stress; the syllable preceding it is pronounced with greater prominence than the other syllables in the word. The symbol (′), as in **grand′moth′-er,** is used to mark secondary stress; a syllable marked for secondary stress is pronounced with less prominence than one marked (′) but with more prominence than those bearing no stress mark at all.

a	act, bat	o͝o	book, put
ā	able, cape	o͞o	ooze, rule
â	air, dare	ou	out, loud
ä	art, calm		
		p	page, stop
b	back, rub	r	read, cry
ch	chief, beach	s	see, miss
d	do, bed	sh	shoe, push
		t	ten, bit
e	ebb, set	th	thin, path
ē	equal, bee	t͟h	that, other
f	fit, puff		
g	give, beg	u	up, love
h	hit, hear	û	urge, burn
		v	voice, live
i	if, big	w	west, away
ī	ice, bite	y	yes, young
		z	zeal, lazy, those
j	just, edge	zh	vision, measure
k	kept, make		
l	low, all	ə	occurs only in unac-cented syllables and in-dicates the sound of
m	my, him		a *in* along
n	now, on		e *in* system
ng	sing, England		i *in* easily
			o *in* gallop
o	box, hot		u *in* circus
ō	over, no		
ô	order, ball		
oi	oil, joy		

A

A **1.** *Cards.* ace. **2.** adulterer; adulteress. **3.** *Electricity.* ampere; amperes. **4.** *Physics.* angstrom. **5.** answer. **6.** *British.* arterial (used with a road number to designate a major highway).

A *Symbol.* **1.** the first in order or in a series. **2.** (in some grading systems) a grade or mark, indicating the quality of a student's work as excellent or superior. **3.** (in some school systems) a symbol designating the first semester of a school year. **4.** *Music.* **a.** the sixth tone in the scale of C major or the first tone in the relative minor scale, A minor. **b.** a string, key, or pipe tuned to this tone. **c.** a written or printed note representing this tone. **d.** (in the fixed system of solmization) the sixth tone of the scale of C major, called *la.* **e.** the tonality having A as the tonic note. **5.** *Physiology.* a major blood group, usually enabling a person whose blood is of this type to donate blood to persons of group A or AB and to receive blood from persons of O or A. **6.** (*sometimes lowercase*) the medieval Roman numeral for 50 or 500. **7.** *Chemistry.* (formerly) argon. **8.** *Chemistry, Physics.* mass number. **9.** *Biochemistry.* **a.** adenine. **b.** alanine. **10.** *Logic.* universal affirmative. **11.** *British.* a designation for a motion picture recommended as suitable for adults. **12.** a proportional shoe width size, narrower than B and wider than AA. **13.** a proportional brassiere cup size, smaller than B and larger than AA. **14.** a quality rating for a corporate or municipal bond, lower than AA and higher than BBB.

a *Measurements.* are; ares.

a *Symbol, Logic.* universal affirmative.

Å *Symbol, Physics.* angstrom.

A- atomic (used in combination): *A-bomb; A-plant.*

A. **1.** Absolute. **2.** Academy. **3.** acre; acres. **4.**

America. **5.** American. **6.** angstrom. **7.** year. [from Latin *annō*, ablative of *annus*] **8.** answer. **9.** before. [from Latin *ante*] **10.** April. **11.** Artillery. **12.** Australia. **13.** Australian.

a. **1.** about. **2.** acre; acres. **3.** active. **4.** adjective. **5.** alto. **6.** ampere; amperes. **7.** year. [from Latin *annō*, ablative of *annus*] **8.** anonymous. **9.** answer. **10.** before. [from Latin *ante*] **11.** *Measurements.* are; ares. **12.** *Sports.* assist; assists. **13.** at.

AA **1.** administrative assistant. **2.** Alcoholics Anonymous. **3.** antiaircraft. **4.** author's alteration.

AA *Symbol.* **1.** a proportional shoe width size, narrower than A and wider than AAA. **2.** the smallest proportional brassiere cup size. **3.** a quality rating for a corporate or municipal bond, lower than AAA and higher than A. **4.** *Electricity.* a battery size for 1.5 volt dry cells: diameter, 0.6 in. (1.4 cm); length, 2 in. (5 cm). **5.** *British.* a designation for motion pictures certified as unsuitable for children under 14 unless accompanied by an adult. Compare **A** (def. 11), **U** (def. 5), **X** (def. 9).

A.A. **1.** Alcoholics Anonymous. **2.** antiaircraft. **3.** antiaircraft artillery. **4.** Associate in Accounting. **5.** Associate of Arts. **6.** author's alteration.

a.a. **1.** always afloat. **2.** author's alteration. Also, **aa**

AAA **1.** Agricultural Adjustment Administration. **2.** Amateur Athletic Association. **3.** American Automobile Association. **4.** antiaircraft artillery. **5.** Automobile Association of America.

AAA *Symbol.* **1.** a proportional shoe width size, narrower than AA. **2.** the highest quality rating for a corporate or municipal bond. **3.** *Electricity.* a battery size for 1.5 volt dry cells: diameter, 0.4 in. (1 cm); length 1.7 in. (4.3 cm).

A.A.A. **1.** Amateur Athletic Association. **2.**

American Automobile Association. **3.** Automobile Association of America.

A.A.A.L. American Academy of Arts and Letters.

A.A.A.S. American Association for the Advancement of Science. Also, **AAAS**

A.A.E. American Association of Engineers.

A.Ae.E. Associate in Aeronautical Engineering.

A.A.E.E. American Association of Electrical Engineers.

AAES American Association of Engineering Societies.

AAF 1. Allied Air Forces. **2.** (in the U.S., formerly) Army Air Forces. Also, **A.A.F.**

A.Agr. Associate in Agriculture.

AAM air-to-air missile.

a&b assault and battery.

A&E Arts and Entertainment (a cable television station).

a&h *Insurance.* accident and health.

a&i *Insurance.* accident and indemnity.

A&M Agricultural and Mechanical (college). Also, **A and M**

A&R (in the recording industry) artists and repertory. Also, **A. & R., A-and-R**

a&r assault and robbery.

a&s *Insurance.* accident and sickness.

AAP Association of American Publishers.

A.A.P.S.S. American Academy of Political and Social Science.

a.a.r. 1. against all risks. **2.** average annual rainfall.

AARP (*pronounced as initials or* ärp), American Association of Retired Persons.

A.A.S. 1. Fellow of the American Academy. [from Latin *Academiae Americanae Socius*] **2.** American Academy of Sciences. **3.** Associate in Applied Science.

A.A.U. Amateur Athletic Union. Also, **AAU**

A.A.U.P. 1. American Association of University Professors. **2.** American Association of University Presses. Also, **AAUP**

A.A.U.W. American Association of University Women.

AB 1. *Nautical.* able seaman. 2. airbase. 3. airborne. 4. *U.S. Air Force.* Airman Basic. 5. Alberta, Canada (for use with ZIP code). 6. antiballistic; antiballistic missile. 7. assembly bill.

AB *Symbol, Physiology.* a major blood group usually enabling a person whose blood is of this type to donate blood to persons of type AB and to receive blood from persons of type O, A, B, or AB.

Ab *Symbol.* 1. *Chemistry.* alabamine. 2. *Immunology.* antibody.

ab. 1. about. 2. *Baseball.* (times) at bat.

A.B. 1. *Nautical.* able seaman. 2. Bachelor of Arts. [from Latin *Artium Baccalaureus*] 3. *Baseball.* (times) at bat.

a.b. *Baseball.* (times) at bat.

ABA 1. Amateur Boxing Association. 2. American Badminton Association. 3. American Bankers Association. 4. American Bar Association. 5. American Basketball Association. 6. American Book Award. 7. American Booksellers Association. 8. Associate in Business Administration. Also, **A.B.A.**

abbr. 1. abbreviate. 2. abbreviated. 3. abbreviation. Also, **abbrev.**

ABC 1. American Broadcasting Company. 2. atomic, biological, and chemical: *ABC warfare.*

A.B.C. 1. Advance Booking Charter. 2. Alcoholic Beverage Control.

abcb air-blast circuit breaker.

ABD all but dissertation: applied to a person who has completed all requirements for a doctoral degree except for the writing of a dissertation. Also, **abd.**

abd 1. abdomen. 2. abdominal.

abd. 1. abdicated. 2. abdomen. 3. abdominal.

A.B.Ed. Bachelor of Arts in Education.

A.B.F.M. American Board of Foreign Missions.

abl. *Grammar.* ablative.

A.B.L.S. Bachelor of Arts in Library Science.
ABM antiballistic missile.
abn airborne.
ABO *Physiology.* ABO system (of blood classification).
A-bomb (ā′bom′), atomic bomb.
abp. archbishop.
abr. 1. abridge. 2. abridged. 3. abridgment.
ABRV Advanced Ballistic Reentry Vehicle.
ABS 1. *Chemistry.* ABS resin: a type of plastic. [*(a)crylanitrile, (b)utadiene,* and *(s)tyrene*] 2. antilock braking system.
abs. 1. absent. 2. absolute. 3. abstract.
A.B.S. 1. American Bible Society. 2. American Bureau of Shipping.
abs. re. *Law.* in the absence of the defendant. [from Latin *absente reo*]
abstr. 1. abstract. 2. abstracted.
abt. about.
abv. above.
AC 1. *Real Estate.* air conditioning. 2. *Electricity.* alternating current.
Ac *Chemistry.* 1. acetate. 2. acetyl.
Ac *Symbol, Chemistry.* actinium.
ac *Electricity.* alternating current.
A/C 1. *Bookkeeping.* **a.** account. **b.** account current. 2. *Real Estate.* air conditioning. Also, **a/c**
A.C. 1. *Real Estate.* air conditioning. 2. *Electricity.* alternating current. 3. before Christ. [from Latin *ante Christum*] 4. Army Corps. 5. Athletic Club.
a.c. 1. *Real Estate.* air conditioning. 2. *Electricity.* alternating current. 3. (in prescriptions) before meals [from Latin *ante cibum*].
ACA 1. American Camping Association. 2. American Canoe Association. 3. American Casting Association.
ACAA Agricultural Conservation and Adjustment Administration.
acad. academy. Also, **Acad.**

AC and U Association of Colleges and Universities. Also, **AC&U**

acb air circuit breaker.

ACC Atlantic Coast Conference.

acc. 1. accelerate. **2.** acceleration. **3.** accept. **4.** acceptance. **5.** accompanied. **6.** accompaniment. **7.** accordant. **8.** according. **9.** account. **10.** accountant. **11.** accounted. **12.** accusative.

ACCD American Coalition of Citizens with Disabilities.

accel. *Music.* accelerando.

accom accommodate.

accomp. 1. accompaniment. **2.** accomplishment.

accrd. accrued.

acct. 1. account. **2.** accountant.

accum. 1. accumulate. **2.** accumulative.

accus. accusative.

ACDA Arms Control and Disarmament Agency.

AC/DC 1. *Electricity.* alternating current or direct current. **2.** *Slang.* sexually responsive to both men and women; bisexual. Also, **A.C./D.C., ac/dc, a-c/d-c, a.c.-d.c.**

acdt accident.

ACE 1. American Council on Education. **2.** Army Corps of Engineers.

acft aircraft.

ACH automated clearinghouse.

ACh *Biochemistry.* acetylcholine.

achiev. achievement.

ack. 1. acknowledge. **2.** acknowledgment.

A.C.L.S. American Council of Learned Societies.

ACLU 1. American Civil Liberties Union. **2.** American College of Life Underwriters. Also, **A.C.L.U.**

ACM Association for Computing Machinery.

ACOC Air Command Operations Center.

ACOG American College of Obstetricians and Gynecologists.

A.C.P. American College of Physicians.

acpt. acceptance.

acq acquisition.

A.C.S. 1. Advanced Communications System. **2.** American Cancer Society. **3.** American Chemical Society. **4.** American College of Surgeons. **5.** autograph card signed. Also, **ACS**

A.C.S.C. Association of Casualty and Surety Companies.

A/cs pay. accounts payable. Also, **a/cs pay.**

A/cs rec. accounts receivable. Also, **a/cs rec.**

acst acoustic.

acsy accessory.

ACT 1. American College Test. **2.** Association of Classroom Teachers. **3.** Australian Capital Territory.

act. 1. acting. **2.** action. **3.** active. **4.** actor. **5.** actual. **6.** actuary.

actg. acting.

ACTH *Biochemistry.* a polypeptide hormone that stimulates the cortex of adrenal glands. [*a(dreno)c(ortico)t(ropic) h(ormone)*]

ACTION (ak′shən), *U.S. Government.* an independent agency that administers domestic volunteer programs. [named by analogy with the acronymic names of other agencies, but itself not an acronym]

actl actual.

ACTP American College Testing Program.

actr actuator.

actvt activate.

ACV 1. Also, **A.C.V.** actual cash value. **2.** air cushion vehicle.

ACW *Radio.* alternating continuous waves.

AD assembly drawing.

Ad Alzheimer's Disease.

a-d *Electronics.* analog-to-digital.

ad. 1. adverb. **2.** advertisement.

A.D. 1. active duty. **2.** in the year of the Lord; since Christ was born. [from Latin *annō*

Domini] **3.** art director. **4.** assembly district. **5.** assistant director. **6.** athletic director. **7.** average deviation.

a.d. 1. after date. **2.** before the day. [from Latin *ante diem*] **3.** autograph document.

ADA 1. adenosine deaminase. **2.** American Dental Association. **3.** American Diabetes Association **4.** Americans for Democratic Action.

A.D.A. 1. American Dental Association. **2.** American Diabetes Association. **3.** Americans for Democratic Action.

ADAD (āʹdad), a coded card or other device that when inserted into a telephone allows the user to reach a number without dialing. [*a(utomatic) telephone) d(ialing-)a(nnouncing) d(evice)*]

ADAMHA Alcohol, Drug Abuse, and Mental Health Administration.

A.D.B. accidental death benefit. Also, **adb.**

ADC 1. advanced developing countries. **2.** Aid to Dependent Children. **3.** Air Defense Command.

A.D.C. aide-de-camp.

ADD attention deficit disorder.

addn. addition.

addnl. additional.

ADF automatic direction finder.

ad fin. to, toward, or at the end. [from Latin *ad finem*]

ADH *Biochemistry.* antidiuretic hormone.

ADHD attention deficit hyperactivity disorder.

ad inf. to infinity; endlessly; without limit. Also, **ad infin.** [from Latin *ad infinitum*]

ad init. at the beginning. [from Latin *ad initium*]

ad int. in the meantime. [from Latin *ad interim* for the time between]

adj. 1. adjacent. **2.** adjective. **3.** adjoining. **4.** adjourned. **5.** adjudged. **6.** adjunct. **7.** adjust. **8.** *Banking.* adjustment. **9.** adjutant.

Adj.A. Adjunct in Arts.

adjt. adjutant.

ADL Anti-Defamation League (of B'nai B'rith). Also, **A.D.L.**

ad lib. 1. at one's pleasure. **2.** *Music.* not obligatory. [from Latin *ad libitum*]

ad loc. at or to the place. [from Latin *ad locum*]

Adm. 1. admiral. **2.** admiralty. Also, **ADM**

adm. 1. administration. **2.** administrative. **3.** administrator. **4.** admission.

admin. administration.

admov. (in prescriptions) **1.** apply. [from Latin *admovē*] **2.** let it be applied. [from Latin *admoveātur*]

ADP 1. *Biochemistry.* an ester of adenosine and pyrophosphoric acid, $C_{10}H_{12}N_5O_3H_3P_2O_7$, serving to transfer energy during glycolysis. [*a(denosine) d(i)p(hosphate)*] **2.** automatic data processing.

ad part. dolent. (in prescriptions) to the painful parts. [from Latin *ad partēs dolentēs*]

adptr adapter.

adrs address.

ADS 1. Alzheimer's Disease Society. **2.** American Dialect Society.

a.d.s. autograph document, signed.

adst. feb. (in prescriptions) when fever is present. [from Latin *adstante febre*]

ADTS Automated Data and Telecommunications Service.

Adv. 1. Advent. **2.** Advocate.

adv. 1. in proportion to value. [from Latin *ad valorem*] **2.** advance. **3.** adverb. **4.** adverbial. **5.** adverbially. **6.** adversus. **7.** advertisement. **8.** advertising. **9.** adviser. **10.** advisory.

ad val. in proportion to value. [from Latin *ad valorem*]

advt. advertisement.

AE 1. account executive. **2.** Actors Equity. **3.** American English.

ae. at the age of. [from Latin *aetātis*]

A.E. 1. Agricultural Engineer. **2.** Associate in Education. **3.** Associate in Engineering.

a.e. *Math.* almost everywhere.

A.E.A. 1. Actors' Equity Association. **2.** Also, **AEA** *British.* Atomic Energy Authority.

A.E. and P. Ambassador Extraordinary and Plenipotentiary.

AEC Atomic Energy Commission.

A.E.C. *Insurance.* additional extended coverage.

A.Ed. Associate in Education.

Ae.E. Aeronautical Engineer.

A.E.F. American Expeditionary Forces; American Expeditionary Force. Also, **AEF**

A.Eng. Associate in Engineering.

aeq. equal. [from Latin *aequālis*]

aero. 1. aeronautic; aeronautical. **2.** aeronautics. **3.** aerospace.

aerodyn aerodynamic.

aeron. aeronautics.

aet. at the age of. Also, **aetat.** [from Latin *aetātis*]

AEW airborne early warning.

AF 1. Air Force. **2.** Anglo-French. **3.** Asian Female.

af 1. audiofidelity. **2.** audiofrequency. **3.** autofocus.

Af. 1. Africa. **2.** African.

A.F. 1. Air Force. **2.** Anglo-French. **3.** audio frequency.

a.f. audio frequency.

A.F.A. Associate in Fine Arts.

AFAIK as far as I know.

A.F.A.M. Ancient Free and Accepted Masons.

AFB Air Force Base.

A.F.B. American Federation for the Blind.

AFBF American Farm Bureau Federation.

AFC 1. American Football Conference. **2.** American Foxhound Club. **3.** Association Football Club. **4.** automatic flight control. **5.** automatic frequency control.

AFCS automatic flight control system.

AFDC Aid to Families with Dependent Children. Also, **A.F.D.C.**

aff. 1. affairs. **2.** affirmative. **3.** affix.

afft. affidavit.

AFGE American Federation of Government Employees.

Afgh. Afghanistan. Also, **Afg.**

A1c airman, first class.

AFL 1. American Federation of Labor. **2.** American Football League.

A.F.L. American Federation of Labor. Also, **A.F. of L.**

AFL-CIO American Federation of Labor and Congress of Industrial Organizations.

AFM 1. American Federation of Musicians. **2.** audio frequency modulation.

AFP *Biochemistry.* alphafetoprotein.

Afr African.

Afr. 1. Africa. **2.** African.

A.-Fr. Anglo-French.

AFS American Folklore Society.

A.F.S. American Field Service.

AFSCME American Federation of State, County, and Municipal Employees.

AFT American Federation of Teachers. Also, **A.F.T.**

aft. afternoon.

AFTRA (af′trə), American Federation of Television and Radio Artists. Also, **A.F.T.R.A.**

Ag *Symbol, Chemistry.* silver. [from Latin *argentum*]

Ag. August.

ag. 1. agricultural. **2.** agriculture.

A.G. 1. Adjutant General. **2.** Attorney General. Also, **AG**

AGA Amateur Gymnastics Association.

AGAC American Guild of Authors and Composers.

AGC 1. advanced graduate certificate. **2.** automatic gain control. Also, **A.G.C.**

AGCA automatic ground-controlled approach.

AGCL automatic ground-controlled landing.

agcy. agency.

Ag.E. Agricultural Engineer.

A.G.E. Associate in General Education.

Agh. (in Afghanistan) afghani.

AGI 1. Also, **agi.** adjusted gross income. **2.** American Geological Institute.

agit. (in prescriptions) shake, stir. [from Latin *agitā*]

AGM air-to-ground missile.

AGMA American Guild of Musical Artists. Also, **A.G.M.A.**

agr. 1. agricultural. **2.** agriculture.

agric. 1. agricultural. **2.** agriculture.

agron. agronomy.

AGS 1. American Gem Society. **2.** American Geographical Society. **3.** American Geriatrics Society.

A.G.S. Associate in General Studies.

agst. against.

Agt. agent. Also, **agt.**

AGU American Geophysical Union.

Ah ampere-hour. Also, **a.h.**

A.H. in the year of the Hegira; since the Hegira (A.D. 622). [from Latin *annō Hejirae*]

AHA American Heart Association.

A.H.A. 1. American Historical Association. **2.** American Hospital Association.

AHAUS Amateur Hockey Association of the United States.

AHE Association for Higher Education.

A.H.E. Associate in Home Economics.

AHF *Biochemistry.* antihemophilic factor.

AHL 1. American Heritage Foundation. **2.** American Hockey League.

AHQ 1. Air Headquarters. **2.** Army Headquarters.

AHRA American Hot Rod Association.

AHS American Humane Society.

AHSA American Horse Shows Association.

AI 1. Amnesty International. **2.** artificial insemination. **3.** artificial intelligence. Also, **A.I.**

A.I.A. 1. American Institute of Architects. **2.** American Insurance Association.

Radio. a system of broadcasting by means of amplitude modulation. **3.** Asian male.

Am *Symbol, Chemistry.* americium.

Am. 1. America. **2.** American.

am amber.

A/m ampere per meter.

A.M. 1. before noon. [from Latin *ante meridiem*] **2.** Master of Arts. [from Latin *Artium Magister*]

a.m. before noon.

A.M.A. 1. American Management Association. **2.** American Medical Association. **3.** American Motorcycle Association.

Amb. Ambassador. Also, **amb.**

AMC American Movie Classics (a cable channel).

A.M.D.G. for the greater glory of God: motto of the Jesuits. Also **AMDG** [from Latin *ad majōrem Dei glōriam*]

A.M.E. 1. Advanced Master of Education. **2.** African Methodist Episcopal.

AMEDS Army Medical Service. Also, **AMedS**

Amer. 1. America. **2.** Also, **Amer** American.

AmerSp American Spanish.

AMEX (am′eks), American Stock Exchange. Also, **Amex**

am/fm (ā′em/ef′em/), (of a radio) able to receive both AM and FM stations. Also, **AM/FM**

AMG Allied Military Government.

ami acute myocardial infarction.

A.M.L.S. Master of Arts in Library Science.

amm antimissile missle.

ammo ammunition.

Amn *Air Force.* airman.

AMNH American Museum of Natural History.

AMORC Ancient Mystic Order Rosae Crucis.

amort. amortization.

AMP *Biochemistry.* a white, crystalline, water-soluble nucleotide, $C_{10}H_{12}N_5O_3H_2PO_4$, obtained by the partial hydrolysis of ATP or of ribonucleic acid. [*a(denosine)* *m(ono)* *p(hosphate)*]

amp. *Electricity.* **1.** amperage. **2.** ampere; amperes.

AMPAS Academy of Motion Picture Arts and Sciences.

ampl amplifier.

AMS **1.** Agricultural Marketing Service. **2.** American Mathematical Society. **3.** American Meteorological Society. **4.** American Musicological Society.

A.M.S. Army Medical Staff.

A.M.S.W. Master of Arts in Social Work.

AMT alternative minimum tax.

amt. amount.

A.M.T. **1.** Associate in Mechanical Technology. **2.** Associate in Medical Technology. **3.** Master of Arts in Teaching.

amu atomic mass unit. Also, **AMU**

A.Mus. Associate in Music.

A.Mus.D. Doctor of Musical Arts.

AMVETS (am′vets′), an organization of U.S. veterans of World War II and more recent wars. [*Am(erican) Vet(eran)s*]

AN Anglo-Norman. Also, **A.-N.**

An *Symbol, Chemistry.* actinon.

an. **1.** above named. **2.** annual. **3.** in the year. [from Latin *annō*]

A.N. **1.** Anglo-Norman. **2.** Associate in Nursing.

A.N.A. **1.** American Newspaper Association. **2.** American Nurses Association. **3.** Association of National Advertisers. Also, **ANA**

anal analysis.

analyt. analytical.

anat. **1.** anatomical. **2.** anatomist. **3.** anatomy.

ANBS Armed Nuclear Bombardment Satellite.

ANC **1.** Also, **A.N.C.** African National Congress. **2.** Army Nurse Corps.

anc automatic noise control.

anc. ancient.

APEX (ā′peks), a type of international air fare offering reduced rates for extended stays that are booked in advance. [*A(dvance) P(urchase) Ex(cursion)*]

aph. *Linguistics.* aphetic.

APHIS Animal and Plant Health Inspection Service.

API American Petroleum Institute. Also, **A.P.I.**

APL 1. allowance parts list. 2. *Computers.* an interactive programming language. [*A P(ro-gramming) L(anguage)*]

APLA American Patent Law Association.

A.P.O. Army & Air Force Post Office. Also, **APO**

app. 1. apparatus. 2. apparent. 3. appendix. 4. *Computers.* application. 5. applied. 6. appointed. 7. approved. 8. approximate.

appar. 1. apparent. 2. apparently.

appd. approved.

appl. 1. appeal. 2. applicable. 3. application. 4. applied.

appmt. appointment.

approp. appropriation.

approx. 1. approximate. 2. approximately.

apprp appropriate.

apprx approximate.

appt. 1. appoint. 2. appointed. 3. appointment.

apptd. appointed.

appx appendix.

APR annual percentage rate. Also, **A.P.R.**

Apr. April.

aprch approach.

aprt airport.

A.P.S. 1. American Peace Society. 2. American Philatelic Society. 3. American Philosophical Society. 4. American Physical Society. 5. American Protestant Society.

A.P.S.A. American Political Science Association.

apt. apartment. Also, **apt**

apu auxiliary power unit.

apv approve.

apvd approved.

apvl approval.

apx. appendix.

AQ *Psychology.* achievement quotient.

aq. water. [from Latin *aqua*]

AQAB Air Quality Advisory Board.

aq. bull. (in prescriptions) boiling water. [from Latin *aqua bulliēns*]

aq. comm. (in prescriptions) common water. [from Latin *aqua commūnis*]

aq. dest. (in prescriptions) distilled water. [from Latin *aqua dēstillāta*]

aq. ferv. (in prescriptions) hot water. [from Latin *aqua fervēns*]

AQL acceptable quality level.

aqstn acquisition.

AR 1. annual return. **2.** Arkansas (for use with ZIP code). **3.** Army Regulation; Army Regulations. **4.** as required.

Ar Arabic.

Ar *Symbol, Chemistry.* argon.

Ar. 1. Arabic. **2.** Aramaic.

ar. 1. arrival. **2.** arrive; arrived; arrives.

A/R account receivable; accounts receivable. Also, **a/r**

A.R. 1. annual return. **2.** Army Regulation; Army Regulations.

a.r. *Insurance.* all risks.

ARA Agricultural Research Administration.

A.R.A. 1. American Railway Association. **2.** Associate of the Royal Academy.

Aram Aramaic. Also, **Aram.**

ARC (ärk), *Pathology.* AIDS-related complex.

ARC American Red Cross. Also, **A.R.C.**

Arc. arcade (approved for postal use).

arc cos *Trigonometry.* arc cosine.

arc cot *Trigonometry.* arc cotangent.

arc csc *Trigonometry.* arc cosecant.

Arch. Archbishop.

arch. 1. archaic. **2.** archaism. **3.** archery. **4.**

archipelago. **5.** architect. **6.** architectural. **7.** architecture. **8.** archive; archives.

archaeol. 1. archaeological. **2.** archaeology.

Archbp. Archbishop.

archd. 1. archdeacon. **2.** archduke. Also, **Archd.**

Arch. E. Architectural Engineer.

archt. architect.

ARCN *Computers.* Attached Resource Computer Network.

A.R.C.S. 1. Associate of the Royal College of Science. **2.** Associate of the Royal College of Surgeons.

ard acute respiratory disease.

ARDS *Pathology.* adult respiratory distress syndrome.

arf acute respiratory failure.

Arg *Biochemistry.* arginine.

Arg. Argentina.

argus advanced research on groups under stress.

arith. 1. arithmetic. **2.** arithmetical.

Ariz. Arizona.

Ark. Arkansas.

ARL Association of Research Libraries.

arl average remaining lifetime.

ARM adjustable-rate mortgage.

Arm Armenian.

Arm. 1. Armenian. **2.** Armorican.

Ar.M. Master of Architecture. [from Latin *Architecturae Magister*]

aro *Commerce.* after receipt of order.

ARP *Stock Exchange.* adjustable-rate preferred.

ARR American Right to Read.

arr. 1. arranged. **2.** arrangement. **3.** *Music.* arranger. **4.** arrival. **5.** arrive; arrived; arrives.

arrgt. arrangement.

ARS 1. advanced record system. **2.** Agricultural Research Service. **3.** American Rescue Service. **4.** American Rose Society.

ART *Linguistics.* article: often used to represent the class of determiners, including words such as *this, that,* and *some* as well as the articles *a, an,* and *the.*

art. 1. artificial. **2.** artillery. **3.** artist.

ARU *Computers.* audio response unit.

A.R.V. 1. AIDS-related virus. **2.** American Revised Version (of the Bible).

ARVN (är′vin), (in the Vietnam War) a soldier in the army of South Vietnam. [*A(rmy) of the) R(epublic of) V(iet) N(am)*]

AS 1. American Samoa (for use with ZIP code). **2.** Anglo-Saxon. **3.** antisubmarine.

As *Symbol, Chemistry.* arsenic.

AS. Anglo-Saxon.

A.S. 1. Anglo-Saxon. **2.** Associate in Science.

A.-S. Anglo-Saxon.

ASA 1. Acoustical Society of America. **2.** American Standards Association. **3.** the numerical exposure index of a photographic film under the system adopted by the American Standards Association.

ASAP as soon as possible. Also, **A.S.A.P., a.s. a.p.**

ASAT (ā′sat′), antisatellite.

ASBM air-to-surface ballistic missile. Also, **A. S.B.M.**

ASC American Society of Cinematographers. Also, **A.S.C.**

ASCAP (as′kap), American Society of Composers, Authors, and Publishers.

ASCE American Society of Civil Engineers.

ASCII (as′kē), a standard code for characters stored in a computer or to be transmitted between computers. [*A(merican) S(tandard) C(ode for) I(nformation) I(nterchange)*]

ASCM antiship capable missile.

ASCP American Society of Clinical Pathologists.

ascr *Electronics.* asymmetrical semiconductor controlled rectifier..

ASCS Agricultural Stabilization and Conservation Service.

ASCU Association of State Colleges and Universities.

ASE American Stock Exchange. Also, **A.S.E.**

ASEAN Association of Southeast Asian Nations. Also, **A.S.E.A.N.**

asgd. assigned.

asgmt. assignment.

asgn assign.

ASHD arteriosclerotic heart disease.

ASI 1. *Aeronautics.* airspeed indicator. **2.** American Safety Institute.

ask amplitude shift keying.

ASL 1. American Shuffleboard League. **2.** American Sign Language. **3.** American Soccer League.

ASLA American Society of Landscape Architects.

ASM air-to-surface missile.

asm assemble.

ASME American Society of Mechanical Engineers.

ASN Army service number.

Asn *Biochemistry.* asparagine.

ASNE American Society of Newspaper Editors.

ASP American selling price.

Asp *Biochemistry.* aspartic acid.

A.S.P.C.A. American Society for the Prevention of Cruelty to Animals.

ASPCC American Society for the Prevention of Cruelty to Children.

ASR 1. airport surveillance radar. **2.** *U.S. Navy.* air-sea rescue.

asr *Teletype.* automatic send-receive.

ass. 1. assistant. **2.** association. **3.** assorted.

assn. association. Also, **Assn.**

assoc. 1. associate. **2.** associated. **3.** association.

ASSR Autonomous Soviet Socialist Republic. Also, **A.S.S.R.**

asst. 1. assistance. **2.** assistant.

asstd. assorted.

Assyr. Assyrian.

AST Atlantic Standard Time. Also, **A.S.T., a. s.t.**

astb *Electronics.* astable.

ASTM American Society for Testing Materials. Also, **A.S.T.M.**

Astronomy. 1. astronomer. **2.** astronomical. **3.** astronomy.

ASU American Students Union.

A.S.V. American Standard Version (of the Bible). Also, **ASV**

A.S.W. Association of Scientific Workers.

ASWG American Steel Wire Gauge.

asym assymmetric.

asymp *Math.* asymptote.

asyn asynchronous.

AT 1. achievement test. **2.** *Military.* antitank.

At ampere-turn.

At *Symbol, Chemistry.* astatine.

at. 1. atmosphere. **2.** atomic. **3.** attorney.

A.T. Atlantic time.

ATA Air Transport Association.

A.T.A. Associate Technical Aide.

atb *Telephones.* all trunks busy.

ATC 1. Air Traffic Control. **2.** Air Transport Command.

atch attach.

ATE equipment that makes a series of tests automatically. [*a(utomatic) t(est) e(quipment)*]

ATF (Bureau of) Alcohol, Tobacco, and Firearms.

ATLA American Trial Lawyers Association.

ATM automated-teller machine.

atm. 1. atmosphere; atmospheres. **2.** atmospheric.

At/m ampere-turns per meter.

at. m. atomic mass.

at. no. atomic number.

ATP *Biochemistry.* an ester of adenosine and triphosphoric acid, $C_{10}H_{12}N_5O_4H_4P_3O_9$. [*a(denosine) t(ri)p(hosphate)*]

atr antitransmit-receive.

ATS *British. Military.* Auxiliary Territorial Service.

A.T.S. **1.** American Temperance Society. **2.** American Tract Society. **3.** American Transport Service.

att. **1.** attached. **2.** attention. **3.** attorney.

att. gen. attorney general.

attn. attention.

attrib. **1.** attribute. **2.** attributive. **3.** attributively.

atty. attorney.

Atty. Gen. Attorney General.

ATV all-terrain vehicle.

at. wt. atomic weight. Also, **at wt**

AU astronomical unit.

Au *Symbol, Chemistry.* gold. [from Latin *aurum*]

au. author.

A.U. *Physics.* angstrom unit. Also, **a.u.**

A.U.A. American Unitarian Association.

A.U.C. **1.** from the founding of the city (of Rome in 753? B.C.). [from Latin *ab urbe conditā*] **2.** in the year from the founding of the city (of Rome). [from Latin *annō urbis conditae*]

aud. **1.** audit. **2.** auditor.

Aug. August.

aug. **1.** augmentative. **2.** augmented.

AUM air-to-underwater missile.

AUS Army of the United States. Also, **A.U.S.**

Aus. **1.** Austria. **2.** Austrian.

Aust. **1.** Austria. **2.** Austria-Hungary. **3.** Austrian.

Austral Australian.

Austral. **1.** Australasia. **2.** Australia. **3.** Australian.

auth. **1.** authentic. **2.** author. **3.** authority. **4.** authorized.

Auth. Ver. Authorized Version (of the Bible).

auto. **1.** automatic. **2.** automobile. **3.** automotive.

AUTODIN (ô′tō din), automatic digital network.

autoxfmr autotransformer.

AUX *Linguistics.* auxiliary verb. Also, **Aux**

aux. auxiliary; auxiliaries. Also, **aux, auxil.**

AV 1. arteriovenous. **2.** atrioventricular. **3.** audiovisual.

av. 1. avenue. **2.** average. **3.** avoirdupois weight.

A-V 1. atrioventricular. **2.** audiovisual.

A/V 1. Also, **a.v.** ad valorem. **2.** audiovisual.

A.V. 1. Artillery Volunteers. **2.** audiovisual. **3.** Authorized Version (of the Bible).

A.V.C. 1. American Veterans' Committee. **2.** automatic volume control. Also, **AVC**

avdp. avoirdupois weight.

Ave. avenue. Also, **ave.**

AVF all-volunteer force.

avg. average.

avlbl available.

AVMA American Veterinary Medical Association.

avn. aviation.

avr automatic voltage regulator.

AW Articles of War.

a.w. 1. actual weight. **2.** (in shipping) all water. **3.** atomic weight. Also, **aw**

AWACS (ā′waks), a detection aircraft, fitted with radar and computers, capable of simultaneously tracking and plotting large numbers of low-flying aircraft. [*A(irborne) W(arning) A(nd) C(ontrol) S(ystem)*]

AWB air waybill.

AWG American Wire Gauge.

AWI Animal Welfare Institute.

AWIS Association of Women in Science.

A.W.L. absent with leave. Also, **a.w.l.**

AWOL (*pronounced as initials or* ā′wôl, ā′wol), away from military duties without permission, but without the intention of deserting. Also, **awol, A.W.O.L., a.w.o.l.** [*A(bsent) W(ith)o(ut) L(eave)*]

AWS American Weather Service.

AWSA American Water-Skiing Association.

ax. 1. axial. 2. axiom.

A.Y.H. American Youth Hostels.

AZ Arizona (for use with ZIP code).

az. 1. azimuth. 2. azure.

AZT *Pharmacology, Trademark.* azidothymidine: an antiviral drug used in the treatment of AIDS.

B

B 1. base: a semiconductor device. **2.** *Chess.* bishop. **3.** black. **4.** *Photography.* bulb. **5.** *Computers.* byte.

B *Symbol.* **1.** the second in order or in a series. **2.** (In some grading systems) a grade or mark, indicating the quality of a student's work as good or better than average. **3.** (In some school systems) a symbol designating the second semester of a school year. **4.** *Physiology.* a major blood group usually enabling a person whose blood is of this type to donate blood to persons of type B or AB and to receive blood from persons of type O or B. **5.** *Music.* **a.** the seventh tone in the scale of C major or the second tone in the relative minor scale, A minor. **b.** a string, key, or pipe tuned to this tone. **c.** a written or printed note representing this tone. **d.** (in the fixed system of solmization) the seventh tone of the scale of C major, called *ti.* **e.** the tonality having B as the tonic note. **6.** (*sometimes lowercase*) the medieval Roman numeral for 300. **7.** *Chemistry.* boron. **8.** a proportional shoe width size, narrower than C and wider than A. **9.** a proportional brassiere cup size, smaller than C and larger than A. **10.** *Physics.* magnetic induction. **11.** bel. **12.** *Electricity.* susceptance. **13.** a designation for a motion picture made on a low budget and meant as the secondary part of a double feature. **14.** a quality rating for a corporate or municipal bond, lower than BB and higher than CCC.

b 1. *Physics.* **a.** bar; bars. **b.** barn; barns. **2.** *Computers.* bit. **3.** black.

B- *U.S. Military.* (in designations of aircraft) bomber: *B-29.*

B. 1. bachelor. **2.** bacillus. **3.** *Baseball.* base; baseman. **4.** bass. **5.** basso. **6.** bay. **7.** Bible. **8.** bolivar. **9.** boliviano. **10.** book. **11.** born.

12. breadth. **13.** British. **14.** brother. **15.** brotherhood.

b. 1. bachelor. **2.** bale. **3.** *Baseball.* base; baseman. **4.** bass. **5.** basso. **6.** bay. **7.** billion. **8.** blend of; blended. **9.** book. **10.** born. **11.** breadth. **12.** brother. **13.** brotherhood.

BA bank acceptance.

Ba *Symbol, Chemistry.* barium.

ba. 1. bath. **2.** bathroom.

B.A. 1. Bachelor of Arts. [from Latin *Baccalaureus Artium*] **2.** *Theater.* bastard amber. **3.** *Baseball.* batting average. **4.** British Academy. **5.** British America. **6.** British Association (for Advancement of Science). **7.** Buenos Aires.

B.A.A. Bachelor of Applied Arts.

B.A.A.E. Bachelor of Aeronautical and Astronautical Engineering.

Bab. Babylon; Babylonia.

BAC blood-alcohol concentration: the percentage of alcohol in the bloodstream.

bact. 1. bacterial. **2.** bacteriology. **3.** bacterium.

BAE 1. Bureau of Agricultural Economics. **2.** Bureau of American Ethnology.

B.A.E. 1. Bachelor of Aeronautical Engineering. **2.** Bachelor of Agricultural Engineering. **3.** Bachelor of Architectural Engineering. **4.** Bachelor of Art Education. **5.** Bachelor of Arts in Education.

B.A.Ed. Bachelor of Arts in Education.

B.A.E.E. Bachelor of Arts in Elementary Education.

B.Ag. Bachelor of Agriculture.

B.Ag.E. Bachelor of Agricultural Engineering.

B.Agr. Bachelor of Agriculture.

B.Ag.Sc. Bachelor of Agricultural Science.

Ba. Is. Bahama Islands.

B.A.Jour. Bachelor of Arts in Journalism.

BAK file (bak), *Computers.* backup file.

BAL 1. *Chemistry.* British Anti-Lewisite: dimercaprol. **2.** *Computers.* Basic Assembly Language.

bal blood alcohol level.

Bal. Baluchistan.

bal. 1. balance. **2.** balancing.

Balt. Baltic.

balun balanced-to-unbalanced network.

B.A.M. 1. Bachelor of Applied Mathematics. **2.** Bachelor of Arts in Music.

B.A.Mus.Ed. Bachelor of Arts in Music Education.

B and B 1. *Trademark.* a brand of liqueur combining Benedictine and brandy. **2.** bed-and-breakfast. Also, **B&B**

B&D bondage and discipline: used in reference to sadomasochistic sexual practices. Also, **B and D**

B&S Brown and Sharp wire gauge.

Bap. Baptist. Also, **Bapt.**

bap. baptized.

B.A.P.C.T. Bachelor of Arts in Practical Christian Training.

B.App.Arts. Bachelor of Applied Arts.

BAR Browning automatic rifle.

Bar. *Bible.* Baruch.

bar. 1. barometer. **2.** barometric. **3.** barrel. **4.** barrister.

B.Ar. Bachelor of Architecture.

B.Arch. Bachelor of Architecture.

B.Arch.E. Bachelor of Architectural Engineering.

barit. baritone.

baro barometer.

barr. barrister.

BART (bärt), Bay Area Rapid Transit.

Bart. Baronet.

B.A.S. 1. Bachelor of Agricultural Science. **2.** Bachelor of Applied Science.

B.A.Sc. 1. Bachelor of Agricultural Science. **2.** Bachelor of Applied Science.

BASIC (bā′sik), *Computers.* a programming language that uses English words, punctuation marks, and algebraic notation. [B(eginner's) A(ll-purpose) S(ymbolic) I(nstruction) C(ode)]

bat. 1. battalion. **2.** battery.

BATF Bureau of Alcohol, Tobacco, and Firearms.

batt. 1. battalion. **2.** battery.

Bav. 1. Bavaria. **2.** Bavarian.

bay *Electronics.* bayonet.

bayc *Electronics.* bayonet candelabra.

bay cand dc *Electronics.* bayonet candelabra double-contact.

bay cand sc *Electronics.* bayonet candelabra single-contact.

BB a quality rating for a corporate or municipal bond, lower than BBB and higher than B.

bb. 1. ball bearing. **2.** *Baseball.* base on balls; bases on balls. **3.** bulletin board.

B/B bottled in bond.

B.B. 1. bail bond. **2.** Blue Book. **3.** B'nai B'rith. **4.** Bureau of the Budget.

b.b. 1. bail bond. **2.** baseboard.

B.B.A. 1. Bachelor of Business Administration. **2.** Big Brothers of America.

BBB Better Business Bureau.

BBB a quality rating for a corporate or municipal bond, lower than A and higher than BB.

B.B.C. British Broadcasting Corporation. Also, **BBC**

bbl. barrel.

bbq barbecue.

bbrg ball bearing.

BBS *Computers.* **1.** bulletin board service. **2.** bulletin board system.

BC 1. British Columbia, Canada (for use with ZIP code). **2.** *Scuba Diving.* buoyancy compensator.

bc 1. *Music.* basso continuo. **2.** between centers. **3.** Also, **bcc** blind carbon copy: used as a notation on the carbon copy of a letter or other document sent to a third person without the addressee's knowledge. **4.** broadcast.

B/C bills for collection.

B.C. 1. Bachelor of Chemistry. **2.** Bachelor of Commerce. **3.** bass clarinet. **4.** battery commander. **5.** before Christ (used in indicating dates). **6.** British Columbia.

BCA Boys' Clubs of America.

bcc blind carbon copy.

BCD 1. *Military.* bad conduct discharge. **2.** *Computers.* binary-coded decimal system.

B.C.E. 1. Bachelor of Chemical Engineering. **2.** Bachelor of Christian Education. **3.** Bachelor of Civil Engineering. **4.** before Christian (or Common) Era.

B.Cer.E. Bachelor of Ceramic Engineering.

bcfsk binary-coded frequency-shift keying.

bch. bunch.

B.Ch. Bachelor of Chemistry.

B.Ch.E. Bachelor of Chemical Engineering.

bci binary-coded information.

B.C.L. Bachelor of Civil Law.

bcn beacon.

BCNU *Pharmacology.* carmustine. [abbreviation of the chemical name *1,3-bis 2-chloroethyl-1-nitrosourea*]

B.Com.Sc. Bachelor of Commercial Science.

B.C.P. 1. Bachelor of City Planning. **2.** Book of Common Prayer.

B.C.S. 1. Bachelor of Chemical Science. **2.** Bachelor of Commercial Science.

Bd *Symbol.* baud.

BD. (in Bahrain) dinar; dinars.

bd. 1. board. **2.** bond. **3.** bound. **4.** bundle.

B/D 1. bank draft. **2.** bills discounted. **3.** *Accounting.* brought down.

b/d barrels per day.

B.D. 1. Bachelor of Divinity. **2.** bank draft. **3.** bills discounted.

B.D.A. 1. Bachelor of Domestic Arts. **2.** Bachelor of Dramatic Art.

bdc bottom dead center.

bde *Military.* brigade.

bd elim band elimination.

B.Des. Bachelor of Design.

bd. ft. board foot; board feet.

bdg binding.

bdgh binding head.

bdl. bundle.

bdle. bundle.

bdrm. bedroom.

bdry boundary.

B.D.S. Bachelor of Dental Surgery.

b.d.s. (in prescriptions) twice a day. [from Latin *bis diē sūmendum*]

BDSA Business and Defense Services Administration.

Be *Symbol, Chemistry.* beryllium.

Bé. *Chemistry.* Baumé: calibrated according to a Baumé scale, used to measure specific gravity of liquids.

B/E bill of exchange. Also, **b.e.**

B.E. **1.** Bachelor of Education. **2.** Bachelor of Engineering. **3.** Bank of England. **4.** bill of exchange. **5.** Board of Education.

bec. because.

B.Ed. Bachelor of Education.

B.E.E. Bachelor of Electrical Engineering.

bef. before.

B.E.F. British Expeditionary Force; British Expeditionary Forces.

Bel. **1.** Belgian. **2.** Belgic. **3.** Belgium.

Belg. **1.** Belgian. **2.** Belgium.

B.E.M. **1.** Bachelor of Engineering of Mines. **2.** British Empire Medal.

benef. beneficiary.

Beng. **1.** Bengal. **2.** Bengali.

B. Engr. Bachelor of Engineering.

B.E.P. Bachelor of Engineering Physics.

ber bit error rate.

Ber. Is. Bermuda Islands.

B.E.S. Bachelor of Engineering Science.

BEShT *Judaism.* Baal Shem-Tov.

BET Black Entertainment Television.

bet. between.

betw between.

BeV (bev), *Physics.* billion electron-volts. Also, **Bev, bev**

BEW Board of Economic Warfare.

BF black female.

bf. *Law.* brief.

B/F *Accounting.* brought forward.

B.F. 1. Bachelor of Finance. **2.** Bachelor of Forestry.

b.f. *Printing.* boldface. Also, **bf**

B.F.A. Bachelor of Fine Arts.

B.F.A.Mus. Bachelor of Fine Arts in Music.

bfo *Electronics.* beat-frequency oscillator.

bfr 1. before. **2.** buffer.

B.F.S. Bachelor of Foreign Service.

BFT biofeedback training. Also, **bft**

B.F.T. Bachelor of Foreign Trade.

bg. 1. background. **2.** bag.

B.G. 1. Birmingham gauge. **2.** brigadier general. Also, **BG**

bge beige.

bGH *Biochemistry, Agriculture.* bovine growth hormone.

Bglr. bugler.

BHA *Chemistry, Pharmacology.* a synthetic antioxidant, $C_{11}H_{16}O_2$. [*b(utylated) h(ydroxy) a(nisole)*]

BHC *Chemistry.* a crystalline, water-soluble, poisonous solid, $C_6H_6Cl_6$. [*b(enzene) h(exa) c(hloride)*]

bhd. bulkhead.

B.H.L. 1. Bachelor of Hebrew Letters. **2.** Bachelor of Hebrew Literature.

Bhn *Metallurgy.* Brinell hardness number.

bhp brake horsepower. Also, **BHP, B.H.P., b.hp., b.h.p.**

BHT *Chemistry, Pharmacology.* an antioxidant, $C_{15}H_{24}O$. [*b(utylated) h(ydroxy)t(oluene)*]

BI *Real Estate.* built-in.

Bi *Symbol, Chemistry.* bismuth.

bi bisexual.

BIA Bureau of Indian Affairs.

BiAF bisexual Asian female.

BiAM bisexual Asian male.

Bib. 1. Bible. **2.** Biblical.

bib. (in prescriptions) drink. [from Latin *bibe*]

BiBF bisexual black female.

Bibl Biblical. Also, **Bibl.**

bibl. 1. biblical. **2.** bibliographical. **3.** bibliography.

BiblHeb Biblical Hebrew.

BiBM bisexual black male.

bicarb. 1. bicarbonate. **2.** bicarbonate of soda.

B.I.D. Bachelor of Industrial Design.

b.i.d. (in prescriptions) twice a day. [from Latin *bis in diē*]

B.I.E. Bachelor of Industrial Engineering.

BiF bisexual female.

Big O *Slang.* orgasm.

BIL Braille Institute Library.

BiM bisexual male.

bin binary.

B.Ind.Ed. Bachelor of Industrial Education.

biog. 1. biographer. **2.** biographical. **3.** biography.

biol. 1. biological. **2.** biologist. **3.** biology.

BIOS (bi'ŏs, -os), *Computers.* firmware that directs many basic functions of the operating system. [*B(asic) I(nput)/O(utput) S(ystem)*]

B.I.S. 1. Bank for International Settlements. **2.** British Information Services.

B.I.T. Bachelor of Industrial Technology.

BiWF bisexual white female.

BiWM bisexual white male.

B.J. Bachelor of Journalism.

Bk *Symbol, Chemistry.* berkelium.

bk 1. back. **2.** *Baseball.* balk; balks. **3.** black.

bk. 1. bank. **2.** book.

bkbndr. bookbinder.

bkcy. bankruptcy.

bkdn breakdown.

bkg. **1.** banking. **2.** bookkeeping. **3.** breakage.

bkgd. background.

bklr. *Printing.* black letter.

bkpg. bookkeeping.

bkpr. bookkeeper.

bkpt. bankrupt.

bks. **1.** banks. **2.** barracks. **3.** books.

bkt. **1.** basket. **2.** bracket. **3.** bucket.

bl. **1.** bale; bales. **2.** barrel; barrels. **3.** black. **4.** block. **5.** blue.

b/l *Commerce.* bill of lading. Also, **B/L**

B.L. **1.** Bachelor of Laws. **2.** Bachelor of Letters. **3.** bill of lading.

b.l. **1.** bill of lading. **2.** *Military.* breech loading.

B.L.A. **1.** Bachelor of Landscape Architecture. **2.** Bachelor of Liberal Arts.

bldg. building.

Bldg.E. Building Engineer.

bldr. builder.

B.L.E. Brotherhood of Locomotive Engineers.

B.Lit. Bachelor of Literature.

B.Litt. Bachelor of Letters.

blk. **1.** black. **2.** block. **3.** bulk.

blkg **1.** blanking. **2.** blocking.

B.LL. Bachelor of Laws.

BLM Bureau of Land Management. Also, **B.L.M.**

blo blower.

BLS Bureau of Labor Statistics.

bls. **1.** bales. **2.** barrels.

B.L.S. **1.** Bachelor of Library Science. **2.** Bureau of Labor Statistics.

BLT a bacon, lettuce, and tomato sandwich. Also, **B.L.T.**

bltin built-in.

Blvd. boulevard. Also, **blvd.**

blw below.

blzd blizzard.

BM **1.** basal metabolism. **2.** *Surveying.* bench mark. **3.** black male. **4.** *Informal.* bowel movement.

bm *Electricity.* break-before-make: a relay contact.

B.M. 1. Bachelor of Medicine. **2.** Bachelor of Music. **3.** British Museum.

B.Mar.E. Bachelor of Marine Engineering.

B.M.E. 1. Bachelor of Mechanical Engineering. **2.** Bachelor of Mining Engineering. **3.** Bachelor of Music Education.

B.M.Ed. Bachelor of Music Education.

B.Met. Bachelor of Metallurgy.

B.Met.E. Bachelor of Metallurgical Engineering.

BMEWS (bē myōōz′), *U.S. Military.* Ballistic Missile Early Warning System.

B.Mgt.E. Bachelor of Management Engineering.

BMI Broadcast Music, Inc.

B.Min.E. Bachelor of Mining Engineering.

BMOC big man on campus. Also, **B.M.O.C.**

BMR basal metabolic rate.

B.M.S. Bachelor of Marine Science.

B.M.T. Bachelor of Medical Technology.

B.Mus. Bachelor of Music.

B.M.V. Blessed Mary the Virgin. [from Latin *Beāta Maria Virgō*]

bn brown.

Bn. 1. Baron. **2.** Battalion.

bn. battalion.

B.N. Bachelor of Nursing.

BNA British North America. Also, **B.N.A.**

BND Germany's national intelligence service. [from German *B(undes)n(achrichten)d(ienst)*]

bnls boneless.

bnr burner.

B.N.S. Bachelor of Naval Science.

bnsh burnish.

bnz bronze.

bo 1. blackout. **2.** *Electronics.* blocking oscillator.

B/o *Accounting.* brought over.

B.O. 1. Board of Ordnance. **2.** *Informal.* body odor. **3.** *Theater.* box office.

b.o. 1. back order. **2.** box office. **3.** branch office. **4.** broker's order. **5.** buyer's option.

BOB Bureau of the Budget.

BOD biochemical oxygen demand.

Bol. Bolivia.

bol. (in prescriptions) bolus (larger than a regular pill).

BOMFOG brotherhood of man, fatherhood of God.

BOQ *U.S. Military.* bachelor officers' quarters.

bor. borough.

bot. 1. botanic; botanical. **2.** botanist. **3.** botany. **4.** bottle.

B.O.T. Board of Trade.

BP 1. beautiful people; beautiful person. **2.** blood pressure.

bp 1. between perpendiculars. **2.** blueprint. **3.** boilerplate.

bp. 1. baptized. **2.** birthplace. **3.** bishop.

B/P *Commerce.* bills payable.

B.P. 1. Bachelor of Pharmacy. **2.** Bachelor of Philosophy. **3.** *Finance.* basis point. **4.** *Archaeology.* before the present: (in radiocarbon dating) in a specified amount of time or at a specified point in time before A.D. 1950. **5.** *Commerce.* bills payable.

b.p. 1. *Finance.* basis point. **2.** below proof. **3.** *Commerce.* bills payable. **4.** *Physics, Chemistry.* boiling point. **5.** the public good [from Latin *bonum publicum*].

bpa bandpass amplifier.

B.P.A. Bachelor of Professional Arts.

BPD barrels per day. Also, **B.P.D.**

B.P.E. Bachelor of Physical Education.

B.Pet.E. Bachelor of Petroleum Engineering.

B.Ph. Bachelor of Philosophy.

B.P.H. Bachelor of Public Health.

B.Pharm. Bachelor of Pharmacy.

B.Phil. Bachelor of Philosophy.

BPI 1. Also, **bpi** *Computers.* **a.** bits per inch. **b.** bytes per inch. **2.** Bureau of Public Inquiries.

bpl. birthplace.

B.P.O.E. Benevolent and Protective Order of Elks.

bps *Computers.* bits per second. Also, **BPS**

BR 1. *Real Estate.* bedroom. **2.** Bureau of Reclamation.

Br *Symbol, Chemistry.* bromine.

Br. 1. branch (in place names). **2.** brick. **3.** Britain. **4.** British.

br. 1. bedroom. **2.** branch. **3.** brass. **4.** brig. **5.** bronze. **6.** brother. **7.** brown.

b.r. *Commerce.* bills receivable. Also, **B.R., B/R**

Braz. 1. Brazil. **2.** Brazilian.

B.R.C.A. Brotherhood of Railway Carmen of America.

B.R.C.S. British Red Cross Society.

brdg bridge.

B.R.E. Bachelor of Religious Education.

brg bearing.

Brig. 1. brigade. **2.** brigadier.

Brig. Gen. brigadier general.

Brit. 1. Britain. **2.** British.

brk brake.

brkg breaking.

brkr *Electricity.* breaker.

brkt bracket.

brng burning.

Bros. brothers. Also, **bros.**

brs brass.

Br. Som. British Somaliland.

BR STD British Standard.

brt 1. bright. **2.** brightness.

B.R.T. Brotherhood of Railroad Trainmen.

BRV Bravo (a cable television station).

brz braze.

BS 1. Bureau of Standards. **2.** *Slang (sometimes vulgar).* bullshit.

b/s 1. bags. **2.** bales. **3.** bill of sale.

B.S. 1. Bachelor of Science. **2.** Bachelor of Surgery. **3.** bill of sale. **4.** *Slang (sometimes vulgar).* bullshit.

b.s. 1. balance sheet. **2.** bill of sale. **3.** *Slang (sometimes vulgar).* bullshit.

B.S.A. 1. Also, **B.S. Agr.** Bachelor of Science in Agriculture. **2.** Bachelor of Scientific Agriculture. **3.** Boy Scouts of America.

B.S.A.A. Bachelor of Science in Applied Arts.

B.S.Adv. Bachelor of Science in Advertising.

B.S.A.E. 1. Also, **B.S.Ae.Eng.** Bachelor of Science in Aeronautical Engineering. **2.** Also, **B.S.Ag.E.** Bachelor of Science in Agricultural Engineering. **3.** Also, **B.S.Arch.E., B.S.Arch. Eng.** Bachelor of Science in Architectural Engineering.

B.S.Arch. Bachelor of Science in Architecture.

B.S.Art.Ed. Bachelor of Science in Art Education.

B.S.B.A. Bachelor of Science in Business Administration.

B.S.Bus. Bachelor of Science in Business.

B.S.Bus.Mgt. Bachelor of Science in Business Management.

B.Sc. Bachelor of Science.

B.S.C. Bachelor of Science in Commerce.

B.S.C.E. Bachelor of Science in Civil Engineering.

B.S.Ch. Bachelor of Science in Chemistry.

B.S.Ch.E. Bachelor of Science in Chemical Engineering.

B.Sch.Music Bachelor of School Music.

B.S.Com. Bachelor of Science in Communications.

B.S.C.P. Brotherhood of Sleeping Car Porters.

B.S.D. Bachelor of Science in Design. Also, **B.S.Des.**

B.S.E. 1. Also, **B.S.Ed.** Bachelor of Science in Education. **2.** Also, **B.S.Eng.** Bachelor of Science in Engineering.

B.S.Ec. Bachelor of Science in Economics.

B.S.E.E. 1. Also, **B.S.E.Engr.** Bachelor of Science in Electrical Engineering. **2.** Bachelor of Science in Elementary Education.

B.S.El.E. Bachelor of Science in Electronic Engineering.

B.S.E.M. Bachelor of Science in Engineering of Mines.

B.S.E.P. Bachelor of Science in Engineering Physics.

B.S.E.S. Bachelor of Science in Engineering Sciences.

B.S.F. Bachelor of Science in Forestry. Also, **B.S.For.**

B.S.F.M. Bachelor of Science in Forest Management.

B.S.F.Mgt. Bachelor of Science in Fisheries Management.

B.S.F.S. Bachelor of Science in Foreign Service.

B.S.F.T. Bachelor of Science in Fuel Technology.

B.S.G.E. Bachelor of Science in General Engineering. Also, **B.S.Gen.Ed.**

B.S.G.Mgt. Bachelor of Science in Game Management.

bsh. bushel; bushels.

B.S.H.A. Bachelor of Science in Hospital Administration.

B.S.H.E. Bachelor of Science in Home Economics. Also, **B.S.H.Ec.**

B.S.H.Ed. Bachelor of Science in Health Education.

bshg bushing.

B.S.Hyg. Bachelor of Science in Hygiene.

B.S.I.E. 1. Also, **B.S.Ind.Ed.** Bachelor of Science in Industrial Education. 2. Also, **B.S. Ind.Engr.** Bachelor of Science in Industrial Engineering.

B.S.Ind.Mgt. Bachelor of Science in Industrial Management.

B.S.I.R. Bachelor of Science in Industrial Relations.

B.S.I.T. Bachelor of Science in Industrial Technology.

B.S.J. Bachelor of Science in Journalism.

bskt. basket.

Bs/L bills of lading.

B.S.L. **1.** Bachelor of Sacred Literature. **2.** Bachelor of Science in Law. **3.** Bachelor of Science in Linguistics.

B.S.L.A. and Nurs. Bachelor of Science in Liberal Arts and Nursing.

B.S.Lab.Rel. Bachelor of Science in Labor Relations.

B.S.L.Arch. Bachelor of Science in Landscape Architecture.

B.S.L.M. Bachelor of Science in Landscape Management.

B.S.L.S. Bachelor of Science in Library Science.

B.S.M. **1.** Bachelor of Sacred Music. **2.** Bachelor of Science in Medicine. **3.** Bachelor of Science in Music.

B.S.M.E. **1.** Bachelor of Science in Mechanical Engineering. **2.** Bachelor of Science in Mining Engineering. **3.** Also, **B.S.Mus.Ed.** Bachelor of Science in Music Education.

B.S.Met. Bachelor of Science in Metallurgy.

B.S.Met.E. Bachelor of Science in Metallurgical Engineering.

bsmt basement. Also, **Bsmt**

B.S.M.T. Bachelor of Science in Medical Technology. Also, **B.S.Med.Tech.**

B.S.N. Bachelor of Science in Nursing.

B.S.N.A. Bachelor of Science in Nursing Administration.

bsns business

BSO *Astronomy.* blue stellar object.

B.S.Orn.Hort. Bachelor of Science in Ornamental Horticulture.

B.S.O.T. Bachelor of Science in Occupational Therapy.

B.S.P. Bachelor of Science in Pharmacy. Also, **B.S.Phar.**, **B.S.Pharm.**

B.S.P.A. Bachelor of Science in Public Administration.

B.S.P.E. Bachelor of Science in Physical Education.

B.S.P.H. Bachelor of Science in Public Health.

B.S.P.H.N. Bachelor of Science in Public Health Nursing.

B.S.P.T. Bachelor of Science in Physical Therapy. Also, **B.S.Ph.Th.**

B.S.Radio-TV. Bachelor of Science in Radio and Television.

B.S.Ret. Bachelor of Science in Retailing.

B.S.R.T. Bachelor of Science in Radiological Technology.

B.S.S. 1. Bachelor of Secretarial Science. **2.** Bachelor of Social Science.

B.S.S.A. Bachelor of Science in Secretarial Administration.

B.S.S.E. Bachelor of Science in Secondary Education.

B.S.S.S. 1. Bachelor of Science in Secretarial Studies. **2.** Bachelor of Science in Social Science.

B.S.T.&I.E. Bachelor of Science in Trade and Industrial Education.

bstb *Electricity, Electronics.* bistable.

B.S.Trans. Bachelor of Science in Transportation.

Bt. Baronet.

bt. 1. boat. **2.** bought.

B.T. 1. Bachelor of Theology. **2.** board of trade.

B.t. *Biology, Agriculture.* Bacillus thuringiensis.

B.T.Ch. Bachelor of Textile Chemistry.

B.T.E. Bachelor of Textile Engineering.

bth bathroom.

B.Th. Bachelor of Theology.

btl. bottle.

btn button.

btn. battalion.

btry. battery.

btry chgr battery charger.

B.T.U. *Physics.* British thermal unit; British thermal units. Also, **BTU, B.t.u., B.th.u., Btu**

BU *Numismatics.* brilliant uncirculated.

bu. 1. bureau. **2.** bushel; bushels.

Bulg. 1. Bulgaria. **2.** Bulgarian. Also, **Bulg**

bull. bulletin. Also, **bul.**

BUN blood urea nitrogen.

Bur. Burma.

bur. bureau.

bus. business.

bush. bushel; bushels.

B.V. 1. Blessed Virgin. [from Latin *Beāta Virgō*] **2.** farewell. [from Latin *bene valē*]

b.v. book value.

B.V.A. Bachelor of Vocational Agriculture.

B.V.D. *Trademark.* a brand of men's underwear. Also, **BVD's**

B.V.E. Bachelor of Vocational Education.

bvg beverage.

B.V.I. British Virgin Islands.

bvl bevel.

B.V.M. Blessed Virgin Mary. [from Latin *Beāta Virgō Maria*]

bvt. 1. brevet. **2.** brevetted.

BW 1. bacteriological warfare. **2.** biological warfare. **3.** (in television, motion pictures, photography, etc.) black and white.

bw *Telecommunications.* bandwidth.

BWC Board of War Communications.

BWG Birmingham Wire Gauge.

B.W.I. British West Indies.

bx base exchange. Also, **BX**

bx. box.

By *Computers.* byte.

BYOB bring your own bottle (in an invitation, to indicate that the host will not provide liquor). Also, **BYO**

byp. bypass. Also, **Byp.**

Byz. Byzantine.

Bz. benzene.

bzr buzzer.

C

C 1. cocaine. **2.** *Electronics.* collector: an electron device. **3.** *Electricity.* common (in diagrams). **4.** *Grammar.* complement. **5.** consonant. **6.** coulomb. **7.** county (used with a number to designate a county road).

C *Symbol.* **1.** the third in order or in a series. **2.** (in some grading systems) a grade or mark, indicating the quality of a student's work as fair or average. **3.** *Music.* **a.** the first tone, or keynote, in the scale of C major or the third tone in the relative minor scale, A minor. **b.** a string, key, or pipe tuned to this tone. **c.** a written or printed note representing this tone. **d.** (in the fixed system of solmization) the first tone of the scale of C major, called *do.* **e.** the tonality having C as the tonic note. **f.** a symbol indicating quadruple time and appearing after the clef sign on a musical staff. **4.** (*sometimes lowercase*) the Roman numeral for 100. **5.** Celsius. **6.** centigrade. **7.** *Electricity.* **a.** capacitance. **b.** a battery size for 1.5 volt dry cells: diameter, 1 in. (2.5 cm); length, 1.9 in. (4.8 cm). **8.** *Chemistry.* carbon. **9.** *Physics.* **a.** charge conjugation. **b.** charm. **10.** *Biochemistry.* **a.** cysteine. **b.** cytosine. **11.** Also, **C-note.** *Slang.* a hundred-dollar bill. **12.** a proportional shoe width size, narrower than D and wider than B. **13.** a proportional brassiere cup size, smaller than D and larger than B. **14.** the lowest quality rating for a corporate or municipal bond. **15.** *Computers.* a high-level programming language. **16.** coulomb.

c 1. calorie. **2.** *Optics.* candle; candles. **3.** carbohydrate; carbohydrates. **4.** (with a year) about: *c1775.* [from Latin *circā, circiter, circum*] **5.** *Physics, Chemistry.* curie; curies. **6.** cycle; cycles.

C- *U.S. Military.* (in designations of aircraft) cargo: *C-124.*

C. 1. calorie. **2.** Cape. **3.** Catholic. **4.** Celsius.

5. Celtic. **6.** Centigrade. **7.** College. **8.** (in Costa Rica and El Salvador) colon; colons. **9.** Congress. **10.** Conservative.

c. 1. calorie. **2.** *Optics.* candle; candles. **3.** carat. **4.** carbon. **5.** carton. **6.** case. **7.** *Baseball.* catcher. **8.** cathode. **9.** cent; cents. **10.** centavo. **11.** *Football.* center. **12.** centigrade. **13.** centime. **14.** centimeter. **15.** century. **16.** chairman; chairperson. **17.** chapter. **18.** chief. **19.** child. **20.** church. **21.** (with a year) about: *c. 1775.* [from Latin *circā, circiter, circum*] **22.** cirrus. **23.** city. **24.** cloudy. **25.** cognate. **26.** color. **27.** gallon. [from Latin *congius*] **28.** copper. **29.** copyright. **30.** corps. **31.** cubic. **32.** (in prescriptions) with. [from Latin *cum*] **33.** cycle; cycles.

C++ *Computers.* a programming language.

CA 1. cable. **2.** California (for use with ZIP code). **3.** chronological age.

Ca *Symbol, Chemistry.* calcium.

ca. 1. cathode. **2.** centiare. **3.** Also, **ca** (with a year) about: *ca. 476* B.C. [def. 3 from Latin *circā*]

C/A 1. capital account. **2.** cash account. **3.** credit account. **4.** current account.

C.A. 1. Central America. **2.** chartered accountant. **3.** *Accounting.* chief accountant. **4.** Coast Artillery. **5.** commercial agent. **6.** consular agent. **7.** controller of accounts. **8.** current assets.

CAA Civil Aeronautics Administration. Also, **C.A.A.**

CAB Civil Aeronautics Board. Also, **C.A.B.**

cab cabinet.

CAC *Real Estate.* central air conditioning.

C.A.C. Coast Artillery Corps.

CAD (kad), computer-aided design.

CAD/CAM (kad/kam/), computer-aided design and computer-aided manufacturing.

CADMAT (kad/mat), computer-aided design, manufacture, and test.

CAE computer-aided engineering.

C.A.F. 1. cost and freight. **2.** cost, assurance, and freight. Also, **c.a.f.**

CAFE (ka fā′, kə-), *n.* a U.S. standard of average fuel consumption for all the cars produced by one manufacturer in a given year. [*C(orporate) A(verage) F(uel) E(conomy)*]

C.A.G.S. Certificate of Advanced Graduate Study.

CAI computer-aided instruction; computer-assisted instruction. Also, **cai**

Cal kilocalorie.

cal 1. calibrate. **2.** calorie.

Cal. California.

cal. 1. calendar. **2.** caliber. **3.** calorie.

calc. calculate.

Calif. California.

CAM (kam), computer-aided manufacturing.

Cam. Cambridge.

cam. camber.

CAMA (kam′ə), *Telecommunications.* centralized automatic message accounting.

Camb. Cambridge.

camflg camouflage.

cAMP *Biochemistry.* cyclic AMP.

camr camera.

Can. 1. Canada. **2.** Canadian.

can. 1. canceled. **2.** canon. **3.** canto.

Canad. Canadian.

canc. 1. cancel. **2.** canceled. **3.** cancellation.

cand candelabra.

C. & F. *Commerce.* cost and freight.

C&I 1. commerce and industry. **2.** commercial and industrial.

c&sc *Printing.* capitals and small capitals.

cand scr candelabra screw.

C and W country-and-western. Also, **C&W**

CanF Canadian French.

Cant. 1. Canterbury. **2.** Cantonese.

cantil cantilever.

canv canvas.

CAP 1. Civil Air Patrol. **2.** Common Agricultural Policy. **3.** computer-aided publishing.

4. *Stock Exchange.* convertible adjustable preferred (stock). Also, **C.A.P.** (for defs. 1, 2, 4).

cap. 1. capacitance, capacitor. **2.** capacity. **3.** (in prescriptions) let the patient take. [from Latin *capiat*] **4.** capital. **5.** capitalize. **6.** capitalized. **7.** capital letter. **8.** chapter. [from Latin *capitulum, caput*] **9.** computer-aided production.

cap. moll. (in prescriptions) soft capsule. [from Latin *capsula mollis*]

caps. 1. capital letters. **2.** (in prescriptions) a capsule [from Latin *capsula*].

cap scr cap screw.

capt. *Military.* captain. Also, **CPT**

CAR computer-assisted retrieval.

car. 1. carat; carats. **2.** cargo.

carb carburetor.

Card. Cardinal.

CARE (kâr), Cooperative for American Relief Everywhere. Also, **Care**

Caricom (kar′i kom′, kâr′-), an economic association formed in 1974 by ten Caribbean nations. Also, **CARICOM** [*Cari(bbean) com(munity)*]

Carol. Carolingian.

carp. carpentry.

carr carrier.

carr cur carrier current.

CAS collision-avoidance system.

cas 1. calculated airspeed. **2.** castle.

C.A.S. Certificate of Advanced Studies.

case computer-aided support equipment.

cas nut castle nut.

CAT 1. clear-air turbulence. **2.** *Medicine.* computerized axial tomography.

cat. 1. catalog; catalogue. **2.** catapult. **3.** catechism.

cate computer-aided test equipment.

cath *Electricity.* cathode.

Cath. 1. (*often lowercase*) cathedral. **2.** Catholic.

CATV community antenna television (a cable television system).

caus. causative.

cav. 1. cavalier. 2. cavalry. 3. cavity.

cax community automatic exchange.

CB 1. Citizens Band (radio). 2. *Military.* construction battalion. 3. continental breakfast.

Cb *Symbol, Chemistry.* columbium.

cb 1. *Electronics.* common base. 2. *Telephones.* common battery.

C.B. 1. Bachelor of Surgery. [from Latin *Chirurgiae Baccalaureus*] 2. *British.* Companion of the Bath.

cbal counterbalance.

CBAT College Board Achievement Test.

CBC 1. Also, **C.B.C.** Canadian Broadcasting Corporation. 2. *Medicine.* complete blood count.

C.B.D. 1. cash before delivery. 2. central business district.

C.B.E. Commander of the Order of the British Empire.

C.B.E.L. Cambridge Bibliography of English Literature. Also, **CBEL**

CBI computer-based instruction.

CBO Congressional Budget Office.

cbore counterbore.

cboreo counterbore other side.

CBS Columbia Broadcasting System.

CBT 1. Chicago Board of Trade. 2. computer-based training.

CBW chemical and biological warfare.

CC *Symbol.* a quality rating for a corporate or municipal bond, lower than CCC and higher than C.

Cc cirrocumulus.

cc 1. carbon copy. 2. close-coupled. 3. closing coil. 4. *Electronics.* common collector. 5. copies. 6. crosscouple. 7. cubic centimeter.

cc. 1. carbon copy. 2. chapters. 3. copies. 4. cubic centimeter. Also, **c.c.**

C.C. 1. carbon copy. 2. cashier's check. 3.

chief clerk. **4.** circuit court. **5.** city council. **6.** city councilor. **7.** civil court. **8.** company commander. **9.** county clerk. **10.** county commissioner. **11.** county council. **12.** county court. Also, **c.c.**

C.C.A. 1. Chief Clerk of the Admiralty. **2.** Circuit Court of Appeals. **3.** County Court of Appeals.

CCC 1. Civilian Conservation Corps. **2.** Commodity Credit Corporation. **3.** copyright clearance center.

CCD 1. *Electronics.* charge-coupled device. **2.** Confraternity of Christian Doctrine.

ccf hundred cubic feet (used of gas).

ccg *Electricity.* constant-current generator.

C.C.I.A. Consumer Credit Insurance Association.

CCITT Consultative Committee for International Telephony and Telegraphy.

CCK *Physiology.* cholecystokinin.

C.Cls. Court of Claims.

CCM counter-countermeasures.

ccm *Electricity.* constant-current modulation.

ccn contract change notice.

cco crystal-controlled oscillator.

CCP Chinese Communist Party.

C.C.P. 1. *Law.* Code of Civil Procedure. **2.** Court of Common Pleas.

CCR Commission on Civil Rights.

ccs 1. *Telephones.* common-channel signaling. **2.** continuous commercial service.

cct *Electricity.* constant-current transformer.

CCTV closed-circuit television.

CCU coronary-care unit.

ccu camera control unit.

ccw counterclockwise.

CD 1. *Finance.* certificate of deposit. **2.** Civil Defense. **3.** Community Development. **4.** compact disk.

Cd *Symbol, Chemistry.* cadmium.

cd 1. candela; candelas. **2.** card. **3.** circuit description. **4.** cold drawn. **5.** Also, **cd.** cord; cords. **6.** current density.

C/D certificate of deposit. Also, **c/d**

C.D. 1. *Finance.* certificate of deposit. **2.** Civil Defense. **3.** civil disobedience. **4.** Congressional District.

c.d. cash discount.

CDC Centers for Disease Control.

cdc cold-drawn copper.

cdel constant delivery.

cdf *Telephones.* combined distributing frame.

cdg coding.

CD-P compact disc-photographic.

cd pl cadmium plate.

Cdr. Commander. Also, **CDR**

cd rdr card reader.

cdrill counterdrill.

CD-ROM (sē′dē′rom′), a compact disk on which digitized read-only data can be stored. [*c(ompact) d(isk) r(ead-)o(nly) m(emory)*]

cds cold-drawn steel.

CDT Central daylight time. Also, **C.D.T.**

CDTA Capital District Transportation Authority.

cdx control-differential transmitter.

Ce *Symbol, Chemistry.* cerium.

ce 1. *Electronics.* common emitter. **2.** communications-electronics.

C.E. 1. Chemical Engineer. **2.** chief engineer. **3.** Christian Era. **4.** Church of England. **5.** Civil Engineer. **6.** common era. **7.** Corps of Engineers.

c.e. 1. buyer's risk. [from Latin *cāveat emptor* may the buyer beware] **2.** compass error.

CEA Council of Economic Advisers.

CEEB College Entrance Examination Board.

C.E.F. Canadian Expeditionary Force.

Cels. Celsius.

Celt. Celtic.

CEM communications electronics meteorological.

cem cement.

CEMA Council for Economic Mutual Assistance.

cemf counter electromotive force.

cen. 1. central. 2. century.

cent. 1. centigrade. 2. central. 3. centum. 4. century.

CEO chief executive officer. Also, **C.E.O.**

cephalom. cephalometry.

cer ceramic.

Cer.E. Ceramic Engineer.

cermet (sûr′met), ceramic-to-metal: a type of seal.

CERN (sârn, sûrn), European Laboratory for Particle Physics; formerly called European Organization for Nuclear Research. [from French *C(onseil) e(uropéen pour la) r(echerche) n(ucléaire)*]

cert. 1. certificate. 2. certification. 3. certified. 4. certify.

certif. 1. certificate. 2. certificated.

CETA (sē′tə), Comprehensive Employment and Training Act.

cet. par. other things being equal. [from Latin *ceteris paribus*]

CF 1. *Baseball.* center field. 2. *Baseball.* center fielder. 3. Christian female. 4. Also, **cf** cubic foot; cubic feet. 5. cystic fibrosis.

Cf *Symbol, Chemistry.* californium.

cf 1. cathode follower. 2. center field. 3. center fielder. 4. centrifugal force. 5. concrete floor.

cf. 1. *Bookbinding.* calf. 2. *Music.* cantus firmus. 3. compare [from Latin *confer*].

c.f. 1. *Baseball.* center field. 2. *Baseball.* center fielder. 3. cost and freight.

c/f *Bookkeeping.* carried forward.

C.F. cost and freight.

CFA chartered financial analyst.

CFAE contractor-furnished aircraft equipment.

cfd cubic feet per day.

CFE contractor-furnished equipment.

CFG Camp Fire Girls.

cfh cubic feet per hour.

C.F.I. cost, freight, and insurance. Also, **c.f.i.**

CFL Canadian Football League.

cfm cubic feet per minute.

CFNP Community Food and Nutrition Programs.

CFO chief financial officer. Also, **C.F.O.**

CFP 1. certified financial planner. **2.** contractor-furnished property.

CFR Code of Federal Regulations.

cfr crossfire.

CFS chronic fatigue syndrome.

cfs 1. cold-finished steel. **2.** cubic feet per second.

CFT *Medicine.* complement fixation test.

CFTC Commodity Futures Trading Commission.

CG Commanding General.

cg centigram; centigrams.

C.G. 1. Captain of the Guard. **2.** center of gravity. **3.** Coast Guard. **4.** Commanding General. **5.** Consul General.

c.g. 1. Captain of the Guard. **2.** center of gravity. **3.** Commanding General. **4.** Consul General.

CGA *Computers.* color graphics adapter.

cgs centimeter-gram-second (system). Also, **CGS, c.g.s.**

ch 1. case harden. **2.** *Surveying, Civil Engineering.* chain; chains. **3.** channel. **4.** chiffonier. **5.** *Electricity.* choke.

Ch. 1. Chaldean. **2.** Chaldee. **3.** *Television.* channel. **4.** chapter. **5.** *Chess.* check. **7.** China. **8.** Chinese. **9.** church.

ch. 1. chair. **2.** chaplain. **3.** chapter. **4.** *Chess.* check. **5.** chief. **6.** child; children. **7.** church.

c.h. 1. candle hours. **2.** clearinghouse. **3.** courthouse. **4.** custom house.

chal challenge.

Chal. 1. Chaldaic. **2.** Chaldean. **3.** Chaldee.

Chald. 1. Chaldaic. **2.** Chaldean. **3.** Chaldee.

cham chamfer.

Chan. **1.** Chancellor. **2.** Chancery. Also, **Chanc.**

chan. channel.

chanc. **1.** chancellor. **2.** chancery.

chap. **1.** Chaplain. **2.** chapter. Also, **Chap.**

char. **1.** character. **2.** charter.

chart. (in prescriptions) paper. [from Latin *charta*]

chart. cerat. (in prescriptions) waxed paper. [from Latin *charta cērāta*]

chas chassis.

Chât. (especially in Bordeaux wines) Château.

Ch.B. Bachelor of Surgery. [from Latin *Chirurgiae Baccalaureus*]

chc choke coil.

chd chord.

Ch.E. Chemical Engineer.

Chem. **1.** chemical. **2.** chemist. **3.** chemistry.

Chem.E. Chemical Engineer.

chg. **1.** change. **2.** charge. Also, **chge.**

chgov changeover.

Chin. **1.** China. **2.** Chinese. Also, **Chin**

Ch. J. Chief Justice.

chk check.

chkb check bit.

chld chilled.

chm. **1.** chairman. **2.** checkmate.

chmbr chamber.

chmn. chairman.

chng change.

choc. chocolate.

chp **1.** chairperson. **2.** chopper.

CHQ Corps Headquarters.

chr chroma.

Chr. **1.** Christ. **2.** Christian.

Chron. *Bible.* Chronicles.

chron. **1.** chronicle. **2.** chronograph. **3.** chronological. **4.** chronology.

chrst characteristic.

chs. chapters.

chw chairwoman.

CI counterintelligence.

Ci curie; curies.

ci 1. cast iron. **2.** circuit interrupter.

C.I. Channel Islands.

CIA Central Intelligence Agency. Also, **C.I.A.**

Cia. Company. Also, **cia.** [from Spanish *Compañía*]

cib. (in prescriptions) food. [from Latin *cibus*]

C.I.C. 1. Combat Information Center. **2.** Commander in Chief. **3.** Counterintelligence Corps.

cid component identification.

C.I.D. Criminal Investigation Department (of Scotland Yard).

c.i.d. *Automotive.* cubic-inch displacement: the displacement of an engine measured in cubic inches. Also, **cid, CID**

Cie. Company. Also, **cie.** [from French *Compagnie*]

C.I.F. *Commerce.* cost, insurance, and freight (the price quoted includes the cost of the merchandise, packing, and freight to a specified destination plus insurance charges). Also, **CIF, c.i.f.**

CIM 1. computer input from microfilm. **2.** computer-integrated manufacturing.

C. in C. Commander in Chief. Also, **C-in-C**

cine cinematographic.

C.I.O. 1. chief investment officer. **2.** Congress of Industrial Organizations. Also, **CIO**

CIP Cataloging in Publication: a program in which a partial bibliographic description of a work appears on the verso of its title page.

cip cast-iron pipe.

Cir. circle (approved for postal use).

cir. 1. about: *cir. 1800.* [from Latin *circā, circiter, circum*] **2.** circle. **3.** circular.

circ (sûrk), circular.

circ. 1. about: *circ. 1800.* [from Latin *circā, circiter, circum*] **2.** circuit. **3.** circular. **4.** circulation. **5.** circumference.

circum. circumference.

CIS *Computers.* CompuServe Information Services.

C.I.S. Commonwealth of Independent States.

CISC (sisk), complex instruction set computer.

cit. 1. citation. 2. cited. 3. citizen. 4. citrate.

C.I.T. counselor in training.

ciu computer interface unit.

Civ. 1. civil. 2. civilian.

CJ Chief Justice.

ck. 1. cask. 2. check. 3. cook. 4. cork.

ckb cork base.

ckbd corkboard.

ckpt cockpit.

ckt circuit.

ckt brkr circuit breaker.

ckt cl circuit closing.

ckt op circuit opening.

CL common law.

Cl *Symbol, Chemistry.* chlorine.

cl 1. center line. 2. centiliter; centiliters. 3. class. 4. closed loop. 5. closing. 6. clutch.

cl. 1. carload. 2. claim. 3. clarinet. 4. class. 5. classification. 6. clause. 7. clearance. 8. clerk. 9. close. 10. closet. 11. cloth.

C/L 1. carload. 2. carload lot. 3. cash letter.

c.l. 1. carload. 2. carload lot. 3. center line. 4. civil law. 5. common law.

CLA College Language Association.

clar. clarinet.

class. 1. classic. 2. classical. 3. classification. 4. classified.

cld. 1. *Stock Exchange.* (of bonds) called. 2. cleared. 3. cooled.

cldy cloudy.

clg 1. ceiling. 2. cooling.

CLI cost-of-living index. Also, **cli**

clin. clinical.

clk. 1. clerk. 2. clock.

clkg caulking.

clkj caulked joint.

cln clean.

clnc clearance.

clnt coolant.

clo. clothing.

clos *Real Estate.* closet.

clp clamp.

clpbd *Real Estate.* clapboard.

clpr clapper.

clp scr clamp screw.

clr. 1. clear. 2. color. 3. cooler. 4. current-limiting resistor.

clrg clearing.

cls classify.

clt cleat.

clthg clothing.

CLU Civil Liberties Union.

C.L.U. Chartered Life Underwriter.

clws. clockwise.

CM 1. Christian male. 2. Common Market. 3. countermeasures.

Cm *Symbol, Chemistry.* curium.

cm 1. Also, **cm.** centimeter; centimeters. 2. *Computers.* core memory. 3. corrective maintenance.

c/m (of capital stocks) call of more.

C.M. *Roman Catholic Church.* Congregation of the Mission.

c.m. 1. church missionary. 2. common meter. 3. corresponding member. 4. court martial.

cm³ *Symbol.* cubic centimeter.

CMA Canadian Medical Association.

C.M.A. certificate of management accounting.

CMC 1. certified management consultant. 2. Commandant of the Marine Corps.

cmd *Computers.* core-memory drive.

cmd. command.

cmdg. commanding.

Cmdr. Commander.

Cmdre Commodore.

CME Chicago Mercantile Exchange.

CMEA Council for Mutual Economic Assistance. See **COMECON.**

cmf coherent memory filter.

cmflr cam follower.

C.M.G. Companion of the Order of St. Michael and St. George.

CMI computer-managed instruction. Also, **cmi**

cmil circular Military.

CML current-mode logic.

cml. commercial.

cmnt comment.

CMOS (sē′môs′, -mos′), *Electronics.* complementary metal oxide semiconductor.

CMP *Biochemistry.* cytidine monophosphate.

cmpd compound.

cmplm complement.

cmplt complete.

cmpns compensate.

cmpnt component.

cmpr compare.

cmps compass.

cmpsg compensating.

cmpsn composition.

cmpst composite.

cmpt compute.

cmptg computing.

cmptr computer.

cmrlr cam roller.

CMS *Printing.* color management system.

cms current-mode switching.

cmshft camshaft.

cmsn commission.

Cmsr Commissioner.

cmte committee.

CMV *Pathology.* cytomegalovirus.

CMYK *Computers, Printing.* cyan, magenta, yellow, black; used for color mixing for printing.

CN 1. change notice. **2.** chloroacetophenone: used as a tear gas.

C/N 1. circular note. **2.** credit note.

cna copper-nickel alloy.

cncl concealed.

cnctrc concentric.

cncv concave.

cnd conduit.

cndct *Electricity.* **1.** conduct. **2.** conductivity. **3.** conductor.

cnds condensate.

cndtn condition.

cnfig configuration.

CNM Certified Nurse Midwife.

CNN Cable News Network (a cable television channel).

CNO Chief of Naval Operations.

CNS central nervous system. Also, **cns**

cnsld consolidate.

cnsltnt consultant.

cnsp conspicuously.

cnstr canister.

cntbd centerboard.

cntd contained.

cntor *Electricity.* contactor.

cnvc convenience.

cnvr conveyor.

cnvt convert.

cnvtb convertible.

cnvtr converter.

cnvx convex.

CO **1.** change order. **2.** Colorado (for use with ZIP code). **3.** Commanding Officer. **4.** conscientious objector.

Co *Symbol, Chemistry.* cobalt.

co **1.** carbon monoxide. **2.** cardiac output. **3.** cutoff. **4.** cutout.

Co. **1.** Company. **2.** County. Also, **co.**

C/O **1.** cash order. **2.** *Commerce.* certificate of origin.

C/o **1.** care of. **2.** *Bookkeeping.* carried over.

c/o **1.** care of. **2.** *Bookkeeping.* carried over. **3.** cash order. **4.** consist of.

C.O. **1.** cash order. **2.** Commanding Officer. **3.** conscientious objector. **4.** correction officer.

c.o. **1.** care of. **2.** *Bookkeeping.* carried over.

COA change of address.

CoA *Biochemistry.* coenzyme A.

coam coaming.

coax (kō′aks), *Electronics.* coaxial (cable).

COBOL (kō′bôl), *Computers.* a programming language. [*Co(mmon) B(usiness-)O(riented) L(anguage)*]

coch. (in prescriptions) a spoonful. [from Latin *cochlear*]

coch. amp. (in prescriptions) a tablespoonful. [from Latin *cochlear amplum* large spoon(ful)]

coch. mag. (in prescriptions) a tablespoonful. [from Latin *cochlear magnum* large spoon(ful)]

coch. med. (in prescriptions) a dessertspoonful. [from Latin *cochlear medium* medium-sized spoon(ful)]

coch. parv. (in prescriptions) a teaspoonful. [from Latin *cochlear parvum* little spoon(ful)]

COD. codex. Also, **cod.**

C.O.D. *Commerce.* cash, or collect, on delivery (payment to be made when delivered to the purchaser). Also, **c.o.d.**

coef coefficient.

COFC container-on-flatcar.

C of C Chamber of Commerce.

coff cofferdam.

C. of S. Chief of Staff.

cog. 1. cognate. 2. cognizant.

coho coherent oscillator.

COIN (koin), counterinsurgency. [*co(unter) in(surgency)*]

COL 1. Computer-Oriented Language. Also, **col** 2. cost of living.

Col. 1. Colombia. 2. Colonel. 3. Colorado. 4. *Bible.* Colossians.

col. 1. (in prescriptions) strain. [from Latin *colā*] 2. collected. 3. collector. 4. college. 5. collegiate. 6. colonial. 7. colony. 8. color. 9. colored. 10. column.

COLA (kō′lə), a clause, especially in union contracts, that grants automatic wage increases to cover the rising cost of living due to inflation. [*c(ost) o(f) l(iving) a(djustment)*]

colat. (in prescriptions) strained. [from Latin *colātus*]

colent. (in prescriptions) let them be strained. Also, **colen.** [from Latin *colentur*]

colet. (in prescriptions) let it be strained. [from Latin *colētur*]

colidar coherent light detection and ranging.

coll. 1. collateral. **2.** collect. **3.** collection. **4.** collective. **5.** collector. **6.** Also, **Coll.** college. **7.** collegiate. **8.** colloquial. **9.** (in prescriptions) an eyewash. [from Latin *collȳrium*]

collab. 1. collaboration. **2.** collaborator.

collat. collateral.

colloq. 1. colloquial. **2.** colloquialism. **3.** colloquially.

collun. (in prescriptions) a nose wash. [from Latin *collunarium*]

collut. (in prescriptions) a mouthwash. [from Latin *collūtorium*]

collyr. (in prescriptions) an eyewash. [from Latin *collȳrium*]

Colo. Colorado.

colog *Math.* cologarithm.

color. (in prescriptions) let it be colored. [from Latin *colōrētur*]

COM (kom), **1.** Comedy Central (a cable channel). **2.** computer output on microfilm.

Com. 1. Commander. **2.** Commission. **3.** Commissioner. **4.** Committee. **5.** Commodore. **6.** Commonwealth.

com. 1. comedy. **2.** comma. **3.** command. **4.** commander. **5.** commerce. **6.** commercial. **7.** commission. **8.** commissioner. **9.** committee. **10.** common. **11.** commonly. **12.** communications.

comb. 1. combination. **2.** combined. **3.** combining. **4.** combustion.

combl combustible.

comd. command.

comdg. commanding.

Comdr. commander. Also, **comdr.**

Comdt. commandant. Also, **comdt.**

COMECON (kom′i kon′), an economic association of Communist countries. Also, **Comecon, CMEA** [*Co(uncil) for M(utual) Econ(omic Assistance)*]

COMEX (kō′meks), Commodity Exchange, New York.

Com. in Chf. Commander in Chief.

coml. commercial.

comm 1. communication. 2. commutator.

comm. 1. commander. 2. commerce. 3. commission. 4. committee. 5. commonwealth. Also, **Comm.**

comp. 1. companion. 2. comparative. 3. compare. 4. compensation. 5. compilation. 6. compiled. 7. compiler. 8. complement. 9. complete. 10. composition. 11. compositor. 12. compound. 13. comprehensive.

compander *Audio.* compressor-expander.

compar. comparative.

compass *Computers.* compiler-assembler.

compd. compound.

Comp. Gen. Comptroller General.

compl complete.

compn compensate.

compt. 1. compartment. 2. Also, **Compt.** comptroller.

comptr comparator.

Comr. Commissioner.

Com·sat (kom′sat′), *Trademark.* a privately owned corporation servicing the global communications satellite system. [*Com(munications) Sat(ellite Corporation)*]

Con. 1. *Religion.* Conformist. 2. Consul.

con. 1. concerto. 2. conclusion. 3. connection. 4. consolidated. 5. consul. 6. continued. 7. against [from Latin *contrā*].

CONAD (kon′ad), Continental Air Defense Command.

conc. 1. concentrate. 2. concentrated. 3. concentration. 4. concerning. 5. concrete.

concl conclusion.

concr concrete.

cond. 1. condenser. **2.** condition. **3.** conditional. **4.** conductivity. **5.** conductor.

conf. 1. (in prescriptions) a confection. [from Latin *confectiō*] **2.** compare. [from Latin *confer*] **3.** conference. **4.** confessor. **5.** confidential. **6.** conformance.

confed. 1. confederacy. **2.** confederate. **3.** confederation. Also, **Confed.**

Cong. 1. Congregational. **2.** Congregationalist. **3.** Congress. **4.** Congressional.

cong. gallon. [from Latin *congius*]

congr congruent.

coni conical.

conj. 1. conjugation. **2.** conjunction. **3.** conjunctive.

conn connect, connector.

Conn. Connecticut.

conn diag connection diagram.

Cons. 1. Conservative. **2.** Constable. **3.** Constitution. **4.** Consul. **5.** Consulting.

cons. 1. consecrated. **2.** conservative. **3.** (in prescriptions) conserve; keep. [from Latin *conservā*] **4.** consolidated. **5.** consonant. **6.** constable. **7.** construction. **8.** constitutional. **9.** construction. **10.** consul. **11.** consulting.

consec consecutive.

consol. consolidated.

conspec construction specification.

consperg. (in prescriptions) dust; sprinkle. [from Latin *consperge*]

Const. Constitution.

const. 1. constable. **2.** constant. **3.** constitution. **4.** constitutional. **5.** construction.

constr. 1. constraint. **2.** construction. **3.** construed.

cont 1. contact. **2.** continue. **3.** continued. **4.** continuous.

Cont. Continental.

cont. 1. containing. **2.** contents. **3.** continent. **4.** continental. **5.** continue. **6.** continued. **7.** contra. **8.** contract. **9.** contraction. **10.** control. **11.** (in prescriptions) bruised [from Latin *contūsus*].

contd. continued.

contemp. contemporary.

contg. containing.

contin. continued.

contr. 1. contract. 2. contracted. 3. contraction. 4. contractor. 5. contralto. 6. contrary. 7. contrasted. 8. control. 9. controller.

cont. rem. (in prescriptions) let the medicines be continued. [from Latin *continuāntur remedia*]

contrib. 1. contribution. 2. contributor.

contro contracting officer.

conv. 1. convention. 2. conventional. 3. convertible. 4. convocation.

convn convection.

COO chief operating officer.

coop. cooperative. Also, **co-op.**

coord coordinate.

COP *Thermodynamics.* coefficient of performance.

Cop. 1. Copernican. 2. Coptic.

cop. 1. copper. 2. copyright; copyrighted.

COPD chronic obstructive pulmonary disease.

cop pl copper plate.

Cor. 1. *Bible.* Corinthians. 2. Coroner.

cor. 1. corner. 2. cornet. 3. coroner. 4. corpus. 5. correct. 6. corrected. 7. correction. 8. correlative. 9. correspondence. 10. correspondent. 11. corresponding.

CORE (kôr, kōr), Congress of Racial Equality. Also, **C.O.R.E.**

Corn. 1. Cornish. 2. Cornwall.

coroll corollary. Also, **corol.**

corp. 1. corporal. 2. corporation. Also, **Corp.**

corpl corporal. Also, **Corpl.**

corpn. corporation.

corr. 1. correct. 2. corrected. 3. correction. 4. correspond. 5. correspondence. 6. correspondent. 7. corresponding. 8. corrugated. 9. corrupt. 10. corrupted. 11. corruption.

correl. correlative.

corresp. correspondence.

corspnd correspond.

cort. (in prescriptions) the bark. [from Latin *cortex*]

cos *Trigonometry.* cosine.

cos. 1. companies. **2.** consul. **3.** consulship. **4.** counties.

C.O.S. cash on shipment. Also, **c.o.s.**

cosh *Trigonometry.* hyperbolic cosine.

cot 1. *Trigonometry.* cotangent. **2.** cotter pin.

coth *Trigonometry.* hyperbolic cotangent.

cov cutoff valve.

covers *Trigonometry.* coversed sine.

cowl cowling.

COWPS Council on Wage and Price Stability.

CP 1. candlepower. **2.** *Pharmacology.* chemically pure.

cP *Physics.* centipoise. Also, **cp**

cp. 1. camp. **2.** center punch. **3.** cerebral palsy. **4.** clock pulse. **5.** command post. **6.** compare. **7.** constant pressure.

C.P. 1. Chief Patriarch. **2.** command post. **3.** Common Pleas. **4.** Common Prayer. **5.** Communist Party.

c.p. 1. chemically pure. **2.** circular pitch. **3.** command post. **4.** common pleas.

C.P.A. 1. certified public accountant. **2.** chartered public accountant.

CPB Corporation for Public Broadcasting. Also, **C.P.B.**

cpch prop controllable-pitch propeller.

CPCU *Insurance.* Chartered Property and Casualty Underwriter. Also, **C.P.C.U.**

cpd. compound.

CPFF cost plus fixed fee.

CPI 1. consumer price index. **2.** cost plus incentive.

cpi characters per inch.

cpl couple.

cpl. corporal. Also, **Cpl.**

cpld coupled.

cplg coupling.

cplr coupler.

cplry capillary.

CPM 1. *Commerce.* cost per thousand. 2. Critical Path Method.

cpm 1. card per minute. 2. *Commerce.* cost per thousand. 3. critical-path method. 4. cycles per minute.

CP/M *Trademark.* Control Program/Microprocessors: a microcomputer operating system.

c.p.m. *Music.* common particular meter.

cpntr carpenter.

CPO chief petty officer. Also, **C.P.O., c.p.o.**

CPR cardiopulmonary resuscitation.

cprs compress.

cprsn compression.

cprsr compressor.

CPS certified professional secretary.

cps 1. *Computers.* characters per second. 2. cycles per second.

cpse counterpoise.

cpt critical-path technique.

cpt. counterpoint.

CPU *Computers.* central processing unit.

cpunch counterpunch.

CQ 1. *Radio.* a signal sent at the beginning of radiograms. 2. *Military.* charge of quarters.

CR 1. conditioned reflex; conditioned response. 2. consciousness-raising. 3. critical ratio.

Cr *Symbol, Chemistry.* chromium.

cr 1. cold rolled. 2. controlled rectifier. 3. control relay. 4. crystal rectifier. 5. current relay.

cr. 1. credit. 2. creditor. 3. crown.

C.R. 1. Costa Rica. 2. *Banking.* credit report.

CRC Civil Rights Commission.

crc *Computers.* cyclical redundancy check.

crclt circulate.

crcmf circumference.

crctn correction.

cre corrosion-resistant.

Cres. crescent (in addresses).

cres corrosion-resistant steel.

CRF *Biochemistry.* corticotropin releasing factor.

crg carriage.

crim. criminal.

crim. con. *Law.* criminal conversation.

criminol. 1. criminologist. **2.** criminology.

crit. 1. critic. **2.** critical. **3.** criticism. **4.** criticized.

crk crank.

crkc crankcase.

CRM counter-radar measures.

crn 1. crane. **2.** crown.

crnmtr chronometer.

cro cathode-ray oscilloscope.

CRP *Biochemistry.* C-reactive protein.

crp crimp.

crpt carpet.

crs 1. coarse. **2.** cold-rolled steel.

crs. 1. creditors. **2.** credits.

crsn corrosion.

crsv corrosive.

crsvr crossover.

CRT cathode-ray tube.

crtg 1. cartridge. **2.** crating.

crv curve.

cryo cryogenic.

crypta cryptanalysis.

crypto cryptography.

cryst. 1. crystalline. **2.** crystallized. **3.** crystallography.

Cs *Symbol, Chemistry.* cesium.

cS *Physics.* centistoke; centistokes. Also, **cs**

cs 1. case; cases. **2.** cast steel. **3.** control switch. **4.** *Computers.* core shift.

C/S cycles per second.

C.S. 1. chief of staff. **2.** Christian Science. **3.** Christian Scientist. **4.** Civil Service. **5.** Confederate States.

c.s. 1. capital stock. **2.** civil service.

CSA Community Services Administration.

C.S.A. Confederate States of America.

CSC Civil Service Commission.

csc *Trigonometry.* cosecant.

CSCE Conference on Security and Cooperation in Europe.

csch *Trigonometry.* hyperbolic cosecant.

csd *Computers.* core-shift drive.

CSEA Civil Service Employees Association.

CSF *Physiology.* cerebrospinal fluid.

csg casing.

cshaft crankshaft.

csk. 1. cask. **2.** countersink.

cskh countersunk head.

C.S.O. 1. Chief Signal Officer. **2.** Chief Staff Officer. Also, **CSO**

CSP C-SPAN (a cable channel).

C-SPAN (sē′span′), Cable Satellite Public Affairs Network (a cable channel).

CSR 1. Certified Shorthand Reporter. **2.** customer service representative.

csr customer signature required.

CST 1. Also, **C.S.T., c.s.t.** Central Standard Time. **2.** convulsive shock therapy.

cstl castellate.

CSW Certified Social Worker. Also, **C.S.W.**

Cswy. causeway.

CT 1. Central time. **2.** Connecticut (for use with ZIP code).

ct 1. control transformer. **2.** current transformer.

Ct. 1. Connecticut. **2.** Count.

ct. 1. carat; carats. **2.** cent; cents. **3.** centum; hundred. **4.** certificate. **5.** county. **6.** Also, **Ct.** court.

C.T. Central time.

CTA commodities trading adviser.

C.T.A. *Law.* with the will annexed. [from Latin *cum testāmentō annexō*]

CTC 1. centralized traffic control. **2.** Citizens' Training Corps.

ctd coated.

ctf certificate.

ctg. 1. Also, **ctge.** cartage. **2.** cartridge. **3.** coating. **4.** cutting.

CTL 1. *Computers.* complementary transistor logic. **2.** core transistor logic.

ctlry cutlery.

ctlst catalyst.

ct/m count per minute.

ctn *Trigonometry.* cotangent.

ctn. carton.

ctnr container.

c to c center to center.

ctr. 1. center. **2.** contour. **3.** cutter.

ctrfgl centrifugal.

ctrg centering.

ctrl central.

ctrlr controller.

ctrst contrast.

CTS Cleveland Transit System.

cts. 1. centimes. **2.** cents. **3.** certificates.

ct/s count per second.

ctshft countershaft.

CTU centigrade thermal unit. Also, **ctu**

ctwlk catwalk.

ctwt counterweight.

cty county.

CU close-up.

Cu *Symbol, Chemistry.* copper. [from Latin *cuprum*]

cu 1. cubic. **2.** *Electronics.* crystal unit.

Cu. cumulus.

cu. 1. cubic. **2.** cumulus.

cub. 1. cubic. **2.** cubicle.

cu. ft. cubic foot; cubic feet.

cu. in. cubic inch; cubic inches.

cuj. (in prescriptions) of which; of any. [from Latin *cūjus*]

culv culvert.

cu m cubic meter.

cum. cumulative.

cu mm cubic millimeter.

cuo copper oxide.

cup cupboard.

cur. 1. currency. **2.** current.

cust. 1. custodian. **2.** custody. **3.** customer.

cu yd cubic yard.

CV 1. cardiovascular. **2.** Also, **C.V.** curriculum vitae.

cv 1. continuously variable. **2.** Also, **cvt.** convertible. **3.** counter voltage.

CVA 1. *Pathology.* cerebrovascular accident. **2.** Columbia Valley Authority.

CVD *Commerce.* countervailing duty.

CVJ *Automotive.* constant-velocity joint.

cvntl conventional.

C.V.O. Commander of the Royal Victorian Order.

cvr cover.

cvrsn conversion.

CVT continuously variable transmission.

CW 1. chemical warfare. **2.** *Radio.* continuous wave.

cw 1. clockwise. **2.** continuous wave.

c/w complete with.

CWA 1. Civil Works Administration. **2.** Communications Workers of America.

CWO *Military.* chief warrant officer.

c.w.o. cash with order.

CWPS Council on Wage and Price Stability.

cwt hundredweight; hundredweights.

cx control transmitter.

CY calendar year.

Cy. county.

cy. 1. capacity. **2.** currency. **3.** cycle; cycles.

CYA *Slang (sometimes vulgar).* cover your ass.

CYC *Biochemistry.* cyclophosphamide.

cyc. cyclopedia.

cyl. 1. cylinder. **2.** cylindrical.

Cym. Cymric.

CYO Catholic Youth Organization.

Cys *Biochemistry.* cysteine.

cytol. 1. cytological. **2.** cytology.

C.Z. Canal Zone. Also, **CZ**

D

D **1.** *Electricity.* debye. **2.** deep. **3.** depth. **4.** *Optics.* diopter. **5.** divorced. **6.** Dutch.

D *Symbol.* **1.** the fourth in order or in a series. **2.** (in some grading systems) a grade or mark, indicating the quality of a student's work as poor or barely passing. **3.** (*sometimes lowercase*) a classification, rating, or the like, indicating poor quality. **4.** *Music.* **a.** the second tone in the scale of C major, or the fourth tone in the relative minor scale, A minor. **b.** a string, key, or pipe tuned to this tone. **c.** a written or printed note representing this tone. **d.** (in the fixed system of solmization) the second tone of the scale of C major, called *re.* **e.** the tonality having D as the tonic note. **5.** (*sometimes lowercase*) the Roman numeral for 500. **6.** *Chemistry.* deuterium. **7.** *Electricity.* **a.** electric displacement. **b.** a battery size for 1.5 volt dry cells: diameter, 1.3 in. (3.3 cm); length, 2.4 in. (6 cm). **8.** *Biochemistry.* aspartic acid. **9.** a proportional shoe width size, narrower than E and wider than C. **10.** a proportional brassiere cup size, larger than C. **11.** *Physics.* darcy.

D- *Symbol, Biochemistry.* (of a molecule) having a configuration resembling the dextrorotatory isomer of glyceraldehyde: always printed as a small capital, roman character (distinguished from *l-*). Cf. *d-.*

d- *Symbol, Chemistry, Biochemistry.* dextrorotatory; dextro- (distinguished from *l-*). Cf. **D-.**

D. **1.** day. **2.** December. **3.** Democrat. **4.** Democratic. **5.** *Physics.* density. **6.** Deus. **7.** *Bible.* Deuteronomy. **8.** Doctor. **9.** dose. **10.** Dutch.

d. **1.** (in prescriptions) give. [from Latin *dā*] **2.** date. **3.** daughter. **4.** day. **5.** deceased. **6.** deep. **7.** degree. **8.** delete. **9.** *British.* pence. [from Latin *denārii*] **10.** *British.* penny. [from Latin *denārius*] **11.** *Physics.* density. **12.**

depth. **13.** deputy. **14.** dialect. **15.** dialectal. **16.** diameter. **17.** died. **18.** dime. **19.** dividend. **20.** dollar; dollars. **21.** dose. **22.** drachma.

DA 1. Department of Agriculture. **2.** *Dictionary of Americanisms.* **3.** a male hairstyle in which the hair is slicked back on both sides to overlap at the back of the head. [euphemistic abbreviation of *duck's ass*]

da *Telecommunications.* don't answer.

d-a *Electronics.* digital-to-analog.

DA. (in Algeria) dinar; dinars.

da. 1. daughter. **2.** day; days.

D/A *Commerce.* **1.** Also, **d/a.** days after acceptance. **2.** deposit account. **3.** documents against acceptance. **4.** documents for acceptance.

D.A. 1. delayed action. **2.** direct action. **3.** District Attorney. **4.** *Commerce.* documents against acceptance. **5.** *Commerce.* documents for acceptance. **6.** doesn't answer; don't answer.

DAB *Dictionary of American Biography.*

D.A.E. *Dictionary of American English.* Also, **DAE**

dag dekagram; dekagrams.

D.Agr. Doctor of Agriculture.

Dak. Dakota.

dal dekaliter; dekaliters.

dam dekameter; dekameters.

Dan. 1. *Bible.* Daniel. **2.** Also, **Dan** Danish.

D and C *Medicine.* a surgical method for the removal of diseased tissue or an early embryo from the lining of the uterus. [*d(ilation) and c(urettage)*]

D&D drug and disease free.

Danl. Daniel.

DAR Defense Aid Reports.

dar 1. *Military.* defense acquisition radar. **2.** digital audio recording.

D.A.R. Daughters of the American Revolution.

DARE (dâr), *Dictionary of American Regional English.*

DARPA (där′pə), Defense Advanced Research Projects Agency.

DAT digital audiotape.

dat. 1. dative. 2. datum.

datacom (dā′tə kom′), data communication.

dau. daughter.

D.A.V. Disabled American Veterans. Also, **DAV**

DB *Radio and Television.* delayed broadcast.

dB *Physics.* decibel; decibels.

D.B. 1. Bachelor of Divinity. 2. Domesday Book.

d.b. daybook.

DBA doing business as. Also, **dba, d.b.a.**

dBa decibels above reference noise, adjusted. Also, **dba**

d/b/a doing business as.

D.B.A. Doctor of Business Administration.

D.B.E. Dame Commander of the Order of the British Empire.

D.Bib. Douay Bible.

dbl. double.

dblr *Electronics.* doubler.

DBMS *Computers.* Data Base Management System.

DBS *Television.* direct broadcast satellite.

DC 1. dental corps. 2. *Electricity.* direct current. 3. District of Columbia (for use with ZIP code).

dc *Electricity.* 1. Also, **d.c.** direct current. 2. double contact.

D.C. 1. *Music.* da capo. 2. *Dictionary of Canadianisms.* 3. *Electricity.* direct current. 4. District of Columbia. 5. Doctor of Chiropractic.

dcd decode.

dcdr decoder.

DCF divorced Christian female.

D.Ch.E. Doctor of Chemical Engineering.

DCHP *Dictionary of Canadianisms on Historical Principles.*

dckg docking.

dcl door closer.

D.C.L. Doctor of Civil Law.

dclr decelerate.

DCM divorced Christian male.

D.C.M. *British.* Distinguished Conduct Medal.

D.Cn.L. Doctor of Canon Law.

DCPA Defense Civil Preparedness Agency.

D.Crim. Doctor of Criminology.

D.C.S. **1.** Deputy Clerk of Sessions. **2.** Doctor of Christian Science. **3.** Doctor of Commercial Science.

DCTL *Computers.* direct-coupled transistor logic.

DD dishonorable discharge.

dd **1.** *Law.* today's date. [from Latin *dē datō*] **2.** deep-drawn. **3.** degree-day. **4.** delayed delivery. **5.** delivered. **6.** *Banking.* demand draft. **7.** double deck. **8.** *Shipbuilding.* dry dock.

dd. delivered.

D/D *Commerce.* days after date.

D.D. **1.** *Banking.* demand draft. **2.** Doctor of Divinity.

dda digital differential analyzer.

D-day (dē′dā′), **1.** a day set for beginning something. **2.** June 6, 1944, the day the Allies invaded W Europe. Also, **D-Day.**

DDD *Telecommunications.* direct distance dialing.

DDP *Computers.* distributed data processing.

DDR German Democratic Republic. [from German *D(eutsche) D(emokratische) R(epublik)*]

DDS *Pharmacology.* dapsone. [*d(iamino)-d(iphenyl) s(ulfone)*]

D.D.S. **1.** Doctor of Dental Science. **2.** Doctor of Dental Surgery.

D.D.Sc. Doctor of Dental Science.

DDT *Chemistry.* a white, crystalline, water-insoluble solid, $C_{14}H_9Cl_5$, used as an insecticide and as a scabicide and pediculicide. [*d(ichloro)d(iphenyl)t(richloroethane)*]

DE 1. Delaware (for use with ZIP code). **2.** destroyer escort.

de digital encoder.

D.E. 1. Doctor of Engineering. **2.** driver education.

DEA Drug Enforcement Administration.

Dec. December.

dec. 1. (in prescriptions) pour off. [from Latin *dēcantā*] **2.** deceased. **3.** decimal. **4.** decimeter. **5.** declension. **6.** decrease. **7.** *Music.* decrescendo.

decaf. decaffeinated.

decd. deceased.

decn decision.

decompn decompression.

decontn decontamination.

decr decrease.

ded. 1. dedicate. **2.** dedicated. **3.** deduct. **4.** deducted. **5.** deduction.

D.Ed. Doctor of Education.

de d in d (in prescriptions) from day to day. [from Latin *dē diē in diem*]

def. 1. defective. **2.** defense. **3.** definition. Also, **def**

DEFCON (def′kon), any of several alert statuses for U.S. military forces. [*def(ense readiness) con(dition)*]

defl deflect.

defs. definitions.

deg. degree; degrees.

deglut. (in prescriptions) may be swallowed; let it be swallowed. [from Latin *dēglutiātur*]

D.E.I. Dutch East Indies.

Del. Delaware.

del. 1. delegate; delegation. **2.** delete; deletion. **3.** he or she drew this [from Latin *delineavit*].

dele delete.

dely. delivery.

dem demodulator.

Dem. 1. Democrat. **2.** Democratic.

dem. 1. demand. **2.** demonstrative. **3.** demurrage.

demod (dē**'**mod), demodulator.

demux (dē**'**muks), *Telecommunications.* demultiplexer.

den denote.

Den. Denmark.

deng diesal engine.

D.Eng. Doctor of Engineering.

D.Eng.S. Doctor of Engineering Science.

dens density.

dent. 1. dental. **2.** dentist. **3.** dentistry,

dep. 1. depart. **2.** department. **3.** departs. **4.** departure. **5.** deponent. **6.** deposed. **7.** deposit. **8.** depot. **9.** deputy.

depr. 1. depreciation. **2.** depression.

dept. 1. department. **2.** deponent. **3.** deputy.

der. 1. derivation. **2.** derivative. **3.** derive. **4.** derived.

deriv. 1. derivation. **2.** derivative. **3.** derive. **4.** derived.

DES *Pharmacology.* diethylstilbestrol.

des designation.

descr 1. describe. **2.** description.

D. ès L. Doctor of Letters. [from French *Docteur ès Lettres*]

D. ès S. Doctor of Sciences. [from French *Docteur ès Sciences*]

destn destination.

DET 1. Also, **Det** *Linguistics.* determiner. **2.** *Pharmacology.* diethyltryptamine.

det. 1. detach. **2.** detachment. **3.** detail. **4.** detector. **5.** determine. **6.** (in prescriptions) let it be given [from Latin *dētur*].

Deut. *Bible.* Deuteronomy.

dev. 1. development. **2.** deviation.

devel. development.

DEW (doo, dyoo), distant early warning.

DF divorced female.

df 1. direction finder. **2.** dissipation factor.

D/F direction finding. Also, **DF**

D.F. 1. Defender of the Faith. [from Latin *Dē-*

fēnsor Fidēī] **2.** Distrito Federal. **3.** Doctor of Forestry.

D.F.A. Doctor of Fine Arts.

D.F.C. Distinguished Flying Cross.

dfl deflating.

D.F.M. Distinguished Flying Medal.

dfr defrost.

dft drift.

dftg drafting.

dftr deflector.

dftsp draftsperson.

dg decigram; decigrams.

D.G. 1. by the grace of God. [from Latin *Dei grātiā*] **2.** Director General.

dgr degrease.

dgs degaussing system.

dgt digit.

dgtl digital.

DH 1. *Racing.* dead heat. **2.** *Baseball.* designated hitter. Also, **dh**

DH. (in Morocco) dirham; dirhams.

D.H. 1. Doctor of Humanics. **2.** Doctor of Humanities.

DHA *Biochemistry.* an omega-3 fatty acid present in fish oils. [*d(ocosa)h(exaenoic) a(cid)*]

D.H.L. 1. Doctor of Hebrew Letters. **2.** Doctor of Hebrew Literature.

dhmy dehumidify.

dhw double-hung window.

dhyr dehydrator.

DI 1. Department of the Interior. **2.** drill instructor.

Di *Symbol, Chemistry.* didymium.

di. diameter. Also, **dia.**

dia. diameter. Also, **dia**

diag 1. diagonal. **2.** diagram.

Dial. 1. dialect. **2.** dialectal. **3.** dialectic. **4.** dialectical.

diaph diaphragm.

dict. 1. dictation. **2.** dictator. **3.** dictionary.

DID 1. data item description. **2.** *Telecommunications.* direct inward dialing.

dieb. alt. (in prescriptions) every other day. [from Latin *diēbus alternīs*]

dieb. secund. (in prescriptions) every second day. [from Latin *diēbus secundīs*]

dieb. tert. (in prescriptions) every third day. [from Latin *diēbus tertiīs*]

diel dielectric.

dif. 1. difference. **2.** different.

diff. 1. difference. **2.** different. **3.** differential.

dig. digest.

dil 1. dilute. **2.** diluted.

dim. 1. dimension. **2.** (in prescriptions) one-half. [from Latin *dimidius*] **3.** diminish. **4.** *Music.* diminuendo. **5.** diminutive.

dimin. 1. diminish. **2.** *Music.* diminuendo. **3.** diminutive.

DIN (din), *Photography.* a designation, originating in Germany, of the speed of a particular film emulsion. [from German *D(eutsche) I(ndustrie) N(ormen)* German industrial standards (later construed as *Das ist Norm* that is (the) standard), registered mark of the German Institute for Standardization]

Din. (in Yugoslavia) dinar; dinars.

d. in p. aeq. (in prescriptions) let it be divided into equal parts. [from Latin *dividātur in partēs aequālēs*]

dio diode.

dioc. 1. diocesan. **2.** diocese.

diopt *Optics.* diopter.

DIP (dip), *Computers.* a packaged chip that connects to a circuit board by means of pins. [*d(ual) i(n-line) p(ackage)*]

dipl. 1. diplomat. **2.** diplomatic.

diplxr *Electronics.* diplexer.

dir. 1. direct. **2.** direction. **3.** directional. **4.** director. **5.** directory. **6.** direxit.

dir cplr *Electronics.* directional coupler.

direc. prop. (in prescriptions) with a proper direction. [from Latin *directiōne prōpriā*]

DIS The Disney Channel (a cable channel).

dis. 1. distance. **2.** distant. **3.** distribute.

disassm disassemble.

disassy disassembly.

disc. 1. disconnect. **2.** discount. **3.** discovered.

disch discharge.

disp 1. dispatcher. **2.** dispenser.

displ displacement.

dist. 1. distance. **2.** distant. **3.** distinguish. **4.** distinguished. **5.** district.

Dist. Atty. district attorney.

Dist. Ct. District Court.

distn distortion.

distr. 1. distribute. **2.** distribution. **3.** distributor.

div 1. *Mathematics, Mechanics.* divergence. **2.** *Music.* divisi.

Div. 1. divine. **2.** divinity.

div. 1. diverter. **2.** divide. **3.** divided. **4.** dividend. **5.** division. **6.** divisor. **7.** divorced.

div. in par. aeq. (in prescriptions) let it be divided into equal parts. [from Latin *dīvidātur in partēs aequālēs*]

DIY *British.* do-it-yourself. Also, **D.I.Y., d.i.y.**

DIYer (dē′ī/wī′ər), *British.* do-it-yourselfer. Also, **DIY'er.**

D.J. 1. Also, **DJ, d.j.** disc jockey. **2.** District Judge. **3.** Doctor of Law [from Latin *Doctor Jūris*].

DJF divorced Jewish female.

DJM divorced Jewish male.

D.Journ. Doctor of Journalism.

D.J.S. Doctor of Juridical Science.

D.J.T. Doctor of Jewish Theology.

DK *Real Estate.* deck.

dk. 1. dark. **2.** deck. **3.** dock.

dkg dekagram; dekagrams.

dkl dekaliter; dekaliters.

dkm dekameter; dekameters.

DL diesel.

dl 1. data link. **2.** daylight. **3.** dead load. **4.** deciliter; deciliters. **5.** drawing list.

D/L demand loan.

dla data link address.

D. Lit. Doctor of Literature.

D. Litt. Doctor of Letters. [from Latin *Doctor Litterārum*]

D.L.O. dead letter office.

dlr. 1. dealer. **2.** Also, **dlr** dollar.

dlrs. dollars. Also, **dlrs**

D.L.S. Doctor of Library Science.

dlvy delivery.

dlx deluxe.

dly 1. delay. **2.** dolly.

DM 1. Deutsche mark. **2.** divorced male.

dm 1. decimeter; decimeters. **2.** demand meter.

DM. direct mail.

Dm. Deutsche mark.

DMA *Computers.* direct memory access.

dmd demodulate.

D.M.D. Doctor of Dental Medicine. [from Latin *Dentāriae Medicinae Doctor* or *Doctor Medicinae Dentālis*]

DMDT *Chemistry.* methoxychlor. [*d(i)m(eth-oxy)d(iphenyl)t(richloroethane)*]

D.M.L. Doctor of Modern Languages.

dmm *Electricity.* digital multimeter.

DMN *Chemistry.* dimethylnitrosamine. Also, **DMNA**

dmp *Computers.* dot-matrix printer.

dmpr damper.

dmr dimmer.

D.M.S. 1. Director of Medical Services. **2.** Doctor of Medical Science.

DMSO a liquid substance, C_2H_6OS, used in industry as a solvent; proposed as an analgesic and anti-inflammatory. [*d(i)m(ethyl)s(ulf)o(xide)*]

DMT *Pharmacology.* dimethyltryptamine.

D. Mus. Doctor of Music.

DMV Department of Motor Vehicles.

dmx data multiplex.

DMZ demilitarized zone.

dn. down.

DNA *Genetics.* deoxyribonucleic acid: an extremely long macromolecule that is the main component of chromosomes and is the material that transfers genetic characteristics.

dna does not apply.

DNase (dē′en′ās, -āz), deoxyribonuclease: any of several enzymes that break down the DNA molecule. Also, **DNAase.**

D.N.B. *Dictionary of National Biography.*

DNC Democratic National Committee.

DNR 1. *Medicine.* do not resuscitate (used in hospitals and other health-care facilities). **2.** Also, **D.N.R.** do not return.

dntl dental.

do. ditto.

D/O delivery order. Also, **d.o.**

D.O. 1. Also, **DO, d.o.** direct object. **2.** Doctor of Optometry. **3.** Doctor of Osteopathy.

DOA dead on arrival. Also, **D.O.A.**

DOB date of birth. Also, **D.O.B., d.o.b.**

DOC Department of Commerce.

doc. 1. data output channel. **2.** document. **3.** Also, **doc** documentation.

DOD 1. Department of Defense. **2.** *Telecommunications.* direct outward diaing.

DOE 1. Department of Energy. **2.** Also, **d.o.e.** depends on experience; depending on experience (used in stating a salary range in help-wanted ads).

DOHC *Automotive.* double overhead camshaft.

DOI Department of the Interior.

DOJ Department of Justice.

DOL Department of Labor.

dol. 1. *Music.* dolce. **2.** dollar.

dols. dollars.

Dom. 1. Dominica. **2.** Dominican.

dom. 1. domain. **2.** domestic. **3.** dominant. **4.** dominion.

D.O.M. to God, the Best, the Greatest. [from Latin *Deō Optimō Maximō*]

d.o.m. *Slang.* dirty old man.

D.O.P. *Photography.* developing-out paper.

Dor. 1. Dorian. **2.** Doric.

DORAN (dôr′an, dōr′-), an electronic device for determining range and assisting navigation. [*Do(ppler) r(ange) a(nd) n(avigation)*]

DOS (dôs, dos), *Computers.* any of several operating systems, especially for microcomputers, that reside wholly on disk storage. [*d(isk) o(perating) s(ystem)*]

DOS Department of State.

DOT 1. Department of Transportation. **2.** *Dictionary of Occupational Titles.*

DOVAP (dō′vap), *Electronics.* a system for plotting the trajectory of a missile or other rapidly moving object by means of radio waves bounced off it. [*Do(ppler) V(elocity) a(nd) P(osition)*]

Dow. dowager.

doz. dozen; dozens.

DP 1. data processing. **2.** displaced person.

dp 1. dashpot: relay. **2.** data processing. **3.** deflection plate. **4.** depth. **5.** dial pulsing. **6.** *Baseball.* double play; double plays. **7.** *Electricity.* double-pole. **8.** dripproof.

D/P documents against payment.

D.P. 1. data processing. **2.** displaced person.

d.p. (in prescriptions) with a proper direction. [from Latin *dīrēctiōne prōpriā*]

D.P.A. Doctor of Public Administration.

DPC Defense Plant Corporation.

dpdt *Electricity.* double-pole double-throw.

dpg damping.

DPH Department of Public Health.

D. Ph. Doctor of Philosophy.

D.P.H. Doctor of Public Health.

dpi *Computers.* dots per inch.

DPL diplomat.

D.P.M. Doctor of Podiatric Medicine.

D.P.P. *Insurance.* deferred payment plan.

D.P.S. Doctor of Public Service.

dpst *Electricity.* double-pole single-throw.

dpstk dipstick.

DPT diphtheria, pertussis, and tetanus: a mixed vaccine used for primary immunization. Also, **DTP**

dpt. 1. department. 2. deponent.

D.P.W. Department of Public Works. Also, **DPW**

dpx duplex.

DQ disqualify.

DR *Real Estate.* dining room.

Dr *Chiefly British.* Doctor.

dr 1. dead reckoning. 2. door. 3. *Electronics.* drain. 4. dram; drams. 5. drill. 6. drive.

Dr. 1. Doctor. 2. Drive (used in street names).

dr. 1. debit. 2. debtor. 3. drachma; drachmas. 4. dram; drams. 5. drawer. 6. drum.

D.R. 1. Daughters of the (American) Revolution. 2. *Navigation.* dead reckoning. 3. Dutch Reformed.

dram detection-radar automatic monitoring.

dram. pers. *Theater.* dramatis personae.

drch. drachma; drachmas. Also, **dr.**

D.R.E. 1. Director of Religious Education. 2. Doctor of Religious Education.

dri dead-reckoning indicator.

drsg dressing.

DRTL *Computers.* diode resistor transistor logic.

D.R.V. (on food labels) Daily Reference Value: the amount of nutrients appropriate for one day.

drvr driver.

drzl drizzle.

Ds *Symbol, Chemistry.* (formerly) dysprosium.

ds 1. diode switch. 2. domestic service.

D.S. 1. *Music.* from the sign. [from Italian *dal segno*] 2. Doctor of Science.

d.s. 1. daylight saving. **2.** *Commerce*. Also, **D/S** days after sight. **3.** document signed.

DSA *Medicine*. digital subtraction angiography.

dsb *Electronics*. double sideband.

dsbl disable.

DSC 1. The Discovery Channel (a cable channel). **2.** Defense Supplies Corporation.

D.Sc. Doctor of Science.

D.S.C. 1. Distinguished Service Cross. **2.** Doctor of Surgical Chiropody.

dscc dessicant.

dscont discontinue.

dscrm *Electronics*. discriminator.

dsd *Computers*. dual-scan display.

dsdd *Computers*. double-side, double-density.

dsgn design.

dshd *Computers*. double-side, high density.

dsl diesel.

dsltr desalter.

dslv dissolve.

D.S.M. 1. Distinguished Service Medal. **2.** Doctor of Sacred Music.

DSNA Dictionary Society of North America.

D.S.O. Distinguished Service Order.

dsp *Computers*. digital signal processing.

D.S.P. died without issue. [from Latin *dēcessit sine prōle*]

dspec design specification.

dspl display.

dspo disposal.

DSR *Medicine*. dynamic spatial reconstructor.

D.S.S. Doctor of Social Science.

dssd *Computers*. double-side, single-density.

DST daylight-saving time.

D.S.T. 1. daylight-saving time. **2.** Doctor of Sacred Theology.

dstlt distillate.

dstng distinguish.

DSU disk storage unit.

D. Surg. Dental Surgeon.

D.S.W. 1. Doctor of Social Welfare. **2.** Doctor of Social Work.

DT *Slang.* detective. Also, **D.T.**

dt 1. decay time. **2.** double throw.

dtd dated.

d.t.d. (in prescriptions) give such doses. [from Latin *dentur tālēs dosēs*]

D.Th. Doctor of Theology. Also, **D.Theol.**

DTL *Computers.* diode transistor logic.

dtl detail.

dtmf *Telecommunications.* dual-tone multifrequency.

DTP 1. desktop publishing. **2.** diphtheria, tetanus, and pertussis. See **DPT.**

dtrbd *Computers.* daughterboard.

dtrs distress.

d.t.'s (dē′tēz′), *Pathology.* delirium tremens.

dtv digital television.

dty cy duty cycle.

Du. 1. Duke. **2.** Dutch.

DUI driving under the influence.

dulc. (in prescriptions) sweet. [from Latin *dulcis*]

dupl duplicate.

duplxr duplexer.

dut *Electronics.* device under test.

D.V. 1. God willing. [from Latin *D(eo) v(olente)*] **2.** Douay Version (of the Bible).

dvc device.

dvl develop.

D.V.M. Doctor of Veterinary Medicine. Also, **DVM**

D.V.M.S. Doctor of Veterinary Medicine and Surgery.

dvr diver.

D.V.S. Doctor of Veterinary Surgery.

dvt deviate.

DW *Real Estate.* dishwasher.

dw 1. dishwasher. **2.** distilled water. **3.** double weight.

D/W *Law.* dock warrant.

dwg drawing.

DWI driving while intoxicated.
dwl dowel.
DWM *Slang.* dead white male.
dwn drawn.
dwr drawer.
DWT deadweight tons; deadweight tonnage.
dwt 1. deadweight tons; deadweight tonnage.
  2. pennyweight; pennyweights.
d.w.t. deadweight tons; deadweight tonnage.
DX *Radio.* distance. Also, **D.X.**
Dx diagnosis.
dx duplex.
Dy *Symbol, Chemistry.* dysprosium.
dyn 1. dynamic. 2. *Physics.* dyne; dynes.
dyn. dynamics. Also, **dynam.**
dynm dynamotor.
dynmm dynamometer.
dynmt dynamite.
DZ drop zone.
dz. dozen; dozens.

E

E 1. east. **2.** eastern. **3.** English. **4.** excellent. **5.** Expressway.

E *Symbol.* **1.** the fifth in order or in a series. **2.** (in some grading systems) a grade or mark, indicating the quality of a student's work is in need of improvement in order to be passing. **3.** *Music.* **a.** the third tone in the scale of C major or the fifth tone in the relative minor scale, A minor. **b.** a string, key, or pipe tuned to this tone. **c.** a written or printed note representing this tone. **d.** (in the fixed system of solmization) the third tone of the scale of C major, called *mi.* **e.** the tonality having E as the tonic note. **4.** (*sometimes lowercase*) the medieval Roman numeral for 250. **5.** *Physics, Electricity.* **a.** electric field. **b.** electric field strength. **6.** *Physics.* energy. **7.** *Biochemistry.* glutamic acid. **8.** *Logic.* universal negative. **9.** a proportional shoe width size, narrower than EE and wider than D.

e 1. electron. **2.** *Physics.* elementary charge.

E. 1. Earl. **2.** Earth. **3.** east. **4.** Easter. **5.** eastern. **6.** engineer. **7.** engineering. **8.** English.

e. 1. eldest. **2.** *Football.* end. **3.** engineer. **4.** engineering. **5.** entrance. **6.** *Baseball.* error; errors.

ea. each.

E.A.A. Engineer in Aeronautics and Astronautics.

ead. (in prescriptions) the same. [from Latin *eādem*]

EAM National Liberation Front, a Greek underground resistance movement and political coalition of World War II. [from Modern Greek *E(thnikō) A(pelevtherōtikò) M(étōpo)*]

EAP employee assistance program.

eax electronic automatic exchange.

EB Epstein-Barr (syndrome).

EBCDIC (eb′sē dik′), *n. Computers.* a code

used for data representation and transfer. [*e(xtended)* *b(inary-)c(oded)* *d(ecimal)* *i(nterchange)* *c(ode)*]

EbN east by north.

EbS east by south.

EBV Epstein-Barr virus.

EC European Community.

E.C. 1. Engineering Corps. **2.** Established Church.

e.c. for the sake of example. [from Latin *exempli causā*]

ECA Economic Cooperation Administration. Also, **E.C.A.**

ECC *Computers.* error-correction code.

ecc eccentric.

Eccl. *Bible.* Ecclesiastes. Also, **Eccles.**

eccl. ecclesiastic; ecclesiastical. Also, **eccles.**

Ecclus. *Bible.* Ecclesiasticus.

ECCM *Military.* electronic countermeasures.

ecd estimated completion date.

ECF extended-care facility.

ECG 1. electrocardiogram. **2.** electrocardiograph.

ech echelon.

ECL *Computers.* emitter-coupled logic.

ECM 1. electronic countermeasures. **2.** European Common Market.

ecn engineering change notice.

eco 1. electron-coupled oscillator. **2.** engineering change notice.

ecol. 1. ecological. **2.** ecology.

E. co·li (ē′ kō′lī), *Escherichia coli,* an anaerobic bacterium.

econ. 1. economic. **2.** economics. **3.** economy.

ecp engineering change proposal.

ecr engineering change request.

ECT electroconvulsive therapy.

ECU (ā ko͞o′ *or, sometimes,* ē′sē′yo͞o′), a money of account of the European Common Market used in international finance.

[*E(uropean) C(urrency) U(nit)*, perhaps with play on *écu*, an old French coin]

E.C.U. English Church Union.

ED Department of Education.

ED$_{50}$ *Pharmacology.* effective dose for 50 percent of the group.

ed. 1. edited. 2. edition. 3. editor. 4. education.

E.D. 1. Eastern Department. 2. election district. 3. *Finance.* ex dividend. 4. executive director.

EDA Economic Development Administration.

edac error detection correction.

EDB *Chemistry.* a colorless liquid, $C_2H_4Br_2$, used as an organic solvent, gasoline additive, pesticide, and soil fumigant. [*e(thylene) d(i)b(romide)*]

Ed.B. Bachelor of Education.

EDC European Defense Community.

Ed.D. Doctor of Education.

EDES Hellenic National Democratic army, a Greek resistance coalition in World War II. [from Modern Greek *E(thnikós) D(ēmokratikós) E(llēnikós) S(yndésmos)*]

edit. 1. edited. 2. edition. 3. editor.

Ed.M. Master of Education.

EDP *Computers.* electronic data processing.

eds. 1. editions. 2. editors.

Ed.S. Education Specialist.

EDT Eastern daylight time. Also, **E.D.T.**

EDTA *Chemistry., Pharmacology.* a colorless compound, $C_{10}H_{16}N_2O_8$, with a variety of medical and other uses. [*e(thylene)-d(iamine)t(etraacetic) a(cid)*]

edtn edition.

edtr editor.

educ. 1. educated. 2. education. 3. educational.

E.E. 1. Early English. 2. electrical engineer. 3. electrical engineering.

e.e. errors excepted.

E.E. & M.P. Envoy Extraordinary and Minister Plenipotentiary.

EEC European Economic Community.

EEG 1. electroencephalogram. 2. electroencephalograph.

EENT *Medicine.* eye, ear, nose, and throat.

EEO equal employment opportunity.

EEOC Equal Employment Opportunity Commission.

eeprom *Electronics.* electronically erasable programmable read-only memory.

EER energy efficiency ratio.

ef emitter follower.

eff. 1. effect. 2. effective. 3. efficiency.

EFI electronic fuel injection.

EFL English as a foreign language.

efl 1. effluent. 2. *Photography.* equivalent focal length.

EFM electronic fetal monitor.

efph equivalent full-power hour.

EFT electronic funds transfer. Also, **EFTS**

EFTA European Free Trade Association.

EFTS electronic funds transfer system.

Eg. 1. Egypt. 2. Egyptian.

e.g. for example; for the sake of example; such as. [from Latin *exemplī grātiā*]

EGA *Computers.* enhanced graphics adapter.

EGmc East Germanic.

EGR *Automotive.* exhaust-gas recirculation.

EHF extremely high frequency. Also, **ehf**

EHS Environmental Health Services.

EHV extra high voltage.

E.I. 1. East Indian. 2. East Indies.

EIA Electronic Industries Association.

E. Ind. East Indian.

EIR Environmental Impact Report.

EIS Environmental Impact Statement.

EISA *Computers.* extended industry standard architecture.

EJ (ē′jā′), 1. electronic journalism. 2. electronic journalist.

ejn ejection.

ejtr ejector.

EKG 1. electrocardiogram. **2.** electrocardio-graph. [from German *E(lectro)k(ardio)g(ramme)*]

el. 1. electroluminescent. **2.** elevation.

E.L.A.S. Hellenic People's Army of Liberation, Greek resistance force in World War II. [from Modern Greek *E(thnikòs) L(aikòs) A(peleutherōtikòs) S(tratós)*]

elb elbow.

elctd electrode.

elctlt electrolyte; electrolytic.

elctrn electron.

elctrochem electrochemical.

Elect. 1. electric. **2.** electrical. **3.** electrician. **4.** electricity. Also, **elec.**

elek electronic.

elem. 1. element; elements. **2.** elementary.

elev. 1. elevation. **2.** elevator.

elex electronics.

ELF extremely low frequency. Also, **elf**

elim eliminate.

ELISA (i li′zə, -sə), **1.** *Medicine.* a diagnostic test for past or current exposure to an infec-tious agent, as the AIDS virus. **2.** *Biology, Medicine.* any similar test using proteins as a probe for the identification of antibodies or antigens. [*e(nzyme-)l(inked) i(mmuno)s(orbent) a(ssay)*]

elix. (in prescriptions) elixir.

Eliz. Elizabethan.

elmech electromechanical.

elng elongate.

e. long. east longitude.

elp elliptical.

elpneu electropneumatic.

elvn elevation.

EM 1. electromagnetic. **2.** electromotive. **3.** electronic mail. **4.** electron microscope. **5.** electron microscopy. **6.** end matched. **7.** En-gineer of Mines. **8.** enlisted man; enlisted men.

Em *Symbol, Physical Chemistry.* emanation.

em 1. electromagnetic. **2.** enlisted men.

E.M. 1. Earl Marshal. **2.** Engineer of Mines.

e-mail (ē′māl′), electronic mail. Also, **E-mail.**

emb emboss.

embryol. embryology.

emer emergency.

E.Met. Engineer of Metallurgy.

emf electromotive force. Also, **EMF, E.M.F., e.m.f.**

EMG 1. electromyogram. **2.** electromyograph. **3.** electromyography.

emi electromagnetic interference.

EMP *Physics.* electromagnetic pulse.

Emp. 1. Emperor. **2.** Empire. **3.** Empress.

emp. (in prescriptions) a plaster. [from Latin *emplastrum*]

e.m.p. (in prescriptions) after the manner prescribed; as directed. [from Latin *ex mōdō praescriptō*]

empl employee.

EMS 1. emergency medical service. **2.** European Monetary System.

ems electromagnetic surveillance.

emsn emission.

EMT emergency medical technician.

emtr *Electronics.* emitter.

EMU 1. Also, **emu** electromagnetic unit; electromagnetic units. **2.** *Aerospace.* extravehicular mobility unit.

emuls. (in prescriptions) an emulsion. [from Latin *ēmulsiō*]

enam enamel.

enbl enable.

enc. 1. enclosed. **2.** enclosure. **3.** encyclopedia.

encap encapsulate.

encd encode.

encl. 1. enclosed. **2.** enclosure.

encsd encased.

ency. encyclopedia. Also, **encyc., encycl.**

end. endorsed.

ENE east-northeast. Also, **E.N.E.**

ENG *Television.* electronic news gathering.

Eng. 1. England. **2.** English.

eng. 1. engine. **2.** engineer. **3.** engineering. **4.** engraved. **5.** engraver. **6.** engraving.

enga engage.

Eng. D. Doctor of Engineering.

engr. 1. engineer. **2.** engraved. **3.** engraver. **4.** engraving.

engrg engineering.

engrv engrave.

engy energy.

enl. 1. enlarge. **2.** enlarged. **3.** enlisted.

enlg enlarge.

enrgz energize.

Ens. Ensign.

ensi (en/sē), equivalent-noise-sideband-input.

ENT *Medicine.* ear, nose, and throat.

entomol. 1. entomological. **2.** entomology. Also, **entom.**

entr 1. enter. **2.** entrance.

enum enumerate, enumeration.

env. envelope.

envr 1. environment. **2.** environmental.

EO executive order.

e.o. ex officio.

EOB Executive Office Building.

EOE 1. equal-opportunity employer. **2.** *Disparaging.* an employee who is considered to have been hired only to satisfy equal-opportunity regulations.

EOF *Computers.* end-of-file.

EOG electrooculogram.

eolm electrooptical light modulator.

eom end of message.

e.o.m. *Chiefly Commerce.* end of the month. Also, **E.O.M.**

EOP Executive Office of the President.

eot end of tape.

EP 1. European plan. **2.** extended play (of phonograph records).

Ep. *Bible.* Epistle.

EPA 1. Environmental Protection Agency. **2.** an omega-3 fatty acid present in fish oils. [*e(icosa)p(entaenoic) a(cid)*]

Eph. *Bible.* Ephesians. Also, **Ephes., Ephs.**

Epiph. Epiphany.

Epis. 1. Episcopal. **2.** Episcopalian. **3.** *Bible.* Epistle.

Episc. 1. Episcopal. **2.** Episcopalian.

Epist. *Bible.* Epistle.

epit. 1. epitaph. **2.** epitome.

EPROM (ē'prom), *Computers.* a memory chip whose contents can be erased and reprogramed. [*e(rasable) p(rogrammable) r(ead)-o(nly) m(emory)*]

EPS earnings per share.

EPT excess-profits tax.

ept external pipe thread.

epu emergency power unit.

EQ educational quotient.

eq. 1. equal. **2.** equation. **3.** equivalent.

eql equal, equally.

eqlz 1. equalize. **2.** equalizer.

eqpt. equipment.

equil equilibrium.

equip. equipment.

equiv. equivalent.

ER 1. efficiency report. **2.** emergency room.

Er *Symbol, Chemistry.* erbium.

E.R. 1. East Riding (Yorkshire). **2.** East River (New York City). **3.** King Edward. [from Latin *Edwardus Rex*] **4.** Queen Elizabeth. [from Latin *Elizabeth Regina*] **5.** emergency room.

ERA 1. Also, **era** *Baseball.* earned run average. **2.** Emergency Relief Administration. **3.** Equal Rights Amendment.

ercg erecting.

erct erection.

ERG electroretinogram.

ERIC Educational Resources Information Center.

ERISA (ə ris'ə), Employee Retirement Income Security Act.

ERP European Recovery Program. Also, **E.R.P.**

errc error correction.

erron. 1. erroneous. 2. erroneously.

ERS Emergency Radio Service. Also, **E.R.S.**

ers 1. erase. 2. erased.

ERTS Earth Resources Technology Satellite.

E.R.V. English Revised Version (of the Bible).

Es *Symbol, Chemistry.* einsteinium.

es electrostatic.

E.S. Education Specialist.

ESA European Space Agency.

Esc. (in Portugal and several other nations) escudo; escudos.

esc. 1. escape. 2. escrow.

escl escalator.

esct escutcheon.

Esd. *Bible.* Esdras.

ESDI (es/dē), *Computers.* enhanced small device interface.

ESE east-southeast. Also, **E.S.E.**

esk engineering sketch.

Esk. Eskimo.

ESL English as a second language.

ESOL (ē/sôl, es/əl), English for speakers of other languages.

ESOP (ē/sop), a plan under which a company's stock is acquired by its employees or workers. [*E(mployee) S(tock) O(wnership) P(lan)*]

ESP extrasensory perception.

esp. especially.

espec. especially.

ESPN the Entertainment Sports Network (a cable channel).

Esq. Esquire. Also, **Esqr.**

ESR 1. erythrocyte sedimentation rate: the rate at which red blood cells settle in a column of blood, serving as a diagnostic test. 2. electron spin resonance.

ess electronic switching system.

EST Eastern Standard Time. Also, **E.S.T., e.s.t.**

est. 1. established. **2.** estate. **3.** estimate. **4.** estimated. **5.** estuary.

estab. established.

Esth. 1. *Bible.* Esther. **2.** Esthonia.

esu electrostatic unit.

Et *Symbol, Chemistry.* ethyl.

E.T. 1. Eastern time. **2.** extraterrestrial. Also, **ET**

e.t. electrical transcription.

E.T.A. estimated time of arrival. Also, **ETA**

et al. (et alʹ, älʹ, ôlʹ), **1.** and elsewhere. [from Latin *et alibi*] **2.** and others. [from Latin *et alii*]

etc. et cetera.

E.T.D. estimated time of departure. Also, **ETD**

Eth. Ethiopia.

ethnog. ethnography.

ethnol. 1. ethnological. **2.** ethnology.

ethol. ethology.

ETI extraterrestrial intelligence.

eti elapsed-time indicator.

ETO (in World War II) European Theater of Operations. Also, **E.T.O.**

e to e end to end.

etr estimated time of return.

Etr. Etruscan.

ETS *Trademark.* Educational Testing Service.

et seq. *plural* **et seqq., et sqq.** and the following. [from Latin *et sequēns*]

et seqq. and those following. Also, **et sqq.** [from Latin *et sequentēs, et sequentia*]

et ux. *Chiefly Law.* and wife. [from Latin *et uxor*]

ETV educational television.

etvm electrostatic transistorized voltmeter.

ety. etymology.

etym. 1. etymological. **2.** etymology. Also, **etymol.**

Eu *Symbol, Chemistry.* europium.

Eur. 1. Europe. **2.** European.

eV *Physics.* electron-volt. Also, **ev**

E.V. English Version (of the Bible).

EVA *Aerospace.* extravehicular activity.

evac evacuation.

eval evaluation.

evap. 1. evaporate. 2. evaporation.

evg. evening.

evm electronic voltmeter.

evom electronic voltohmmeter.

EW 1. electronic warfare. 2. enlisted women.

Ex. *Bible.* Exodus.

ex. 1. examination. 2. examined. 3. example. 4. except. 5. exception. 6. exchange. 7. excursion. 8. executed. 9. executive. 10. express. 11. extra.

exam. 1. examination. 2. examined. 3. examinee. 4. examiner.

Exc. Excellency.

exc. 1. excellent. 2. except. 3. exception. 4. he or she printed or engraved (this). [from Latin *excudit*] 5. excursion.

exch. 1. exchange. 2. exchequer. Also **Exch.**

excl. 1. exclamation. 2. excluding. 3. exclusive.

exclam. 1. exclamation. 2. exclamatory.

excsv excessive.

exctr exciter.

excud. he or she printed or engraved (this). [from Latin *excudit*]

Ex. Doc. executive document.

exec. 1. executive. 2. executor.

exer exercise.

exh 1. exhaust. 2. exhibit.

ex int. *Stock Exchange.* ex interest.

ex lib. from the library of. [from Latin *ex libris*]

Exod. *Bible.* Exodus.

ex off. by virtue of office or position. [from Latin *ex officio*]

exor. executor.

exp 1. expand. 2. expansion. 3. experiment. 4. expose. 5. expulsion.

exp. 1. expenses. 2. experience. 3. expired.

    4. exponential. **5.** export. **6.** exported. **7.** exporter. **8.** express.

exped expedite.

expen expendable.

exp jt expansion joint.

expl 1. explain. **2.** explanation.

expld explode.

expln explosion.

expnt 1. exponent. **2.** exponential.

expo exposition.

expr express.

expsr exposure.

expt. experiment.

exptl. experimental.

Expy. expressway.

exr. executor.

exstg existing.

ext. 1. extension. **2.** exterior. **3.** external. **4.** extinct. **5.** extinguish. **6.** extra. **7.** extract.

extd. 1. extended. **2.** extrude.

extm extreme.

extn. 1. extension. **2.** external.

extnr extinguisher.

extr. 1. exterior. **2.** extract.

eylt eyelet.

eypc eyepiece.

Ez. *Bible.* Ezra. Also, **Ezr.**

Ezek. *Bible.* Ezekiel.

F

F 1. Fahrenheit. **2.** female. **3.** *Genetics.* filial. **4.** firm. **5.** franc; francs. **6.** French.

F *Symbol.* **1.** the sixth in order or in a series. **2.** (in some grading systems) a grade or mark that indicates academic work of the lowest quality; failure. **3.** *Music.* **a.** the fourth tone in the scale of C major or the sixth tone in the relative minor scale, A minor. **b.** a string, key, or pipe tuned to this tone. **c.** a written or printed note representing this tone. **d.** (in the fixed system of solmization) the fourth tone of the scale of C major, called *fa.* **e.** the tonality having F as the tonic note. **4.** (*sometimes lowercase*) the medieval Roman numeral for 40. **5.** *Math* **a.** field. **b.** function (of). **6.** (*sometimes lowercase*) *Electricity.* farad. **7.** *Chemistry.* fluorine. **8.** (*sometimes lowercase*) *Physics.* **a.** force. **b.** frequency. **c.** fermi. **9.** *Biochemistry.* phenylalanine.

f 1. firm. **2.** *Photography.* f-number. **3.** *Music.* forte.

f *Symbol, Optics.* focal length.

F- *Military.* (in designations of aircraft) fighter: *F-105.*

F. 1. Fahrenheit. **2.** February. **3.** Fellow. **4.** (in Hungary) forint; forints. **5.** franc; francs. **6.** France. **7.** French. **8.** Friday.

f. 1. (in prescriptions) make. [from Latin *fac*] **2.** farad. **3.** farthing. **4.** father. **5.** fathom. **6.** feet. **7.** female. **8.** feminine. **9.** (in prescriptions) let them be made. [from Latin *fiant*] **10.** (in prescriptions) let it be made. [from Latin *fiat*] **11.** filly. **12.** fine. **13.** fluid (ounce). **14.** folio. **15.** following. **16.** foot. **17.** form. **18.** formed of. **19.** franc. **20.** from. **21.** *Math.* function (of). **22.** (in the Netherlands) guilder; guilders.

f/ *Photography.* f-number. Also, **f/, f:**

fa 1. final assembly. **2.** forced air.

FAA Federal Aviation Administration.

F.A.A.A.S. 1. Fellow of the American Academy of Arts and Sciences. **2.** Fellow of the American Association for the Advancement of Science.

fab fabricate.

fabx fire alarm box.

fac. 1. facsimile. **2.** factor. **3.** factory. **4.** faculty.

facil facility.

F.A.C.P. Fellow of the American College of Physicians. Also, **FACP**

FACS 1. *Biology.* fluorescence-activated cell sorter. **2.** Also, **F.A.C.S.** Fellow of the American College of Surgeons.

facsim. facsimile.

FAdm Fleet Admiral.

Fahr. Fahrenheit (thermometer). Also, **Fah.**

F.A.L.N. Armed Forces of National Liberation: a militant underground organization whose objective is independence for Puerto Rico. Also, **FALN** [from Spanish *F(uerzas) A(rmadas) de) L(iberación) N(acional)*]

FAM The Family Channel (a cable television station).

fam. 1. familiar. **2.** family.

F.A.M. Free and Accepted Masons. Also, **F. & A.M.**

F. & T. *Insurance.* fire and theft.

FAO Food and Agriculture Organization.

F.A.Q. *Australian.* fair average quality. Also, **f. a.q.**

f/a ratio fuel-air ratio.

FAS 1. fetal alcohol syndrome. **2.** Foreign Agricultural Service.

F.A.S. *Commerce.* free alongside ship: without charge to the buyer for goods delivered alongside ship. Also, **f.a.s., fas**

FASB Financial Accounting Standards Board.

fath. fathom.

fax (faks), facsimile.

f.b. 1. freight bill. **2.** *Sports.* fullback.

F.B.A. Fellow of the British Academy.

FBI *U.S. Government.* Federal Bureau of Investigation.

fbk firebrick.

fbm foot board measure.

FBO for the benefit of. Also, **F/B/O**

fbr fiber.

fbrbd fiberboard.

FC foot-candle; footcandles. Also, **fc**

fc 1. *Computers.* ferrite core. 2. file cabinet. 3. fire control.

f.c. 1. *Baseball.* fielder's choice. 2. *Printing.* follow copy.

FCA Farm Credit Administration.

FCC *U.S. Government.* Federal Communications Commission.

fcg facing.

FCIA Foreign Credit Insurance Association.

FCIC Federal Crop Insurance Corporation.

fcp. foolscap.

fcr fuse current rating.

fcs. francs.

fcsg focusing.

fcsle forecastle.

fctn function.

fctnl functional.

fcty factory.

fcy. fancy.

fd feed.

F.D. 1. Defender of the Faith. [from Latin *Fidei Defensor*] 2. fire department. 3. focal distance.

fdb field dynamic braking.

fdbk feedback.

fdc 1. fire department connection. 2. *Computers.* floppy-disk controller.

fdd *Computers.* floppy-disk drive.

fddl frequency-division data link.

Fdg *Banking.* funding.

FDIC Federal Deposit Insurance Corporation.

fdm frequency-division multiplex.

fdn foundation.

fdp *Hardware.* full dog point.

FDR Franklin Delano Roosevelt.

fdr 1. feeder. **2.** finder. **3.** fire door.

fdry foundry.

fd svc food service.

fdx *Telecommunications.* full duplex.

Fe *Symbol, Chemistry.* iron. [from Latin *ferrum*]

fe. he or she has made it. [from Latin *fecit*]

FEB Fair Employment Board.

Feb. February.

Fed. Federal.

fed. 1. federal. **2.** federated. **3.** federation.

fedn. federation.

Fed. Res. Bd. Federal Reserve Board.

Fed. Res. Bk. Federal Reserve Bank.

felr feeler.

FeLV feline leukemia virus.

fem. 1. female. **2.** feminine.

FEMA Federal Emergency Management Agency.

FEPA Fair Employment Practices Act.

FEPC Fair Employment Practices Commission.

FERA Federal Emergency Relief Administration.

FERC Federal Energy Regulatory Commission.

FET 1. *Banking.* federal estate tax. **2.** *Electronics.* field-effect transistor.

F.E.T. Federal Excise Tax.

fext fire extinguisher.

ff 1. flip-flop. **2.** folios. **3.** (and the) following (pages, verses, etc.). **4.** *Music.* fortissimo.

FFA Future Farmers of America.

F.F.A. *Commerce.* free from alongside (ship). Also, **f.f.a.**

FFC 1. Foreign Funds Control. **2.** free from chlorine.

F.F.I. free from infection.

ffilh *Hardware.* flat fillister head.

ffrr full frequency-range recording.

F.F.V. First Families of Virginia.

ffwd fast forward.

f.g. *Basketball, Football.* field goal; field goals.

fgd forged.

fgn. foreign.

FGP Foster Grandparent Program.

FGT federal gift tax.

fgy foggy.

FH *Pathology.* familial hypercholesterolemia.

fh fire hose.

FHA 1. Farmers' Home Administration. **2.** Federal Housing Administration. **3.** Future Homemakers of America.

FHLB Federal Home Loan Bank.

FHLBA Federal Home Loan Bank Administration.

FHLBB Federal Home Loan Bank Board.

FHLBS Federal Home Loan Bank System.

FHLMC Federal Home Loan Mortgage Corporation.

FHWA Federal Highway Administration.

fhy fire hydrant.

F.I. Falkland Islands.

FIA Federal Insurance Administration.

fict. fiction.

fid. fiduciary.

FIDO (fī/dō), *Aeronautics.* a system for evaporating the fog above airfield runways. [*f(og) i(nvestigation) d(ispersal) o(perations)*]

FIFO (fī/fō), *n.* **1.** *Commerce.* first-in, first-out. **2.** *Computers.* a storage and retrieval technique, in which the first item stored is also the first item retrieved.

fig. 1. figurative. **2.** figuratively. **3.** figure; figures.

FIIG (fig), Federal Item Identification Guide.

fil 1. filament. **2.** *Hardware.* fillister.

filh *Hardware.* fillister head.

filt. (in prescriptions) filter. [from Latin *filtrā*]

Fin. 1. Finland. **2.** Finnish.

fin. 1. finance. **2.** financial. **3.** finish.

fin. sec. financial secretary.

F.I.O. *Commerce.* free in and out: a term of

contract in which a ship charterer pays for loading and unloading.

FIT *Banking.* Federal Insurance Tax.

fk fork.

FL 1. Florida (for use with ZIP code). **2.** foreign language.

fL *Optics.* foot-lambert.

fl 1. *Sports.* flanker. **2.** flashing. **3.** flat. **4.** flush. **5.** focal length.

Fl. 1. Flanders. **2.** Flemish.

fl. 1. floor. **2.** florin; florins. **3.** flourished. [from Latin *flōruit*] **4.** fluid. **5.** (in the Netherlands) guilder; guilders. [from Dutch *florin*]

Fla. Florida.

flav. (in prescriptions) yellow. [from Latin *flāvus*]

F.L.B. Federal Land Bank.

fld. 1. field. **2.** fluid.

fldg folding.

fl dr fluid dram; fluid drams.

fldt floodlight.

fldxt (in prescriptions) fluidextract. [from Latin *fluidextractum*]

FLETC Federal Law Enforcement Training Center.

flex flexible.

flg 1. flange. **2.** flooring.

flh flathead.

fll frequency-locked loop.

flld full load.

flm flame.

flmb flammable.

flmt flush mount.

fln fuel line.

FLOPS (flops), *Computers.* floating-point operations per second.

flor. flourished. [from Latin *flōruit*]

flot flotation.

fl. oz. fluid ounce; fluid ounces.

flr 1. failure. **2.** filler. **3.** floor.

FLRA Federal Labor Relations Authority.

flrt flow rate.

flry flurry.

flt 1. flashlight. **2.** flight. **3.** float.

fltg floating.

fltr 1. filter. **2.** flutter.

fluor fluorescent.

flusoch fluted socket head.

flv flush valve.

flw flat washer.

flwp followup.

flywhl flywheel.

FM 1. Federated States of Micronesia (approved for postal use). **2.** *Electronics.* frequency modulation: a method of impressing a signal on a radio carrier wave. **3.** *Radio.* a system of radio broadcasting by means of frequency modulation.

Fm *Symbol, Chemistry.* fermium.

fm 1. *Symbol, Physics.* femtometer. **2.** field manual.

fm. 1. fathom; fathoms. **2.** from.

f.m. (in prescriptions) make a mixture. [from Latin *fiat mistūra*]

FMB Federal Maritime Board.

FMC Federal Maritime Commission.

FMCS Federal Mediation and Conciliation Service.

fmcw frequency-modulated continuous wave.

F.Mk. finmark; Finnish markka. Also, **FMk**

fmla formula.

fmr former.

fmw *Computers.* firmware.

fn footnote.

fnd found.

FNMA Federal National Mortgage Association.

fnsh finish.

fo. 1. *Electricity.* fast-operate: a type of relay. **2.** foldout. **3.** folio.

F.O. 1. field officer. **2.** foreign office. **3.** *Military.* forward observer.

f.o.b. *Commerce.* free on board: without charge to the buyer for goods placed on board a carrier at the point of shipment. Also, **F.O.B.**

FOBS fractional orbital bombardment system. Also, **F.O.B.S.**

foc focal.

F.O.E. Fraternal Order of Eagles.

FOIA Freedom of Information Act.

fol. 1. folio. 2. (in prescriptions) a leaf. [from Latin *folium*] 3. followed. 4. following.

foll. following.

For. Forester.

for. 1. foreign. 2. forester. 3. forestry.

F.O.R. *Commerce.* free on rails. Also, **f.o.r.**

fort. 1. fortification. 2. fortified.

FORTRAN (fôr′tran), *Computers.* a programming language used mainly in science and engineering. [*for(mula) tran(slation)*]

F.O.S. *Commerce.* 1. free on station. 2. free on steamer. Also, **f.o.s.**

F.O.T. *Commerce.* free on truck. Also, **f.o.t.**

fouo for official use only.

4WD four-wheel drive.

fp 1. faceplate. 2. *Music.* forte-piano. 3. *Football.* forward pass.

F.P. *Physics.* foot-pound; foot-pounds.

f.p. 1. fireplug. 2. foolscap. 3. foot-pound; foot-pounds. 4. *Music.* forte-piano. 5. freezing point. 6. fully paid.

FPC 1. Federal Power Commission. 2. fish protein concentrate.

FPHA Federal Public Housing Authority.

Fpl *Real Estate.* fireplace.

fpl fire plug.

fpm feet per minute. Also, **ft/min, ft./min.**

FPO *Military.* 1. field post office. 2. fleet post office.

fprf fireproof.

fps 1. Also, **ft/sec** feet per second. 2. *Physics.* foot-pound-second.

f.p.s. 1. Also, **ft./sec.** feet per second. 2. *Physics.* foot-pound-second. 3. frames per second.

fpsps feet per second per second. Also, **ft/s²**

FPT freight pass-through.

fpt female pipe thread.

FR 1. *Real Estate.* family room. **2.** freight release.

Fr *Symbol, Chemistry.* francium.

fr 1. failure rate. **2.** *Electricity.* fast release: a type of relay. **3.** field reversing.

Fr. 1. Father. **2.** franc; francs. **3.** France. **4.** *Religion.* frater. **5.** Frau: the German form of address for a married woman. **6.** French. **7.** Friar. **8.** Friday.

fr. 1. fragment. **2.** franc; francs. **3.** from.

frac fractional.

frag fragment.

F.R.A.S. Fellow of the Royal Astronomical Society.

FRB 1. Federal Reserve Bank. **2.** Federal Reserve Board. Also, **F.R.B.**

frbd freeboard.

FRC Federal Radio Commission.

FRCD *Finance.* floating-rate certificate of deposit.

F.R.C.P. Fellow of the Royal College of Physicians.

F.R.C.S. Fellow of the Royal College of Surgeons.

freq. 1. frequency. **2.** frequent. **3.** frequentative. **4.** frequently.

freqm frequency meter.

frequ frequency.

fres fire-resistant.

F.R.G. Federal Republic of Germany.

F.R.G.S. Fellow of the Royal Geographical Society.

Fri. Friday.

frict friction.

Fris. Frisian. Also, **Fris**

Frl. Fräulein: the German form of address for an unmarried woman.

frm frame.

FRN *Finance.* floating-rate note.

frnc furnace.

frng fringe.

front. frontispiece.

frpl *Real Estate.* fireplace.

FRS Federal Reserve System.

Frs. Frisian.

frs. francs.

F.R.S. Fellow of the Royal Society.

F.R.S.L. Fellow of the Royal Society of Literature.

F.R.S.S. Fellow of the Royal Statistical Society.

frt. 1. freight. 2. front.

frwk framework.

frz freeze.

frzr freezer.

FS Federal Specification.

fs 1. field service. 2. fire station. 3. functional schematic.

f.s. foot-second; foot-seconds.

FSA Farm Security Administration

fsbl 1. feasible. 2. fusible.

fsc full scale.

FSH *Biochemistry.* follicle-stimulating hormone.

fsk frequency-shift keying.

FSLIC Federal Savings and Loan Insurance Corporation.

fsm field-strength meter.

FSN Federal Stock Number.

FSO foreign service officer.

FSR Field Service Regulations.

fssn fission.

fstnr fastener.

fsz full size.

FT full time.

Ft. (in Hungary) forint; forints.

ft. foot; feet.

ft³ *Symbol.* cubic foot; cubic feet.

FTC *U.S. Government.* Federal Trade Commission.

ftc fast time constant.

ftd fitted.

ftg 1. fitting. **2.** footing.

fth. fathom; fathoms. Also, **fthm.**

ft./hr. feet per hour.

fthrd female thread.

ft-L *Optics.* foot-lambert.

ft-lb *Physics.* foot-pound.

ft./min. feet per minute.

FTP *Computers.* File Transfer Protocol.

ft-pdl *Physics.* foot-poundal.

ft./sec. feet per second.

FTZ free-trade zone.

fu fuse.

fuhld fuseholder.

ful fulcrum.

fund fundamental.

funl funnel.

fur. furlong; furlongs.

furl. furlough.

furn 1. furnish. **2.** furniture.

fuslg fuselage.

fut. future.

fv flux valve.

f.v. on the back of the page. [from Latin *foliō versō*]

FVC *Medicine.* forced vital capacity.

FWA Federal Works Agency.

FWD 1. Also, **4WD** four-wheel drive. **2.** front-wheel drive.

fwd. 1. foreword. **2.** forward.

F.W.I. French West Indies.

fwv full wave.

Fwy. freeway.

FX foreign exchange.

fx. 1. fracture. **2.** fractured.

fxd fixed.

fxtr fixture.

FY fiscal year.

FYI for your information.

fz fuze.

G

G **1.** *Slang.* grand: one thousand dollars. **2.** (*sometimes lowercase*) *Aerospace.* gravity: a unit of acceleration.

G **1.** gay. **2.** *Psychology.* general intelligence. **3.** German. **4.** good.

G *Symbol.* **1.** the seventh in order or in a series. **2.** *Music.* **a.** the fifth tone in the scale of C major or the seventh tone in the relative minor scale, A minor. **b.** a string, key, or pipe tuned to this tone. **c.** a written or printed note representing this tone. **d.** (in the fixed system of solmization) the fifth tone of the scale of C major, called *sol.* **e.** the tonality having G as the tonic note. **3.** (*sometimes lowercase*) the medieval Roman numeral for 400. **4.** *Electricity.* **a.** conductance. **b.** gauss. **5.** *Physics.* constant of gravitation; law of gravity. **6.** *Biochemistry.* **a.** glycine. **b.** guanine. **7.** a rating assigned to a motion picture by the Motion Picture Association of America indicating that the film is suitable for general audiences, or children as well as adults.

g **1.** *Psychology.* general intelligence. **2.** good. **3.** gram; grams. **4.** *Electronics.* grid.

g *Symbol, Physics.* **1.** acceleration of gravity. **2.** gravity.

G. **1.** General. **2.** German. **3.** (in Haiti) gourde; gourdes. **4.** (specific) gravity. **5.** Gulf.

g. **1.** gauge. **2.** gender. **3.** general. **4.** generally. **5.** genitive. **6.** going back to. **7.** gold. **8.** grain; grains. **9.** gram; grams. **10.** *Sports.* guard. **11.** *British.* guinea; guineas. **12.** gun.

GA **1.** Gamblers Anonymous. **2.** General American. **3.** general of the army. **4.** Georgia (for use with ZIP code).

Ga *Symbol, Chemistry.* gallium.

Ga. Georgia.

G.A. **1.** General Agent. **2.** General Assembly.

3. Also, **g.a.**, **G/A** *Insurance.* general average.

G.A.A. Gay Activists' Alliance.

GABA (gab′ə), *Biochemistry.* a neurotransmitter of the central nervous system that inhibits its excitatory responses. [*g(amma-)a(mino)-b(utyric) a(cid)*]

G/A con. *Insurance.* general average contribution.

G/A dep. *Insurance.* general average deposit.

GAE General American English.

GAI guaranteed annual income.

Gal. *Bible.* Galatians.

gal. gallon; gallons.

gal/h *Symbol.* gallons per hour.

gall gallery.

gal/min *Symbol.* gallons per minute.

gals. gallons.

gal/s *Symbol.* gallons per second.

galv galvanic.

galvnm galvanometer.

galvs galvanized steel.

galy galley.

GAM 1. graduate in Aerospace Mechanical Engineering. **2.** ground-to-air missile.

G&AE *Accounting.* general and administrative expense.

G and T gin and tonic. Also, **g and t**

GAO General Accounting Office.

GAPL Ground-to-Air Data Link.

gar. garage. Also, **gar**

G.A.R. Grand Army of the Republic.

gas gasoline.

GASP Gravity-assisted Space Probe.

GAT 1. *Military.* Ground Attack Tactics. **2.** Ground-to-Air Transmitter.

GATT (gat), General Agreement on Tariffs and Trade.

G.A.W. guaranteed annual wage.

gaz. 1. gazette. **2.** gazetteer.

GB 1. *Computers.* gigabyte: 1000 megabytes.

2. *Finance.* Gold Bond. **3.** (on CB radio) good-bye. **4.** Great Britain.

Gb *Electricity.* gilbert.

G.B. Great Britain.

G.B.E. Knight Grand Cross of the British Empire or Dame Grand Cross of the British Empire.

GBF gay black female.

gbg garbage.

GBM gay black male.

GBO *Commerce.* goods in bad order.

GBS *Radiography.* Gall Bladder Series.

Gc 1. gigacycle; gigacycles. **2.** gigacycles per second.

GCA Girls' Clubs of America.

g-cal gram calorie. Also, **g-cal.**

G.C.B. Grand Cross of the Bath.

GCC Gulf Cooperation Council.

G.C.D. 1. *Math.* greatest common denominator. **2.** greatest common divisor. Also, **g.c.d.**

GCE *British.* General Certificate of Education.

G.C.F. *Math.* greatest common factor; greatest common divisor. Also, **g.c.f.**

GCG *Military.* Guidance Control Group.

G.C.M. *Math.* greatest common measure. Also, **g.c.m.**

GCPS gigacycles per second. Also, **Gc/s, Gc/sec**

GCR *Military.* ground-controlled radar.

G.C.T. Greenwich Civil Time.

GCU *Aerospace.* Ground Control Unit.

GD 1. *Real Estate.* garbage disposal. **2.** General Delivery.

Gd *Symbol, Chemistry.* gadolinium.

gd. 1. good. **2.** guard.

G.D. 1. Grand Duchess. **2.** Grand Duke.

Gde. (in Haiti) gourde; gourdes.

GDI *Slang.* God Damned Independent.

gdlk grid leak.

Gdn guardian.

gdn garden.

gdnc guidance.

Gdns. gardens.

GDP gross domestic product.

GDR German Democratic Republic. Also, **G.D.R.**

gds. goods.

GE *Medicine.* gastroenterology.

Ge *Symbol, Chemistry.* germanium.

g.e. *Bookbinding.* gilt edges.

GEB Guiding Eyes for the Blind.

geb. born. [from German *geboren*]

GED 1. general educational development. **2.** general equivalency diploma.

GEF 1. Gauss Error Function. **2.** *Military.* ground equipment failure.

GEM giant earth mover.

Gen. 1. *Military.* General. **2.** Genesis. **3.** Geneva.

gen. 1. gender. **2.** general. **3.** generator. **4.** genitive. **5.** genus.

genit. genitive.

genl general.

Genl. General.

Gen. Mtg. *Banking.* general mortgage.

Gent. gentleman; gentlemen. Also, **gent.**

Geo. George.

geod. 1. geodesy. **2.** geodetic.

geog. 1. geographer. **2.** geographic; geographical. **3.** geography.

geol. 1. geologic; geological. **2.** geologist. **3.** geology.

geom. 1. geometric; geometrical. **2.** geometry.

GEOS Geodetic Earth Orbiting Satellite.

Ger. 1. German. **2.** Germany.

ger. 1. gerund. **2.** gerundive.

Gestapo (gə stä′pō), the German secret police under Hitler. [from German *Ge(heime) Sta(ats)po(lizei)* secret state police]

GeV *Physics.* gigaelectron volt. Also, **Gev**

GF gay female.

gfci ground-fault circuit interrupter.

GFE government-furnished equipment.

GFR German Federal Republic.

G.F.T.U. General Federation of Trade Unions.

GG 1. gamma globulin. **2.** great gross.

GGR great gross.

GH growth hormone.

GHA Greenwich hour angle.

GHF gay Hispanic female.

GHM gay Hispanic male.

GHz *Physics.* gigahertz; gigahertzes.

GI (jēˈīˈ), a member of the U.S. armed forces, especially an enlisted soldier. Also, **G.I.** [originally abbreviation of *galvanized iron,* used in U.S. Army bookkeeping in entering articles (e.g., trash cans) made of it; later extended to all articles issued (as an assumed abbreviation of *government issue*) and finally to soldiers themselves]

Gi *Electricity.* gilbert; gilberts.

gi. gill; gills.

G.I. 1. galvanized iron. **2.** gastrointestinal. **3.** general issue. **4.** government issue. Also, **GI, g.i.**

Gib. Gibraltar.

GIGO (giˈgō), *Computers.* a rule of thumb stating that when faulty data are fed into a computer, the information that emerges will also be faulty. [*g(arbage) i(n) g(arbage) o(ut)*]

GILMER guardian of impressive letters and master of excellent replies.

GIRLS (gûrlz), Generalized Information Retrieval and Listing System.

GI's (jēˈīzˈ), **the GI's,** *Slang.* diarrhea. Also, **G.I.'s, G.I.s** [probably for *GI shits*]

GJ *Informal.* grapefruit juice.

GJF gay Jewish female.

GJM gay Jewish male.

Gk Greek. Also, **Gk.**

Gl *Symbol, Chemistry.* glucinum.

gl gold.

gl. 1. glass; glasses. **2.** gloss.

g/l grams per liter.

GLB gay, lesbian, bisexual.

glb *Math.* greatest lower bound.

Gld. guilder; guilders.

GLF Gay Liberation Front.

Gln *Biochemistry.* glutamine.

GLO *Slang.* get the lead out.

gloss. glossary.

GLOW Gross Lift-Off Weight.

GLP Gross Lawyer Product.

glpg glowplug.

glsry glossary.

Glu *Biochemistry.* glutamic acid.

glv globe valve.

Gly *Biochemistry.* glycine.

glyc. (in prescriptions) glycerite. [from Latin *glyceritum*]

glycn glycerine.

glz glaze.

GM 1. gay male. **2.** General Manager. **3.** General Medicine. **4.** Greenwich Meridian.

gm. 1. gram; grams. **2.** guided missile.

G.M. 1. General Manager. **2.** Grand Marshal. **3.** Grand Master. Also, **GM**

G.M.&S. general, medical, and surgical.

GMAT 1. *Trademark.* Graduate Management Admissions Test. **2.** Greenwich Mean Astronomical Time.

GMB *British.* Grand Master of the Bath.

gmbl gimbal.

Gmc Germanic. Also, **Gmc.**

GMP *Biochemistry.* a ribonucleotide constituent of ribonucleic acid. [g(uanosine) m(ono) p(hosphate)]

GMT Greenwich Mean Time. Also, **G.M.T.**

gmtry geometry.

gmv guaranteed minimum value.

GMW gram-molecular weight.

gn green.

G.N. Graduate Nurse.

gnd *Electricity.* ground.

GNI *Economics.* Gross National Income.

gnltd granulated.

GNMA Government National Mortgage Association.

GNP gross national product. Also, **G.N.P.**

GnRH gonadotropin releasing hormone.

G.O. 1. general office. **2.** general order. Also, **g.o.**

GOES Geostationary Operational Environmental Satellite.

G.O.K. *Medicine.* God Only Knows.

GOO Get Oil Out.

G.O.P. Grand Old Party (an epithet of the Republican party since 1880). Also, **GOP**

Goth. Gothic. Also, **Goth, goth.**

Gov. governor.

gov. 1. government. **2.** governor.

Govt. government. Also, **govt.**

GP 1. Galactic Probe. **2.** General Purpose.

gp 1. general purpose. **2.** glide path.

gp. group. Also, **Gp.**

G.P. 1. General Practitioner. **2.** General Purpose. **3.** Gloria Patri. **4.** Graduate in Pharmacy. **5.** Grand Prix.

GPA grade point average.

gpad gallons per acre per day.

gpcd gallons per capita per day.

gpd gallons per day.

gph 1. gallons per hour. **2.** graphite.

gpi ground-position indicator.

gpib *Computers.* general-purpose interface bus.

gpm 1. gallons per mile. **2.** gallons per minute.

G.P.O. 1. general post office. **2.** Government Printing Office. Also, **GPO**

GPRF gay Puerto Rican female.

GPRM gay Puerto Rican male.

GPS *Aerospace, Navigation.* Global Positioning System.

gps gallons per second.

GPU General Postal Union; Universal Postal Union.

GPU (gä′pā′ōō′, jē′pē′yōō′), (in the Soviet Union) the secret-police organization (1922–23) functioning under the NKVD. Also, **G.P.U.** [from Russian *G(osudárstvennoe) p(olitícheskoe) u(pravlénie)* state political directorate]

GQ General Quarters.

gr 1. gear. **2.** grain. **3.** gram; grams. **4.** gross.

Gr. 1. Grecian. **2.** Greece. **3.** Greek.

gr. 1. grade. **2.** grain; grains. **3.** gram; grams. **4.** grammar. **5.** gravity. **6.** great. **7.** gross. **8.** group.

G.R. King George. [from Latin *Geōrgius Rēx*]

grad. 1. *Math.* gradient. **2.** graduate. **3.** graduated.

gram. 1. grammar. **2.** grammarian. **3.** grammatical.

gran 1. granite. **2.** granular; granulated.

GRAS (gras), generally recognized as safe: a status label assigned by the FDA to a listing of substances not known to be hazardous and thus approved for use in foods.

Gr. Br. Great Britain. Also, **Gr. Brit.**

grbx gearbox.

grd 1. grind. **2.** guard.

grdl griddle.

grdtn graduation.

GRE Graduate Record Examination.

GRF growth hormone releasing factor.

GRI Government Reports Index.

gro. gross.

grom grommet.

grp group.

grph graphic.

grs grease.

grshft gearshaft.

grtg grating.

grtr grater.

GRU (in the former Soviet Union) the Chief Intelligence Directorate of the Soviet General Staff, a military intelligence organization founded in 1920 and functioning as a complement to the KGB. Also, **G.R.U.** [from Russian G(lávnoe) r(azvédyvatel'noe) u(pravlénie)]

Grv. grove.

grv groove.

gr. wt. gross weight.

GS 1. General Schedule (referring to the Civil Service job classification system). **2.** general staff. **3.** German silver.

gs ground speed.

G.S. 1. general secretary. **2.** general staff. Also, **g.s.**

GSA 1. General Services Administration. **2.** Girl Scouts of America. Also, **G.S.A.**

G.S.C. General Staff Corps.

GSE ground-support equipment.

Gsil German silver.

gskt gasket.

GSL Guaranteed Student Loan.

G spot (jē′spot′), Gräfenberg spot: a patch of tissue in the vagina purportedly excitable and erectile. Also, **G-spot.**

GSR 1. galvanic skin reflex. **2.** galvanic skin response.

gsr glide slope receiver.

GST Greenwich Sidereal Time.

G-suit (jē′soot′), Aerospace. anti-G suit: a flier's or astronaut's suit. Also, **g-suit.** [g(ravity) suit]

GT 1. Game Theory. **2.** gigaton; gigatons. **3.** grand theft **4.** Automotive. grand touring: a car type.

gt. 1. gilt. **2.** great. **3.** (in prescriptions) a drop [from Latin gutta].

Gt. Br. Great Britain. Also, **Gt. Brit.**

g.t.c. 1. good till canceled. **2.** good till countermanded. Also, **G.T.C.**

gtd. guaranteed.

GTG ground-to-ground.

GTO Automotive. Gran Turismo Omologato: a car style (grand touring).

GTP Biochemistry. an ester that is an important metabolic cofactor and precursor in the biosynthesis of cyclic GMP. [*g(uanosine) t(ri) p(hosphate)*]

gtrb gas turbine.

GTS gas turbine ship.

gtt. (in prescriptions) drops. [from Latin *guttae*]

GU 1. genitourinary. **2.** Guam (for use with ZIP code).

guar guarantee.

GUGB the Chief Directorate for State Security: the former Soviet Union's secret police organization (1934–1941) functioning as part of the NKVD. Also, **G.U.G.B.** [from Russian *G(lávnoe) u(pravlénie) g(osudárstvennoi) b(ezopásnosti)*]

GUI (gōō′ē), *Computers.* graphical user interface.

Gui. Guiana.

Guin. Guinea.

gun. gunnery.

GUT *Physics.* grand unification theory.

gut gutter.

g.v. 1. gravimetric volume. **2.** gigavolt; gigavolts.

gvl gravel.

GVW gross vehicle weight; gross vehicular weight.

GW gigawatt; gigawatts. Also, **Gw**

GWF gay white female.

GWh Gigawatt-hour.

GWM gay white male.

Gy *Physics.* gray: a measure of radiation absorption.

gy gray.

GYN 1. gynecological. **2.** gynecologist. **3.** gynecology. Also, **gyn.**

gyp gypsum.

GySgt *Marine Corps.* gunnery sergeant.

GZ ground zero.

H

H **1.** hard. **2.** *Grammar.* head. **3.** *Electricity.* henry. **4.** *Slang.* heroin. **5.** high.

H *Symbol.* **1.** the eighth in order or in a series. **2.** (*sometimes lowercase*) the medieval Roman numeral for 200. **3.** *Chemistry.* hydrogen. **4.** *Biochemistry.* histidine. **5.** *Physics.* **a.** enthalpy. **b.** horizontal component of the earth's magnetic field. **c.** magnetic intensity. **6.** *Music.* the letter used in German to indicate the tone B.

H¹ *Symbol, Chemistry.* protium. Also, **¹H, Hᵃ**

H² *Symbol, Chemistry.* deuterium. Also, **²H, Hᵇ**

H³ *Symbol, Chemistry.* tritium. Also, **³H, Hᶜ**

h hard.

h *Symbol, Physics.* Planck's constant.

H. (in prescriptions) an hour. [from Latin *hōra*]

h. **1.** harbor. **2.** hard. **3.** hardness. **4.** heavy sea. **5.** height. **6.** hence. **7.** high. **8.** *Baseball.* hit; hits. **9.** horns. **10.** hour; hours. **11.** hundred. **12.** husband. Also, **H.**

Ha *Symbol, Chemistry.* hahnium.

ha hectare; hectares.

h.a. **1.** *Gunnery.* high angle. **2.** in this year [from Latin *hōc annō*].

Hab. *Bible.* Habakkuk.

HAC House Appropriations Committee.

Hag. *Bible.* Haggai.

Hal *Chemistry.* halogen.

H&A Health and Accident.

haust. (in prescriptions) draught. [from Latin *haustus*]

Haw. Hawaii.

HAWK (hôk), **1.** have alimony, will keep. **2.** Homing All the Way Killer (small missile).

haz hazardous.

Hb *Symbol, Biochemistry.* hemoglobin.

h.b. *Sports.* halfback.

H.B.M. His Britannic Majesty; Her Britannic Majesty.

HBO Home Box Office (a cable television channel).

H-bomb (āch′bom′), hydrogen bomb.

HBP high blood pressure.

HBV hepatitis B.

H.C. **1.** Holy Communion. **2.** House of Commons.

h.c. for the sake of honor. [from Latin *honōris causā*]

hce human-caused error.

H.C.F. *Math.* highest common factor. Also, **h.c.f.**

hCG human chorionic gonadotropin.

H.C.M. His Catholic Majesty; Her Catholic Majesty.

H. Con. Res. House concurrent resolution.

HCR highway contract route.

hcs high-carbon steel.

hd. **1.** hand. **2.** hard. **3.** head.

h.d. **1.** heavy duty. **2.** (in prescriptions) at bedtime [from Latin *hōra dēcubitūs*]

hdbk. handbook.

hdcp handicap.

hdd *Computers.* hard-disk drive.

hdg heading.

hdkf. handkerchief.

HDL high-density lipoprotein.

hdl handle.

hdlg handling.

hdlng headlining.

hdn harden.

hdns hardness.

H. Doc. House document.

HDPE high-density polyethylene.

hdqrs. headquarters.

hdr header.

hdshk *Computers.* handshake.

hdst headset.

HDTV high-definition television.

hdw. hardware. Also, **hdwe, hdwr.**

hdwd hardwood.

hdx *Telecommunications.* half duplex.

HE high explosive. Also, **he**.

He *Symbol, Chemistry.* helium.

H.E. 1. high explosive. **2.** His Eminence. **3.** His Excellency; Her Excellency.

HEAO High Energy Astrophysical Observatory.

Heb Hebrew.

Heb. 1. Hebrew. **2.** *Bible.* Hebrews. Also, **Hebr.**

herp. herpetology. Also, **herpet.**

herpetol. 1. herpetological. **2.** herpetology.

het heterodyne.

HETP *Chemistry.* hexaethyl tetraphosphate.

HEW Department of Health, Education, and Welfare.

hex. 1. *Math.* hexadecimal (number system). **2.** hexagon. **3.** hexagonal.

hex hd hexagonal head.

hex soch hexagonal socket head.

HF 1. high frequency. **2.** Hispanic female.

Hf *Symbol, Chemistry.* hafnium.

hf. half.

hf. bd. *Printing.* half-bound.

hfe human-factors engineering.

HG 1. High German. **2.** *British.* Home Guard.

Hg *Symbol, Chemistry.* mercury. [from Latin *hydrargyrum,* from Greek *hydrárgyros* literally, liquid silver]

hg hectogram; hectograms.

H.G. 1. High German. **2.** His Grace; Her Grace.

hGH human growth hormone.

hgr hanger.

hgt. height.

hgwy. highway.

H.H. 1. His Highness; Her Highness. **2.** His Holiness.

hhd hogshead; hogsheads.

HH.D. Doctor of Humanities.

HHFA Housing and Home Finance Agency.

H-hour (āch′ou°r′, -ou′ər), the time, usually unspecified, set for the beginning of a planned attack.

HHS Department of Health and Human Services.

HI Hawaii (for use with ZIP code).

H.I. 1. Hawaiian Islands. 2. *Meteorology.* heat index.

HIF human-initiated failure.

hi-fi (hi'fi'), high fidelity. Also, **hi fi**

H.I.H. His Imperial Highness; Her Imperial Highness.

H.I.M. His Imperial Majesty; Her Imperial Majesty.

Hind Hindustani.

Hind. 1. Hindi. 2. Hindu. 3. Hindustan. 4. Hindustani.

hint high intensity.

HIP (āch'i'pē' *or, sometimes,* hip), Health Insurance Plan.

hipar high-power acquisition radar.

hipot high potential.

His *Biochemistry.* histidine.

hist. 1. histology. 2. historian. 3. historical. 4. history.

HIV human immunodeficiency virus; AIDS virus.

H.J. here lies. [from Latin *hic jacet*]

H.J. Res. House joint resolution.

H.J.S. here lies buried. [from Latin *hic jacet sepultus*]

HK Hong Kong.

hksw *Telephones.* hookswitch.

hl 1. haul. 2. hectoliter; hectoliters.

H.L. House of Lords.

HLA *Immunology.* human leukocyte antigen.

HLBB Home Loan Bank Board.

hlcl helical.

hlcptr helicopter.

hldg holding.

hldn holddown.

hldr holder.

hll *Computers.* high-level language.

hlpr helper.

HLTL *Computers.* high-level transistor logic.

HLTTL *Computers.* high-level transistor-transistor logic.

HM Hispanic male.

hm hectometer; hectometers.

H.M. Her Majesty; His Majesty.

hma *Computers.* high-memory area.

HMAS Her Majesty's Australian Ship; His Majesty's Australian Ship.

hmc harmonic.

HMCS Her Majesty's Canadian Ship; His Majesty's Canadian Ship.

hmd humidity.

HMF Her Majesty's Forces; His Majesty's Forces.

HMMV humvee: a military vehicle. Also, **HMMWV.** [*H(igh)-M(obility) M(ultipurpose) W(heeled) V(ehicle)*]

HMO health maintenance organization.

hmr hammer.

H.M.S. 1. Her Majesty's Service; His Majesty's Service. **2.** Her Majesty's Ship; His Majesty's Ship.

hnd cont hand control.

hndrl handrail.

hndst handset.

hndwl handwheel.

hng hinge.

hntg hunting.

HO (hō), (in police use) habitual offender.

Ho *Symbol, Chemistry.* holmium.

ho. house.

H.O. 1. Head Office. **2.** Home Office.

HOLC Home Owners' Loan Corporation. Also, **H.O.L.C.**

Hon. 1. Honorable. **2.** Honorary.

hon. 1. honor. **2.** honorable. **3.** honorably. **4.** honorary.

Hond. Honduras.

hor. 1. horizon. **2.** horizontal. **3.** horology.

hor. interm. (in prescriptions) at intermediate hours. [from Latin *hōrā intermediis*]

horol. horology.

hor. som. (in prescriptions) at bedtime. [from Latin *hōrā somni* at the hour of sleep]

hort. 1. horticultural. **2.** horticulture.

hor. un. spatio (in prescriptions) at the end of one hour. [from Latin *hōrae ūnius spatiō*]

horz horizontal.

Hos. *Bible.* Hosea.

hosp. hospital.

HOV high-occupancy vehicle.

hp 1. high pass. **2.** horsepower.

H.P. 1. *Electricity.* high power. **2.** high pressure. **3.** horsepower. Also, **h.p., HP**

HPER Health, Physical Education, and Recreation.

hpot helical potentiometer.

hps high-pressure steam.

HPV human papilloma virus.

H.Q. headquarters. Also, **h.q., HQ**

HR 1. *Baseball.* home run; home runs. **2.** House of Representatives.

Hr. Herr: the German form of address for a man.

hr. hour; hours. Also, **h.**

H.R. House of Representatives. Also, **HR**

h.r. *Baseball.* home run; home runs. Also, **hr**

HRA Health Resources Administration.

H-R diagram *Astronomy.* Hertzsprung-Russell diagram.

H.R.E. 1. Holy Roman Emperor. **2.** Holy Roman Empire.

H. Rept. House report.

H. Res. House resolution.

hrg hearing.

H.R.H. His Royal Highness; Her Royal Highness.

H.R.I.P. here rests in peace. [from Latin *hic requiēscit in pāce*]

hrs. 1. hot-rolled steel. **2.** hours.

hrzn horizon.

HS 1. *Medicine.* Herpes Simplex. **2.** laid here. [from Latin *Hic situs*]

hs high speed.

H.S. 1. High School. **2.** *British.* Home Secretary.

h.s. 1. in this sense. [from Latin *hōc sensū*] **2.** (in prescriptions) at bedtime. [from Latin *hōrā somni* at the hour of sleep]

hse house.

hsg housing.

H.S.H. His Serene Highness; Her Serene Highness.

hshld household.

HSI heat stress index.

H.S.M. His Serene Majesty; Her Serene Majesty.

hss high-speed steel.

HST Hawaii Standard Time. Also, **H.S.T., h.s.t.**

hsth hose thread.

HSV-1 herpes simplex virus: usually associated with oral herpes. Also, **HSV-I.**

HSV-2 herpes simplex virus: usually causing genital herpes. Also, **HSV-II.**

HT 1. *Sports.* halftime. **2.** halftone. **3.** Hawaii time. **4.** *Electricity.* high tension. **5.** high tide. **6.** at this time. [from Latin *hōc tempŏre*] **7.** under this title. [from Latin *hōc titulō*]

ht. height.

h.t. at this time. [from Latin *hōc tempŏre*]

htd heated.

htg heating.

HTLV *Pathology.* human T-cell lymphotropic virus.

HTLV-1 *Pathology.* human T-cell lymphotropic virus type 1. Also, **HTLV-I.**

HTLV-2 *Pathology.* human T-cell lymphotropic virus type. Also, **HTLV-II.**

HTLV-3 *Pathology.* human T-cell lymphotropic virus type 3; AIDS virus. Also, **HTLV-III.**

HTML *Computers.* HyperText Markup Language.

htr heater.

Hts. Heights.

ht tr heat-treat.

HUAC (hyoo′ak), House Un-American Activities Committee.

HUD (hud), Department of Housing and Urban Development.

HUM humanities.

huricn hurricane.

husb. husbandry.

H.V. 1. high velocity. **2.** Also, **h.v., hv** high voltage. **3.** high volume.

HVAC heating, ventilating, and air conditioning.

HVDC high-voltage direct current.

HVP hydrolyzed vegetable protein. Also, **H.V.P.**

hvps high-voltage power supply.

hvy. heavy.

HW 1. half wave. **2.** *Real Estate.* hardwood. **3.** high water. **4.** hot water (heat).

HWM high-water mark. Also, **H.W.M., h.w.m.**

hwy highway. Also, **Hwy, hwy.**

hy. *Electricity.* (formerly) henry.

hyb hybrid.

hyd. 1. hydrant. **2.** hydraulics. **3.** hydrostatics.

hydm hydrometer.

hydr hydraulic.

hydraul. hydraulics.

hydrelc hydroelectric.

HYDROPAC (hi′drə pak′), an urgent warning of navigational dangers in the Pacific Ocean, issued by the U.S. Navy Hydrographic Office.

hydros. hydrostatics.

hyp. 1. hypotenuse. **2.** hypothesis. **3.** hypothetical.

hypoth. 1. hypothesis. **2.** hypothetical.

Hz hertz; hertzes.

I

I interstate (used with a number to designate an interstate highway): *I-95.*

I *Symbol.* **1.** the ninth in order or in a series. **2.** (*sometimes lowercase*) the Roman numeral for 1. **3.** *Chemistry.* iodine. **4.** *Biochemistry.* isoleucine. **5.** *Physics.* isotopic spin. **6.** *Electricity.* current. **7.** *Logic.* particular affirmative.

i *Symbol, Math.* **1.** the imaginary number. **2.** a unit vector on the *x*-axis of a coordinate system.

I. **1.** Independent. **2.** Indian. **3.** Iraqi. **4.** Island; Islands. **5.** Isle; Isles. **6.** Israeli.

i. **1.** imperator. **2.** incisor. **3.** interest. **4.** intransitive. **5.** island. **6.** isle; isles.

IA Iowa (for use with ZIP code).

ia **1.** immediately available. **2.** impedance angle. **3.** international angstrom.

Ia. Iowa.

i.a. in absentia.

IAAF International Amateur Athletic Federation.

IAB **1.** Industry Advisory Board. **2.** Inter-American Bank.

IAC Industry Advisory Commission.

IACA Independent Air Carriers Association.

IACB International Association of Convention Bureaus.

IADB **1.** Inter-American Defense Board. **2.** Inter-American Development Bank.

IAEA International Atomic Energy Agency.

IAG International Association of Gerontology.

IAIA Institute of American Indian Arts.

IAMAW International Association of Machinists and Aerospace Workers.

IAS **1.** *Aeronautics.* indicated air speed. **2.** Institute for Advanced Study.

ias indicate airspeed.

IAT international atomic time.

IATA International Air Transport Association.

IATSE International Alliance of Theatrical Stage Employees (and Moving Picture Machine Operators of the U.S. and Canada).

iaw in accordance with.

ib. **1.** in the same book, chapter, page, etc. [from Latin *ibidem*] **2.** instruction book.

IBA **1.** Independent Bankers Association. **2.** International Bar Association.

IBC **1.** International Broadcasting Corporation. **2.** international business company.

IBD inflammatory bowel disease.

IBEW International Brotherhood of Electrical Workers.

IBF international banking facilities.

ibid. (ib′id), in the same book, chapter, page, etc. [from Latin *ibidem*]

IBR infectious bovine rhinotracheitis.

I.B.T.C.W.H. International Brotherhood of Teamsters, Chauffeurs, Warehousemen, and Helpers of America.

IC **1.** immediate constituent. **2.** *Computers, Electronics.* integrated circuit. **3.** intensive care.

I.C. Jesus Christ. [from Latin *I(ēsus) C(hristus)*]

ICA **1.** International Communication Agency (1978–82). **2.** International Cooperation Administration.

ICAO International Civil Aviation Organization.

icas intermittent commercial and amateur service.

ICBM intercontinental ballistic missile. Also, **I.C.B.M.**

ICC Indian Claims Commission.

I.C.C. **1.** International Control Commission. **2.** Interstate Commerce Commission. Also, **ICC**

Icel. **1.** Iceland. **2.** Icelandic. Also, **Icel**

ICF *Physics.* inertial confinement fusion: an experimental method for producing controlled thermonuclear energy.

ICJ International Court of Justice.

ICM Institute of Computer Management.

icm 1. intercom. **2.** intercommunication.

ICR 1. Institute of Cancer Research. **2.** Institute for Cooperative Research.

ICRC International Committee of the Red Cross.

icrm ice cream.

ICS International College of Surgeons.

ICSE International Committee for Sexual Equality.

ICSH *Biochemistry, Pharmacology.* interstitial-cell stimulating hormone.

ICU intensive care unit.

icw interrupted continuous wave.

ID (i/dē/), a means of identification, as a card or bracelet.

ID 1. Idaho (for use with ZIP code). **2.** Also, **i.d., id** inside diameter.

id 1. inside diameter. **2.** internal diameter.

ID. (in Iraq) dinar; dinars.

Id. Idaho.

id. idem: the same as previously given.

I.D. 1. identification. **2.** identity. **3.** *Military.* Infantry Division. **4.** Intelligence Department.

IDA 1. Industrial Development Agency. **2.** Institute for Defense Analysis.

IDB 1. Industrial Development Board. **2.** industrial development bond.

IDE *Computers.* integrated drive electronics: hard-drive interface.

ident 1. identical. **2.** identification.

idf *Telephones.* intermediate distributing frame.

IDP 1. integrated data processing. **2.** International Driving Permit.

IDR 1. Institute for Dream Research. **2.** international drawing rights.

idrty indirectly.

idx index.

IE Indo-European.

I.E. 1. Indo-European. **2.** Industrial Engineer.

i.e. that is. [from Latin *id est*]

IEC International Electrotechnical Commission.

I.E.E.E. (ī′ trip′əl ē′), Institute of Electrical and Electronics Engineers. Also, **IEEE**

IEP Individualized Educational Program.

IES Illuminating Engineering Society.

if 1. inside frosted (of a light bulb). **2.** intermediate frequency.

IFA *Medicine.* immunofluorescence assay.

IFALP International Federation of Air Line Pilots Associations.

IFC 1. International Finance Corporation. **2.** International Fisheries Commission **3.** International Freighting Corporation.

IFF 1. *Military.* Identification, Friend or Foe: a system to distinguish between friendly and hostile aircraft. **2.** Institute for the Future.

iff *Math.* if and only if.

IFIP (if′ip), International Federation for Information Processing.

I.F.L.W.U. International Fur and Leather Workers′ Union.

IFN *Biochemistry, Pharmacology.* interferon.

ifr instrument flight rules.

IFS International Foundation for Science.

I.F.S. Irish Free State.

IG *Electronics.* ignitor: an electron device.

Ig *Immunology.* immunoglobulin.

I.G. 1. Indo-Germanic. **2.** Inspector General.

IgA *Immunology.* immunoglobulin A.

IgE *Immunology.* immunoglobulin E.

IGFET insulated-gate field-effect transistor.

IgG *Immunology.* immunoglobulin G.

IgM *Immunology.* immunoglobulin M.

ign. 1. ignition. **2.** unknown [from Latin *ignōtus*].

igt ingot.

IGY International Geophysical Year.

IHL International Hockey League.

ihp indicated horsepower. Also, **IHP**

IHS 1. Jesus. [from Latin, from Greek: partial transliteration of the first three letters of *Iē-*

soûs Jesus] **2.** Jesus Savior of Men. [from Latin *Iēsus Hominum Salvātor*] **3.** in this sign (the cross) shalt thou conquer. [from Latin *In Hōc Signō Vincēs*] **4.** in this (cross) is salvation. [from Latin *In Hōc Salūs*]

IL Illinois (for use with ZIP code).

Il *Symbol, Chemistry.* illinium.

il. 1. illustrated. **2.** illustration.

ILA 1. International Law Association. **2.** International Longshoremen's Association. Also, **I.L.A.**

ILAS Instrument Landing Approach System.

I.L.G.W.U. International Ladies' Garment Workers' Union. Also, **ILGWU**

Ill. Illinois.

ill. 1. illustrated. **2.** illustration. **3.** illustrator. **4.** most illustrious [from Latin *illustrissimus*].

illum illuminate.

illus. 1. illustrated. **2.** illustration. Also, **illust.**

ILO International Labor Organization. Also, **I.L.O.**

I.L.P. Independent Labour Party.

ILS 1. *Aeronautics.* instrument landing system. **2.** Integrated Logistic Support.

ILTF International Lawn Tennis Federation.

I.L.W.U. International Longshoremen's and Warehousemen's Union.

im intermodulation.

I.M. Isle of Man.

imag imaginary.

IMCO Inter-Governmental Maritime Consultive Organization.

imd intermodulation distortion.

IMF International Monetary Fund. Also, **I.M.F.**

imit. 1. Also, **imit** imitation. **2.** imitative.

immed immediate.

immunol. immunology.

IMP *Bridge.* international match point.

Imp. 1. Emperor. [from Latin *Imperātor*] **2.** Empress. [from Latin *Imperātrix*]

imp. 1. impact. **2.** imperative. **3.** imperfect. **4.** imperial. **5.** impersonal. **6.** implement. **7.**

import. **8.** important. **9.** imported. **10.** importer. **11.** imprimatur. **12.** in the first place. [from Latin *imprimis*] **13.** imprint. **14.** improper. **15.** improved. **16.** improvement.

impd impedance.

imper. imperative.

imperf. imperfect.

impers. impersonal.

impf. imperfect.

imp. gal. imperial gallon.

impl implement.

implr impeller.

imprg impregnate.

imprl imperial.

improv 1. improvement. **2.** improvisation.

imprsn impression.

impv. imperative.

imrs immersion.

IN Indiana (for use with ZIP code).

In *Symbol, Chemistry.* indium.

in. inch; inches.

in³ *Symbol.* cubic inch; cubic inches.

INA 1. international normal atmosphere. **2.** Israeli News Agency.

inbd inboard.

Inc. incorporated.

inc. 1. engraved. [from Latin *incisus*] **2.** inclosure. **3.** included. **4.** including. **5.** inclusive. **6.** income. **7.** incorporated. **8.** increase. **9.** incumbent.

incand incandescent.

incin incinerator.

incl. 1. inclosure. **2.** including. **3.** inclusive.

incln inclined.

incls inclosure.

incm incoming.

incmpl incomplete.

incnd incendiary.

incog incognito.

incoh incoherent.

incor. 1. Also, **incorp.** incorporated. **2.** incorrect.

incorr. incorrect. Also, **incor.**

incpt intercept.

incr. 1. increase. 2. increased. 3. increasing. 4. increment.

incrt increment.

IND *Pharmacology.* investigative new drug.

Ind. 1. India. 2. Also, **Ind** Indian. 3. Indiana. 4. Indies.

ind. 1. independence. 2. independent. 3. index. 4. indicate. 5. indicated. 6. indicative. 7. indicator. 8. indigo. 9. indirect. 10. industrial. 11. industry.

in d. (in prescriptions) daily. [from Latin *in diēs*]

I.N.D. in the name of God. [from Latin *in nōmine Dei*]

Ind.E. Industrial Engineer.

indef. indefinite.

indep independent.

indic. 1. indicating. 2. indicative. 3. indicator.

individ. individual. Also, **indiv.**

indl industrial.

indn induction.

indt indent.

indtry industry.

induc. induction.

indus. 1. industrial. 2. industry.

indv individual.

INF European-based U.S. nuclear weapons that were capable of striking the Soviet Union and Soviet ones that could hit Western Europe. [*I(ntermediate-range) N(uclear) F(orces)*]

inf 1. *Math.* greatest lower bound. [from Latin *infimum*] 2. infinite. 3. infinity.

Inf. 1. infantry. 2. infuse [from Latin *infunde*].

in f. in the end; finally. [from Latin *in fine*]

infin. infinitive.

info (in′fō), information.

INH *Pharmacology, Trademark.* a brand of isoniazid.

inher. inheritance.

in. Hg *Meteorology.* inch of mercury.

init. Also, **init** initial.

inject. (in prescriptions) an injection. [from Latin *injectiō*]

inl inlet.

in loc. cit. in the place cited. [from Latin *in locō citātō*]

in mem. in memoriam.

inn. *Sports.* inning.

inop inoperative.

inorg. inorganic.

INP International News Photos.

inp input.

inq inquiry.

inr inner.

I.N.R.I. Jesus of Nazareth, King of the Jews. [from Latin *Iēsūs Nazarēnus, Rēx Iūdaeōrum*]

INS 1. Immigration and Naturalization Service. **2.** Also, **I.N.S.** International News Service. **3.** Integrated Navigation System.

ins. 1. inches. **2.** *Chiefly British.* inscribed. **3.** inside. **4.** inspector. **5.** insulated. **6.** insurance. **7.** insure.

in./sec. inches per second.

insep. inseparable. Also, **insep**

insol. insoluble.

insp. 1. inspection. **2.** inspector.

inst. 1. instant. **2.** instantaneous. **3.** Also, **Inst.** institute. **4.** Also, **Inst.** institution. **5.** instructor. **6.** instrument. **7.** instrumental.

instl 1. install. **2.** installation.

instm instrumentation.

instr. 1. instruct. **2.** instructor. **3.** instrument. **4.** instrumental.

insuf insufficient.

insul 1. insulate. **2.** insulation.

int. 1. intelligence. **2.** interest. **3.** interim. **4.** interior. **5.** interjection. **6.** internal. **7.** international. **8.** interpreter. **9.** interval. **10.** intransitive.

intchg interchangeable.

intcom intercommunication.

intcon interconnection.

integ 1. integral. 2. integrate.

integrg integrating.

intel intelligence.

INTELSAT (in tel′sat′, in′tel-), International Telecommunications Satellite Consortium.

inten intensity.

Intens *Grammar.* intensifier. Also, **intens**

intens. 1. intensifier. 2. intensive.

inter. 1. intermediate. 2. interrogation. 3. interrogative.

interj. interjection.

internat. international.

Interpol (in′tər pōl′), International Criminal Police Organization.

interrog. 1. interrogation. 2. interrogative.

intfc *Computers.* interface.

intk intake.

intl. 1. internal. 2. Also, **intnl.** international.

intlk interlock.

intlz initialize.

intmd intermediate.

intmt intermittent.

intpr interpret.

intr. 1. interior. 2. intransitive. 3. introduce. 4. introduced. 5. introducing. 6. introduction. 7. introductory.

intrans. intransitive.

in trans. in transit. [from Latin *in trānsitū*]

Int. Rev. Internal Revenue.

intrf interference.

intrg interrogate.

intro introduction.

intrpl interpolate.

intrpt interrupt.

intsct intersect.

intstg interstage.

intvl interval.

inv. 1. he or she invented it. [from Latin *invenit*] 2. invented. 3. invention. 4. inventor. 5. inventory. 6. investment. 7. invoice.

invs inverse.

invt. 1. inventory. **2.** invert.

invtr inverter.

Io *Symbol, Chemistry.* ionium.

Io. Iowa.

I/O 1. inboard-outboard. **2.** Also **i/o** *Computers.* input/output.

I.O. indirect object. Also, **IO, i.o.**

IOC International Olympic Committee. Also, **I.O.C.**

I.O.F. Independent Order of Foresters.

IOM interoffice memo.

I.O.O.F. Independent Order of Odd Fellows.

IOU a written acknowledgment of a debt, especially an informal one. Also, **I.O.U.** [representing *I owe you*]

IPA 1. International Phonetic Alphabet. **2.** International Phonetic Association. **3.** International Press Association. Also, **I.P.A.**

IPB illustrated parts breakdown.

i.p.h. 1. *Printing.* impressions per hour. **2.** inches per hour. Also, **iph**

IPI International Patent Institute.

IPL information processing language. Also, **ipl**

IPM integrated pest management.

ipm inches per minute. Also, **i.p.m.**

IPO initial public offering.

ipr inches per revolution. Also, **i.p.r.**

ips inches per second. Also, **i.p.s.**

IQ *Psychology.* intelligence quotient.

i.q. the same as. [from Latin *idem quod*]

IR 1. information retrieval. **2.** infrared. **3.** intelligence ratio.

Ir Irish.

Ir *Symbol, Chemistry.* iridium.

ir 1. infrared. **2.** insulation resistance.

Ir. 1. Ireland. **2.** Irish.

I.R. 1. immediate reserve. **2.** infantry reserve. **3.** intelligence ratio. **4.** internal revenue.

IRA 1. individual retirement account. **2.** Irish Republican Army. Also, **I.R.A.**

IRB 1. Industrial Relations Bureau. **2.** industrial revenue bond.

IRBM intermediate range ballistic missile. Also, **I.R.B.M.**

IRC 1. Internal Revenue Code. **2.** International Red Cross.

Ire. Ireland.

IRO 1. International Refugee Organization. **2.** International Relief Organization.

IRQ *Computers.* interrupt request.

irreg. 1. irregular. **2.** irregularly.

irrglr irregular.

IRS Internal Revenue Service.

Is. 1. *Bible.* Isaiah. **2.** Island; Islands. **3.** Isle; Isles.

is. 1. island; islands. **2.** isle; isles.

ISA Instrument Society of America.

Isa. *Bible.* Isaiah.

ISBA International Seabed Authority.

ISBN International Standard Book Number.

ISDN integrated-services digital network.

isgn insignia.

isl. 1. island. **2.** isle. Also, **Isl.**

isln isolation.

isls. islands. Also, **Isls.**

ISO 1. incentive stock option. **2.** in search of. **3.** *Photography.* International Standardization Organization.

iso isometric.

isol isolate.

isos isosceles.

ISR Institute for Sex Research.

Isr. 1. Israel. **2.** Israeli.

iss issue.

ISSN International Standard Serial Number.

IST 1. insulin shock therapy. **2.** International Standard Thread (metric).

Isth. isthmus. Also, **isth.**

ISV International Scientific Vocabulary.

It Italian.

It. 1. Italian. **2.** Italy.

I.T.A. Initial Teaching Alphabet. Also, **i.t.a.**

Ital. 1. Italian. **2.** Italic. **3.** Italy.

ital. 1. italic; italics. **2.** italicized.

ITC 1. International Trade Commission. **2.** investment tax credit.

ITO International Trade Organization.

ITU International Telecommunication Union.

I.T.U. International Typographical Union.

ITV instructional television.

IU 1. immunizing unit. **2.** Also, **I.U.** international unit.

IUD intrauterine device.

IUS *Rocketry.* inertial upper stage.

IV (ī′vē′), *Medicine.* an intravenous device.

IV *Medicine.* **1.** intravenous. **2.** intravenous drip. **3.** intravenous injection. **4.** intravenously.

I.V. initial velocity.

i.v. 1. increased value. **2.** initial velocity. **3.** invoice value.

IVF in vitro fertilization.

I.W. Isle of Wight.

i.w. 1. inside width. **2.** isotopic weight.

IWC International Whaling Commission.

I.W.W. Industrial Workers of the World. Also, **IWW**

J

J 1. *Cards.* jack. Also, **J. 2.** Jewish. **3.** *Physics.* joules.

J *Symbol.* **1.** the tenth in order or in a series, or, when *I* is omitted, the ninth. **2.** (*sometimes lowercase*) the medieval Roman numeral for 1. **3.** *Physics.* angular momentum.

j *Symbol.* **1.** *Math.* a unit vector on the y-axis of a coordinate system. **2.** *Engineering.* the imaginary number

J. 1. *Cards.* jack. Also, **J 2.** Journal. **3.** Judge. **4.** Justice.

JA 1. joint account. **2.** Joint Agent. **3.** Judge Advocate. **4.** Junior Achievement. Also, **J.A.**

Ja. January.

J.A.C. Junior Association of Commerce.

J.A.G. Judge Advocate General. Also, **JAG**

Jam. Jamaica.

Jan. January.

Jap. 1. Japan. **2.** Japanese.

Japn 1. Japan. **2.** Japanese. Also, **Japn**

Jas. *Bible.* James.

Jav. Javanese.

jb junction box.

JC 1. junior college. **2.** juvenile court.

J.C. 1. Jesus Christ. **2.** Julius Caesar. **3.** *Law.* jurisconsult. [from Latin *jūris cōnsultus*]

J.C.B. 1. Bachelor of Canon Law. [from Latin *Jūris Canonici Baccalaureus*] **2.** Bachelor of Civil Law. [from Latin *Jūris Civilis Baccalaureus*]

J.C.C. Junior Chamber of Commerce.

J.C.D. 1. Doctor of Canon Law. [from Latin *Jūris Canonici Doctor*] **2.** Doctor of Civil Law. [from Latin *Jūris Civilis Doctor*]

JCI Jaycees International.

JCL *Computers.* job control language.

J.C.L. Licentiate in Canon Law. [from Latin *Jūris Canonici Licentiātus*]

J.C.S. Joint Chiefs of Staff. Also, **JCS**

jct. junction. Also, **jctn.**

JD *Informal.* **1.** juvenile delinquency. **2.** juvenile delinquent.

JD. (in Jordan) dinar; dinars.

J.D. 1. *Astronomy.* Julian Day. **2.** Doctor of Jurisprudence; Doctor of Law. [from Latin *Jūris Doctor*] **3.** Doctor of Laws. [from Latin *Jūrum Doctor*] **4.** Justice Department. **5.** *Informal.* **a.** juvenile delinquency. **b.** juvenile delinquent.

JDC Juvenile Detention Center.

JDL Jewish Defense League.

Je. June.

Jer. 1. *Bible.* Jeremiah. **2.** Jersey.

JFET (jāʹfet), junction field-effect transistor.

JFK John Fitzgerald Kennedy.

jg junior grade. Also, **j.g.**

⸱HS IHS (defs. 1, 2).

J.H.S. junior high school.

JJ. 1. Judges. **2.** Justices.

jk jack.

jkt jacket.

jl journal.

Jl. 1. Journal. **2.** July.

jn join.

Jno. John.

jnr. junior.

jnt. joint.

Jo. Bapt. John the Baptist.

JOBS (jobz), Job Opportunities in the Business Sector.

Jo. Div. John the Divine.

Jo. Evang. John the Evangelist.

Josh. *Bible.* Joshua.

jour. 1. journal. **2.** journeyman.

journ. journalism.

JP 1. jet propulsion. **2.** Justice of the Peace.

J.P. Justice of the Peace. Also, **j.p.**

JPEG (jāʹpeg), Joint Photographic Experts Group.

Jpn. 1. Japan. **2.** Japanese. Also, **Jpn**

Jr. 1. Journal. **2.** Junior.

jr. junior.

JRC Junior Red Cross.

JSC Johnson Space Center.

J.S.D. Doctor of the Science of Law; Doctor of Juristic Science.

jt. joint.

Ju. June.

Jud. *Bible.* **1.** Judges. **2.** Judith (Apocrypha).

jud. **1.** judge. **2.** judgment. **3.** judicial. **4.** judiciary.

Judg. *Bible.* Judges.

Jul. July.

Jun. **1.** June. **2.** Junior.

Junc. Junction. Also, **junc.**

Jur. D. Doctor of Law. [from Latin *Jūris Doctor*]

jurisp. jurisprudence. Also, **juris.**

Jur. M. Master of Jurisprudence.

just. justification.

juv. juvenile.

JV **1.** joint venture. **2.** junior varsity. Also, **J.V.**

jwlr. jeweler.

J.W.V. Jewish War Veterans.

Jy jansky; janskies.

Jy. July.

K

K 1. *Chess.* king. **2.** *Physics.* Kelvin. **3.** the number 1000: *The salary is $20K.* [abbreviation of *kilo-*] **4.** *Electronics.* cathode. **5.** *Music.* Köchel listing. **6.** kindergarten: *a K–12 boarding school.* **7.** *Real Estate.* kitchen.

K *Symbol.* **1.** the eleventh in order or in a series, or, when *I* is omitted, the tenth. **2.** *Chemistry.* potassium. [from Latin *kalium*] **3.** *Computers.* **a.** the number 1024 or 2^{10}. **b.** kilobyte. **4.** *Baseball.* strikeout; strikeouts. **5.** *Physics.* kaon. **6.** *Biochemistry.* lysine.

K *Ecology.* carrying capacity.

k *Symbol.* **1.** *Math.* a vector on the z-axis, having length 1 unit. **2.** *Physics.* Boltzmann constant.

K. 1. kip; kips (monetary unit). **2.** Knight. **3.** (in Malawi or Zambia) kwacha.

k. 1. *Electricity.* capacity. **2.** karat. **3.** kilogram; kilograms. **4.** kindergarten. **5.** *Chess.* king. **6.** knight. **7.** knot. **8.** kopeck.

kA *Electricity.* kiloampere; kiloamperes.

Kan. Kansas. Also, **Kans., Kas.**

KB 1. *Chess.* king's bishop. **2.** *Computers.* kilobyte; kilobytes.

Kb *Computers.* kilobit; kilobits.

kB *Computers.* kilobyte; kilobytes.

kb *Computers.* kilobar; kilobars.

K.B. 1. King's Bench. **2.** Knight Bachelor.

kbar (kā′bär), kilobar; kilobars.

K.B.E. Knight Commander of the British Empire.

KBP *Chess.* king's bishop's pawn.

kc 1. kilocycle; kilocycles. **2.** kilocurie; kilocuries.

K.C. 1. Kansas City. **2.** King's Counsel. **3.** Knight Commander. **4.** Knights of Columbus.

K.C.B. Knight Commander of the Bath.

kCi kilocurie; kilocuries.

K.C.M.G. Knight Commander of the Order of St. Michael and St. George.

Kčs. koruna; korunas. [from Czech *k(oruna) č(esko)s(lovenská)*]

kc/s kilocycles per second. Also, **kc/sec**

K.C.S.I. Knight Commander of the Order of the Star of India.

K.C.V.O. Knight Commander of the (Royal) Victorian Order.

KD 1. kiln-dried. **2.** Also, **k.d.** *Commerce.* knocked-down.

KD. (in Kuwait) dinar; dinars.

Ken. Kentucky.

kG kilogauss; kilogausses.

kg kilogram; kilograms.

kg. 1. keg; kegs. **2.** kilogram; kilograms.

K.G. 1. Knight of the Garter. **2.** (in police use) known gambler.

KGB Committee for State Security: the intelligence and internal-security agency of the former Soviet Union. Also, **K.G.B.** [from Russian *K(omitét) g(osudárstvennoĭ) b(ezopásnosti)*]

kgf kilogram-force.

kg-m kilogram-meter; kilogram-meters.

KGPS kilograms per second. Also, **kgps**

Kh Knoop hardness.

Khn Knoop hardness number.

kHz kilohertz.

Ki. *Bible.* Kings.

KIA killed in action. Also, **K.I.A.**

KIAS knot indicated airspeed.

kil. kilometer; kilometers.

kip-ft one thousand foot-pounds.

KISS (kis), keep it simple, stupid.

K.J.V. King James Version (of the Bible).

K.K.K. Ku Klux Klan. Also, **KKK**

KKt *Chess.* king's knight.

KKtP *Chess.* king's knight's pawn.

kl kiloliter; kiloliters. Also, **kl.**

km kilometer; kilometers.

km. 1. kilometer; kilometers. **2.** kingdom.

kMc kilomegacycle; kilomegacycles.

km/sec kilometers per second.

KN *Chess.* king's knight.

kn knot; 1 nautical mile.

kn. (in Germany and Austria) kronen.

KNP *Chess.* king's knight's pawn.

kn sw knife switch.

Knt. Knight.

KO (kā′ō′, kā′ō′), *Slang.* a knockout, especially in boxing. Also, **ko, K.O., k.o., kayo.** [*k(nock) o(ut)*]

K. of C. Knights of Columbus.

K. of P. Knights of Pythias.

kop. kopeck.

KP *Chess.* king's pawn.

K.P. 1. *Military.* kitchen police. 2. Knight of the Order of St. Patrick. 3. Knights of Pythias.

kpc kiloparsec; kiloparsecs.

kph kilometers per hour. Also, **k.p.h.**

KR *Chess.* king's rook.

Kr *Symbol, Chemistry.* krypton.

Kr. 1. (in Sweden and the Faeroe Islands) krona; kronor. 2. (in Iceland) króna; krónur. 3. (in Denmark and Norway) krone; kroner.

kr. 1. (in Germany and Austria) kreutzer. 2. (in Sweden and the Faeroe Islands) krona; kronor. 3. (in Iceland) króna; krónur. 4. (in Denmark and Norway) krone; kroner.

KRP *Chess.* king's rook's pawn.

krs (in Turkey) kurus.

krsn kerosene.

KS Kansas (for use with ZIP code).

ksi one thousand pounds per square inch. [*k(ilo) + s(quare) i(nch)*]

ksr *Telecommunications.* keyboard send and receive.

Kt *Chess.* knight. Also, **Kt.**

Kt. knight.

kt. 1. karat; karats. 2. kiloton; kilotons. 3. knot; knots.

K.T. 1. Knights Templars. **2.** Knight of the Order of the Thistle.

Kt. Bach. knight bachelor.

kV kilovolt; kilovolts. Also, **kv**

K.V. *Music.* Köchel-Verzeichnis, the chronological listing of Mozart's works.

kVA kilovolt-ampere; kilovolt-amperes. Also, **kva**

kVAhm kilovolt-ampere hour meter.

kW kilowatt; kilowatts. Also, **kw.**

kWh kilowatt-hour. Also, **kwhr, K.W.H.**

KWIC (kwik), of or designating an alphabetical concordance of the principal terms in a text showing every occurrence of each term surrounded by a few words of the context. [*k(ey)-w(ord)-i(n)-c(ontext)*]

kwy keyway.

KY Kentucky (for use with ZIP code).

Ky. Kentucky.

kybd keyboard.

kypd keypad.

L

L **1.** *Optics.* lambert; lamberts. **2.** language. **3.** large. **4.** Latin. **5.** left. **6.** length. **7.** *British.* pound; pounds. [from Latin *libra*] **8.** long: denoting a size longer than regular, esp. for suits and coats. **9.** longitude. **10.** *Theater.* stage left.

L *Symbol.* **1.** the 12th in order or in a series, or, if *I* is omitted, the 11th. **2.** (*sometimes lowercase*) the Roman numeral for 50. **3.** *Electricity.* inductance. **4.** *Physics.* kinetic potential. **5.** *Biochemistry.* leucine. **6.** *Economics.* liquid assets. **7.** liter; liters.

l **1.** large. **2.** liter; liters. **3.** long.

L- **1.** *Chemistry.* levo-. **2.** *U.S. Military.* (in designations of light aircraft) liaison: *L-15.*

L- *Symbol, Biochemistry.* (of a molecule) having a configuration resembling the levorotatory isomer of glyceraldehyde: printed as a small capital, roman character. Compare *l-*.

l- *Symbol, Optics, Chemistry, Biochemistry.* levorotatory; levo-. Compare **L-**.

L. **1.** Lady. **2.** Lake. **3.** large. **4.** Latin. **5.** latitude. **6.** law. **7.** left. **8.** (in Honduras) lempira; lempiras. **9.** (in Romania) leu; lei. **10.** (in Bulgaria) lev; leva. **11.** book. [from Latin *liber*] **12.** Liberal. **13.** (in Italy) lira; lire. **14.** place. [from Latin *locus*] **15.** Lord. **16.** Low. **17.** lumen. **18.** *Theater.* stage left.

l. **1.** large. **2.** latitude. **3.** law. **4.** leaf. **5.** league. **6.** left. **7.** length. **8.** *plural* **ll.,** line. **9.** link. **10.** (in Italy) lira; lire. **11.** liter; liters. **12.** long.

LA Louisiana (for use with ZIP code).

La *Symbol, Chemistry.* lanthanum.

La. Louisiana.

l/a letter of authority.

L.A. **1.** Latin America. **2.** Law Agent. **3.** Library Association. **4.** Local Agent. **5.** Los Angeles.

Lab. **1.** Laborite. **2.** Labrador.

lab. **1.** labor. **2.** laboratory. **3.** laborer.

LAC leading aircraftsman.

LACW leading aircraftswoman.

LAD language acquisition device.

LaF Louisiana French.

lag lagging.

LAK cell *Immunology.* lymphokine-activated killer cell.

Lam. *Bible.* Lamentations.

lam. laminated.

LAN (lan), local area network.

lang. language.

laq lacquer.

laser (lā′zər), *Electronics.* light amplification by stimulated emission of radiation.

LASH (lash), an ocean-going vessel equipped with special cranes and holds for lifting and stowing cargo-carrying barges. [*l(ighter) a(board) sh(ip)*]

Lat. Latin.

lat. latitude.

latl lateral.

lau laundry.

LAV lymphadenopathy-associated virus.

lav lavatory.

lb *Telecommunications.* local battery.

lb. *plural* **lbs., lb.** pound. [from Latin *libra,* plural *librae*]

L.B. 1. landing barge. **2.** light bomber. **3.** bachelor of letters; bachelor of literature. [from Latin *Litterārum Baccalaureus; Literārum Baccalaureus*] **4.** local board.

lb. ap. *Pharmacology.* pound apothecary's.

L bar. angle iron. Also, **L beam.**

lb. av. pound avoirdupois.

lbf *Physics.* pound-force.

LBJ Lyndon Baines Johnson.

lbl label.

LBO *Finance.* leveraged buyout.

lbr lumber.

lbry library.

lb. t. pound troy.

lbyr labyrinth.

LC 1. inductance-capacitance. **2.** landing craft.

L/C letter of credit. Also, **l/c**

L.C. Library of Congress.

l.c. 1. left center. **2.** letter of credit. **3.** in the place cited. [from Latin *locō citātō*] **4.** *Printing.* lowercase.

l.c.a. lowercase alphabet.

LCD *Electronics.* liquid-crystal display.

L.C.D. *Math.* least common denominator; lowest common denominator. Also, **l.c.d.**

L.C.F. *Math.* lowest common factor. Also, **l.c.f.**

L chain *Immunology.* light chain.

LCI *Military.* a type of landing craft used in World War II. [*L(anding) C(raft) I(nfantry)*]

lcl local.

L.C.L. *Commerce.* less than carload lot. Also, **l.c.l.**

L.C.M. least common multiple; lowest common multiple. Also, **l.c.m.**

LCR inductance-capacitance-resistance.

LCT *Military.* a type of landing craft used in World War II. [*L(anding) C(raft) T(ank)*]

LD 1. praise (be) to God. [from Latin *laus Deō*] **2.** learning disability. **3.** learning-disabled. **4.** lethal dose. **5.** long distance (telephone call). **6.** Low Dutch.

LD. (in Libya) dinar; dinars.

Ld. 1. limited. **2.** Lord.

ld 1. leading. **2.** line drawing.

ld. load.

L.D. Low Dutch.

LD$_{50}$ *Pharmacology.* median lethal dose.

LDC less developed country. Also, **L.D.C.**

ldg. 1. landing. **2.** loading.

LDH *Biochemistry.* lactate dehydrogenase.

LDL *Biochemistry.* low-density lipoprotein.

ldmk landmark.

Ldp. 1. ladyship. **2.** lordship.

LDPE *Chemistry.* low-density polyethylene.

ldr ladder.

L.D.S. 1. Latter-day Saints. **2.** praise (be) to

God forever. [from Latin *laus Deō semper*] **3.** Licentiate in Dental Surgery.

l.e. *Football.* left end.

lect. 1. lecture. **2.** lecturer.

LED *Electronics.* light-emitting diode.

legis. 1. legislation. **2.** legislative. **3.** legislature.

LEM (lem), lunar excursion module.

LEP 1. *Physics.* large electron-positron collider. **2.** limited English proficiency.

Lett. Lettish.

Lev. *Bible.* Leviticus.

lex. 1. lexical. **2.** lexicon.

LF 1. *Baseball.* left field. **2.** *Baseball.* left fielder. **3.** low frequency.

lf 1. *Baseball.* left field. **2.** *Baseball.* left fielder. **3.** *Printing.* lightface. **4.** line feed.

l.f. *Baseball.* **1.** left field. **2.** left fielder.

lfb *Sports.* left fullback.

LG Low German. Also, **L.G.**

lg. 1. large. **2.** length. **3.** long.

l.g. *Football.* left guard.

lgc logic.

lge. large. Also, **lge**

L. Ger. 1. Low German. **2.** Low Germanic.

LGk Late Greek. Also, **LGk, L.Gk.**

lgsltd legislated.

lgsltr legislature.

lgstcs logistics.

lgth. length.

LH *Biochemistry, Physiology.* luteinizing hormone.

lh *Sports.* left halfback.

l.h. 1. left hand; left-handed. **2.** lower half. Also, **L.H.**

l.h.b. *Sports.* left halfback.

L.H.D. 1. Doctor of Humane Letters. **2.** Doctor of Humanities. [from Latin *Litterārum Humāniōrum Doctor*]

lhdr left-hand drive.

Li *Symbol, Chemistry.* lithium.

li *Surveying.* link; links.

L.I. **1.** *British.* light infantry. **2.** Long Island.

Lib. Liberal.

lib. **1.** book. [from Latin *liber*] **2.** librarian. **3.** library.

lic. **1.** license. **2.** licensed.

Lieut. lieutenant.

Lieut. Col. lieutenant colonel.

Lieut. Comdr. lieutenant commander.

LIF Lifetime (a cable television channel).

LIFO (li′fō), **1.** *Commerce.* last-in, first-out. **2.** *Computers.* a data storage and retrieval technique, in which the last item stored is the first item retrieved. [*l(ast) i(n) f(irst) o(ut)*]

lim. limit.

lin. **1.** lineal. **2.** linear. **3.** liniment.

lin ft linear foot; linear feet.

liq. **1.** liquid. **2.** liquor. **3.** (in prescriptions) solution. [from Latin *liquor*]

LISP (lisp), *Computers.* a programming language that processes data in the form of lists. [*lis(t) p(rocessing)*]

Lit. (in Italy) lira; lire.

lit. **1.** liter; liters. **2.** literal. **3.** literally. **4.** literary. **5.** literature.

Lit.B. Bachelor of Letters; Bachelor of Literature. [from Latin *Lit(t)erārum Baccalaureus*]

Lit.D. Doctor of Letters; Doctor of Literature. [from Latin *Lit(t)erārum Doctor*]

Lith. **1.** Lithuania. **2.** Also, **Lith** Lithuanian.

lith. **1.** lithograph. **2.** lithographic. **3.** lithography.

lithol. lithology.

Litt. B. Bachelor of Letters; Bachelor of Literature. [from Latin *Lit(t)erārum Baccalaureus*]

Litt. D. Doctor of Letters; Doctor of Literature. [from Latin *Lit(t)erārum Doctor*]

Litt.M. Master of Letters. [from Latin *Lit(t) erārum Magister*]

Lk. *Bible.* Luke.

lkd locked.

lkg looking.

lkge linkage.

lknt locknut.

lkr locker.

LL 1. Late Latin. 2. Low Latin. Also, **L.L.**

ll. 1. lines. 2. low level.

l.l. 1. in the place quoted. [from Latin *locō laudātō*] 2. loose-leaf.

L. Lat. 1. Late Latin. 2. Low Latin.

LLB Little League Baseball.

LL.B. Bachelor of Laws. [from Latin *Lēgum Baccalaureus*]

LL.D. Doctor of Laws. [from Latin *Lēgum Doctor*]

LL.M. Master of Laws. [from Latin *Lēgum Magister*]

llti long lead-time item.

LM (*often* lem), lunar module.

lm 1. list of material. 2. *Optics.* lumen; lumens.

L.M. 1. Licentiate in Medicine. 2. Licentiate in Midwifery. 3. Lord Mayor.

lm-hr *Optics.* lumen-hour; lumen-hours.

LMT local mean time.

lmtr limiter.

lm/W *Symbol.* lumen per watt.

Ln. lane.

ln logarithm (natural).

lndry rm *Real Estate.* laundry room.

LNG liquefied natural gas.

lnrty linearity.

lntl lintel.

LO lubrication order.

loc. locative.

loc. cit. (lok′ sit′), in the place cited. [from Latin *locō citātō*]

loep list of effective pages.

lof local oscillator frequency.

log. logarithm.

logamp logarithmic amplifier.

LOGO (lō′gō), *Computers.* a programming language widely used to teach children how to use computers. [from Greek *lógos* word, spelled as if an acronym]

lon. longitude.

Lond. London.

long. 1. longitude. **2.** longitudinal.

L.O.O.M. Loyal Order of Moose.

LOP *Navigation.* line of position.

loq. he speaks; she speaks. [from Latin *loquitur*]

loran (lôr′an, lōr′-), *Electronics.* long-range navigation.

lo-res (lō′rez′), *Computers.* low-resolution.

lot. (in prescriptions) a lotion. [from Latin *lōtiō*]

lox (loks), liquid oxygen.

LP long-playing: a phonograph record played at 33⅓ r.p.m.

L.P. *Printing.* **1.** long primer. **2.** low pressure. Also, **l.p.**

LPG liquefied petroleum gas. Also called **LP gas.**

LPGA Ladies Professional Golf Association.

lphldr lampholder.

lpm *Computers.* lines per minute. Also, **LPM**

LPN licensed practical nurse.

lprsvr life preserver.

L.P.S. Lord Privy Seal.

lptv low-power television.

lpw lumen per watt.

LQ letter-quality.

lqp *Computers.* letter-quality printer.

LR 1. *Real Estate.* living room. **2.** long range. **3.** lower right.

Lr *Symbol, Chemistry.* lawrencium.

L.R. Lloyd's Register.

LRAM long-range attack missile.

LRBM long-range ballistic missile.

lrg. large.

LRT light-rail transit.

LS 1. left side. **2.** letter signed. **3.** library science. **4.** lightship.

ls loudspeaker.

L.S. 1. Licentiate in Surgery. **2.** Linnaean Society. **3.** Also, **l.s.** the place of the seal, as on a document [from Latin *locus sigilli*].

LSA 1. Leukemia Society of America. **2.** Linguistic Society of America.

LSAT *Trademark.* Law School Admission Test.

lsb 1. least significant bit. **2.** lower sideband.

l.s.c. in the place mentioned above. [from Latin *locā suprā citātō*]

LSD 1. *U.S. Navy.* a seagoing amphibious ship capable of carrying and launching assault landing craft. [*l(anding) s(hip) d(eck)*] **2.** *Pharmacology.* lysergic acid diethylamide: a powerful psychedelic drug. **3.** *Math.* least significant digit.

L.S.D. *British.* pounds, shillings, and pence. Also, **£.s.d.**, **l.s.d.** [from Latin *librae, solidi, dēnāriī*]

LSI *Electronics.* large-scale integration.

LSM a type of military landing ship. [*l(anding) s(hip) m(edium)*]

L.S.S. Lifesaving Service.

LST an oceangoing military ship, used for landing troops and heavy equipment on beaches. [*l(anding) s(hip) t(ank)*]

l.s.t. local standard time.

lt 1. Also, **lt.** light. **2.** *Electricity.* low-tension.

Lt. lieutenant.

L.T. 1. long ton. **2.** *Electricity.* low-tension.

l.t. 1. *Football.* left tackle. **2.** local time. **3.** long ton.

LTA (of an aircraft) lighter-than-air.

Lt. Col. Lieutenant Colonel. Also **LTC**

Lt. Comdr. Lieutenant Commander. Also, **Lt. Com.**

Ltd. limited. Also, **ltd**, **ltd.**

ltg lighting.

Lt. Gen. Lieutenant General. Also, **LTG**

Lt. Gov. Lieutenant Governor.

L.Th. Licentiate in Theology.

lthr leather.

Lt. Inf. *Military.* light infantry.

LTJG *U.S. Navy.* Lieutenant Junior Grade.

LTL *Commerce.* less-than-truckload lot.

LTR long-term relationship.

ltr. 1. letter. **2.** lighter.

ltrprs letterpress.

lt-yr light-year; light-years.

lub *Math.* least upper bound.

lub. 1. lubricant. **2.** lubricating. **3.** lubrication.

lubo lubricating oil.

lubt lubricant.

luf lowest usable frequency.

LULAC League of United Latin-American Citizens.

lum luminous.

Luth. Lutheran.

Lux. Luxembourg.

LV. (in Bulgaria) lev; leva.

lv. 1. leave; leaves. **2.** (in France) livre; livres.

lvl level.

LVN licensed vocational nurse.

lvr 1. lever. **2.** louver.

LW low water.

l/w lumen per watt; lumens per watt.

l.w.m. low water mark.

lwop leave without pay.

lwp leave with pay.

lwr lower.

LWV League of Women Voters. Also, **L.W.V.**

lwyr lawyer.

lx *Optics.* lux.

lyr layer.

lyt layout.

LZ landing zone.

M

M 1. mach. **2.** *Music.* major. **3.** male. **4.** married. **5.** Medieval. **6.** medium. **7.** mega-: one million. [from Greek *mégas* large, great] **8.** Middle. **9.** modal auxiliary. **10.** modifier. **11.** *Economics.* monetary aggregate. **12.** *British.* motorway (used with a road number).

M *Symbol.* **1.** the thirteenth in order or in a series, or, when *I* is omitted, the twelfth. **2.** (*sometimes lowercase*) the Roman numeral for 1,000. **3.** *Electricity.* magnetization. **4.** *Biochemistry.* methionine.

m 1. *Physics.* mass. **2.** *Finance.* (of bonds) matured. **3.** medieval. **4.** medium. **5.** meter; meters. **6.** middle. **7.** *Music.* minor.

m *Symbol, Electricity.* magnetic pole strength.

M- *U.S. Military.* (used to designate the production model of military equipment, as the M-1 rifle.)

m- *Chemistry.* meta-: least hydrated (of a series); designating the meta position in the benzene ring.

M. 1. Majesty. **2.** Manitoba. **3.** (in Finland) markka; markkaa. **4.** Marquis. **5.** *Music.* measure. **6.** medicine. **7.** medium. **8.** meridian. **9.** noon. [from Latin *merídiēs*] **10.** Monday. **11.** *plural* **MM.** Monsieur. **12.** mountain.

m. 1. male. **2.** (in Germany) mark; marks. **3.** married. **4.** masculine. **5.** *Physics.* mass. **6.** medium. **7.** noon. [from Latin *merídiēs*] **8.** meter. **9.** middle. **10.** mile. **11.** minute. **12.** (in prescriptions) mix. [from Latin *misce*] **13.** modification of. **14.** *Physics, Math.* modulus. **15.** molar. **16.** month. **17.** moon. **18.** morning. **19.** mouth.

m³ *Symbol.* cubic meter.

MA 1. Massachusetts (for use with ZIP code). **2.** *Psychology.* mental age.

mA *Electricity.* milliampere; milliamperes.

ma master.

M.A. 1. Master of Arts. [from Latin *Magister Artium*] **2.** *Psychology.* mental age. **3.** Military Academy.

MAA master-at-arms.

M.A.Arch. Master of Arts in Architecture.

MAb *Immunology.* monoclonal antibody.

mac maintenance allocation chart.

Mac. *Bible.* Maccabees.

M.Ac. Master of Accountancy.

Macc. *Bible.* Maccabees.

Maced. Macedonia.

Mach *Physics.* mach number.

mach. 1. machine. **2.** machinery. **3.** machinist.

MAD (mad), Mutual Assured Destruction.

Mad. Madam.

MADD (mad), Mothers Against Drunk Driving.

Madm. Madam.

M.A.E. 1. Master of Aeronautical Engineering. **2.** Master of Art Education. **3.** Master of Arts in Education.

M.A.Ed. Master of Arts in Education.

M.Aero.E. Master of Aeronautical Engineering.

mag. 1. magazine. **2.** magnet. **3.** magnetic. **4.** magnetism. **5.** magneto. **6.** magnitude. **7.** (in prescriptions) large. [from Latin *magnus*]

magamp magnetic amplifier.

M.Ag.Ec. Master of Agricultural Economics.

M.Ag.Ed. Master of Agricultural Education.

magn *Electronics.* magnetron.

magtd magnitude.

mah mahogany.

maint maintenance.

Maj. Major.

Maj. Gen. Major General.

Mal. *Bible.* **1.** Malachi. **2.** Malayan.

M.A.L.D. Master of Arts in Law and Diplomacy.

malf malfunction.

M.A.L.S. 1. Master of Arts in Liberal Studies. **2.** Master of Arts in Library Science.

mam milliammeter.

Man. 1. Manila. 2. Manitoba.

man. manual.

manf manifold.

MAO *Biochemistry.* monoamine oxidase.

MAOI *Biochemistry.* monoamine oxidase inhibitor.

MAO inhibitor *Biochemistry.* monoamine oxidase inhibitor.

MAP modified American plan.

MAPI *Computers.* Messaging Application Programming Interface.

Mar. March.

mar. 1. maritime. 2. married.

M.A.R. Master of Arts in Religion.

MARC (märk), a standardized system developed by the Library of Congress for producing and transmitting records. [*ma(chine) r(eadable) c(atologing)*]

March. Marchioness.

M.Arch. Master of Architecture.

M.Arch.E. Master of Architectural Engineering.

Mar.E. Marine Engineer.

marg. 1. margin. 2. marginal.

Mar.Mech.E. Marine Mechanical Engineer.

Marq. 1. Marquess. 2. Marquis.

MARS (marz), 1. Military Affiliated Radio System. 2. multiple-access retrieval system.

mas. masculine.

masc. masculine.

maser (mā′zər), *Electronics.* microwave amplification by stimulated emission of radiation.

MASH (mash), mobile army surgical hospital.

mas. pil. (in prescriptions) a pill mass. [from Latin *massa pilulāris*]

Mass. Massachusetts.

mat. 1. *Ecclesiastical.* matins. 2. *Finance.* maturity.

M.A.T. Master of Arts in Teaching.

Mat.E. Materials Engineer.

math 1. mathematical. 2. mathematics.

matl material.

MATS (mats), Military Air Transport Service.

Matt. *Bible.* Matthew.

MATV master antenna television system.

MAX Cinemax (a cable television channel).

max. maximum.

MB 1. Manitoba, Canada (for use with ZIP code). **2.** *Computers.* megabyte; megabytes.

Mb *Computers.* megabit; megabits.

mb *Physics.* **1.** millibar; millibars. **2.** millibarn; millibarns.

M.B. *Chiefly British.* Bachelor of Medicine. [from Latin *Medicinae Baccalaureus*]

M.B.A. Master of Business Administration. Also, **MBA**

mbb *Electricity.* make-before-break.

mbd (of oil) million barrels per day.

MBE Multistate Bar Examination.

M.B.E. Member of the Order of the British Empire.

mbl mobile.

Mbm one thousand feet, board measure.

mbm *Computers.* magnetic bubble memory.

MBO management by objective.

mbr member.

MBTA Massachusetts Bay Transportation Authority.

MByte *Computers.* megabyte: 1 million bytes.

MC 1. Marine Corps. **2.** master of ceremonies. **3.** Medical Corps. **4.** Member of Congress.

Mc 1. *Physics, Chemistry.* megacurie; megacuries. **2.** *Electricity.* megacycle.

mC 1. *Electricity.* millicoulomb; millicoulombs. **2.** *Physics, Chemistry.* millicurie; millicuries.

mc 1. *Electricity.* megacycle. **2.** *Optics.* metercandle. **3.** *Physics, Chemistry.* millicurie; millicuries. **4.** *Electricity.* momentary contact.

M.C. 1. Master Commandant. **2.** master of ceremonies. **3.** Medical Corps. **4.** Member of Congress. **5.** Member of Council. **6.** *British.* Military Cross.

MCAT Medical College Admission Test.

M.C.E. Master of Civil Engineering.

Mcf one thousand cubic feet. Also, **mcf, MCF**

Mcfd thousands of cubic feet per day.

M.Ch.E. Master of Chemical Engineering.

MChin Middle Chinese.

mchry machinery.

mCi *Physics, Chemistry.* millicurie; millicuries.

M.C.J. Master of Comparative Jurisprudence.

mcm 1. *Computers.* magnetic-core memory. **2.** thousand circular mils.

MCP male chauvinist pig.

M.C.P. Master of City Planning.

M.C.R. Master of Comparative Religion.

mcw *Electronics.* modulated continuous wave.

MD 1. Maryland (for use with ZIP code). **2.** Doctor of Medicine. [from Latin *Medicinae Doctor*] **3.** Middle Dutch. **4.** months after date. **5.** muscular dystrophy.

Md *Music.* right hand. [from Italian *mano destra* or French *main droite*]

Md *Symbol, Chemistry.* mendelevium.

md mean deviation.

Md. Maryland.

M/D months after date. Also, **m/d**

M.D. 1. Doctor of Medicine. [from Latin *Medicinae Doctor*] **2.** Middle Dutch.

MDA *Pharmacology.* an amphetamine derivative, $C_{10}H_{13}NO_2$. [*m(ethylene) d(ioxy)a(mphetamine)*]

MDAA Muscular Dystrophy Association of America.

MDAP Mutual Defense Assistance Program.

M.Des. Master of Design.

mdf *Telephones.* main distributing frame.

mdl 1. middle. **2.** minimum detectable level. **3.** module.

Mdlle. Mademoiselle.

mdm medium.

Mdm. Madam.

MDMA an amphetamine derivative, $C_{11}H_{15}NO_2$. [*m(ethylene) d(ioxy)m(eth)a(mphetamine)*]

Mdme. Madame.

mdn median.

mdnt. midnight.

mdnz modernize.

MDR minimum daily requirement.

mdse. merchandise.

MDT 1. mean downtime. 2. Also, **M.D.T.** Mountain Daylight Time.

ME 1. Maine (for use with ZIP code). 2. Middle East. 3. Middle English.

Me *Chemistry.* methyl.

Me. Maine.

M.E. 1. (*often lowercase*) managing editor. 2. Master of Education. 3. Master of Engineering. 4. Mechanical Engineer. 5. Medical Examiner. 6. Methodist Episcopal. 7. Middle English. 8. Mining Engineer.

meas. 1. measurable. 2. measure. 3. measurement.

mech. 1. mechanical. 2. mechanics. 3. mechanism.

med. 1. medical. 2. medicine. 3. medieval. 4. medium.

M.Ed. Master of Education.

Medit. Mediterranean.

Med.Sc.D. Doctor of Medical Science.

MEG *Medicine.* magnetoencephalogram.

meg 1. *Electricity.* megacycle. 2. megohm; megohms.

MEGO (mē′gō), my eyes glaze over.

MEK *Chemistry.* methyl ethyl ketone.

mem. 1. member. 2. memoir. 3. memorandum. 4. memorial. 5. memory.

M.Eng. Master of Engineering.

M.E.P. Master of Engineering Physics.

m.e.p. mean effective pressure.

M.E.P.A. Master of Engineering and Public Administration.

mEq milliequivalent.

mer. 1. meridian. 2. meridional.

merc. 1. mercantile. 2. mercurial. 3. mercury.

Messrs. (mes′ərz), plural of **Mr.**

Met *Biochemistry.* methionine.

met. 1. metal. **2.** metallurgical. **3.** metaphor. **4.** metaphysics. **5.** meteorology. **6.** metropolitan.

metal. 1. metallurgical. **2.** metallurgy.

metall. 1. metallurgical. **2.** metallurgy.

metaph. 1. metaphysical. **2.** metaphysics.

metaphys. metaphysics.

Met.E. metallurgical engineer.

meteor. 1. meteorological. **2.** meteorology.

meteorol. 1. Also, **metrl** meteorological. **2.** meteorology.

Meth. Methodist.

MeV (mev), *Physics.* million electron volts; megaelectron volt. Also, **Mev, mev**

Mex. 1. Mexican. **2.** Mexico.

MexSp Mexican Spanish.

mez mezzanine.

MF 1. married female. **2.** medium frequency. **3.** Middle French.

mF *Electricity.* millifarad; millifarads.

mf 1. medium frequency. **2.** microfilm. **3.** *Electricity.* millifarad; millifarads.

mf. *Music.* mezzo forte. **2.** *Electricity.* microfarad.

m/f male or female: used especially in classified ads. Also, **M/F**

M.F. 1. Master of Forestry. **2.** Middle French.

MFA Museum of Fine Arts.

M.F.A. Master of Fine Arts.

mfd. manufactured.

mfg. manufacturing.

m/f/h male, female, handicapped: used especially in classified ads. Also, **M/F/H**

M.F.H. master of foxhounds.

MFlem Middle Flemish.

MFM *Computers.* modified frequency modulation: hard-drive interface.

M.For. Master of Forestry.

mfr. 1. manufacture. **2.** manufacturer.

M.Fr. Middle French.

M.F.S. 1. Master of Food Science. **2.** Master of Foreign Service. **3.** Master of Foreign Study.

mfsk multiple-frequency shift-keying.

M.F.T. Master of Foreign Trade.

MG 1. machine gun. **2.** major general. **3.** military government. **4.** *Pathology.* myasthenia gravis.

Mg *Music.* left hand. [from French *main gauche*]

Mg *Symbol, Chemistry.* magnesium.

mg 1. milligram; milligrams. **2.** motor-generator.

mGal milligal; milligals.

MGB the Ministry of State Security in the U.S. S.R. (1946–53). [from Russian, for *Ministér-stvo gosudárstvennoĭ bezopásnosti*]

mgd millions of gallons per day.

mgf magnify.

MGk. Medieval Greek. Also, **MGk**

mgl mogul.

mgmt management.

mgn 1. magneto. **2.** margin.

MGr. Medieval Greek.

mgr. 1. manager. **2.** Monseigneur. **3.** Monsignor. Also, **Mgr.**

mgt. management.

MGy Sgt master gunnery sergeant.

MH Marshall Islands (approved for postal use).

mH *Electricity.* millihenry; millihenries. Also, **mh**

M.H. Medal of Honor.

M.H.A. Master in Hospital Administration; Master of Hospital Administration.

MHC *Biochemistry.* major histocompatibility complex.

MHD *Physics.* magnetohydrodynamics.

mhd 1. magnetohydrodynamic. **2.** masthead.

M.H.E. Master of Home Economics.

MHG Middle High German. Also, **M.H.G.**

M.H.R. Member of the House of Representatives.

M.H.W. mean high water. Also, **MHW, mhw, m.h.w.**

MHz megahertz. Also, **mhz**

mHz millihertz.

MI Michigan (for use with ZIP code).

MI *Pathology.* myocardial infarction.

mi mile; miles.

mi. 1. mile; miles. 2. *Finance.* mill; mills.

M.I. 1. Military Intelligence. 2. Mounted Infantry.

MIA *Military.* missing in action.

M.I.A. 1. Master of International Affairs. 2. *Military.* missing in action.

mic 1. micrometer. 2. microphone.

Mic. *Bible.* Micah.

Mich. 1. Michaelmas. 2. Michigan.

MICR *Electronics.* magnetic ink character recognition.

micr microscope.

micros. microscopy.

Mid. Midshipman.

mid. middle.

M.I.D. Master of Industrial Design.

midar (mi′där), microwave detection and ranging.

MIDI (mid′ē), *Electronics.* Musical Instrument Digital Interface.

MIDN Midshipman.

Midn. Midshipman.

M.I.E. Master of Industrial Engineering.

MiG (mig), any of several Russian fighter aircraft. Also, **Mig, MIG** [named after Artem *Mi(koyan)* and Mikhail *G(urevich),* aircraft designers]

mil. 1. military. 2. militia.

milit. military.

M.I.L.R. Master of Industrial and Labor Relations.

MIL-STD military standard.

min minim; minims.

min. 1. mineralogical. 2. mineralogy. 3.

minim. **4.** minimum. **5.** mining. **6.** minor. **7.** minuscule. **8.** minute; minutes.

M.Ind.E. Master of Industrial Engineering.

Min.E. Mineral Engineer.

mineral. 1. mineralogical. **2.** mineralogy.

Mining Eng. Mining Engineer.

Minn. Minnesota.

mintr miniature.

MIP monthly investment plan.

MIPS (mips), *Computers.* million instructions per second: a measure of computer speed.

mir mirror.

MIr. Middle Irish. Also, **M.Ir.**

MIRV (mûrv), multiple independently targetable reentry vehicle. Also, **M.I.R.V.**

MIS 1. management information system. **2.** *Electronics.* metal-insulated semiconductor.

misc. 1. miscellaneous. **2.** miscellany.

Misc. Doc. miscellaneous document.

Miss. Mississippi.

miss. 1. mission. **2.** missionary.

mist. (in prescriptions) a mixture. [from Latin *mistūra*]

MITC mortgage investment tax credit.

mitt. (in prescriptions) send. [from Latin *mitte*]

mixt. mixture.

M.J. Master of Journalism.

mk. 1. (in Germany) mark. **2.** (in Finland) markka.

mkr marker.

MKS meter-kilogram-second. Also, **mks**

MKSA meter-kilogram-second-ampere. Also, **mksa**

mkt. market.

mktg. marketing.

ML Medieval Latin. Also, **M.L.**

mL *Optics.* millilambert; millilamberts.

ml milliliter; milliliters.

ml. 1. mail. **2.** milliliter; milliliters.

MLA Modern Language Association.

M.L.A. 1. Master of Landscape Architecture. **2.** Modern Language Association.

M.L.Arch. Master of Landscape Architecture.

MLB Maritime Labor Board.

MLD 1. median lethal dose. **2.** minimum lethal dose.

mldg molding.

MLF Multilateral Nuclear Force.

MLG. Middle Low German. Also, **M.L.G.**

Mlle. Mademoiselle. Also, **Mlle**

Mlles. Mesdemoiselles.

MLR minimum lending rate.

MLS *Real Estate.* Multiple Listing Service.

M.L.S. Master of Library Science.

MLU *Psycholinguistics.* mean length of utterance.

MLW mean low water.

MM married male.

mM millimole; millimoles.

mm millimeter; millimeters.

MM. Messieurs.

mm. 1. *Music.* measures. **2.** thousands. [from Latin *millia*] **3.** millimeter; millimeters.

M.M. 1. Master Mason. **2.** Master Mechanic. **3.** Master of Music.

mm³ *Symbol.* cubic millimeter.

MMA Metropolitan Museum of Art.

Mme. Madame.

M.M.E. 1. Master of Mechanical Engineering. **2.** Master of Mining Engineering. **3.** Master of Music Education.

Mmes. Mesdames.

M.Met.E. Master of Metallurgical Engineering.

mmf *Electricity.* magnetomotive force. Also, **m.m.f.**

M.Mgt.E. Master of Management Engineering.

mm Hg millimeter of mercury. Also, **mmHg**

mmho *Electricity.* millimho; millimhos.

MMPI *Psychology.* Minnesota Multiphasic Personality Inventory.

M.M.Sc. Master of Medical Science.

MMT 1. *Astronomy.* Multiple Mirror Telescope.

2. *Chemistry.* $C_9H_7MnO_3$, a gasoline additive. [*m(ethylcyclopentadienyl) m(anganese) t(ricarbonyl)*]

mmu memory-management unit.

M.Mus. Master of Music.

M.Mus.Ed. Master of Music Education.

MN Minnesota (for use with ZIP code).

Mn *Symbol, Chemistry.* manganese.

mn main.

M.N. Master of Nursing.

M.N.A. Master of Nursing Administration.

M.N.A.S. Member of the National Academy of Sciences.

mncpl municipal.

M.N.E. Master of Nuclear Engineering.

mnfrm *Computers.* mainframe.

mng managing.

Mngr. Monsignor.

mngr. manager.

mnl manual.

Mnr. manor.

mnrl mineral.

M.N.S. Master of Nutritional Science.

mnstb *Electronics.* monostable.

M.Nurs. Master of Nursing.

MO 1. method of operation. **2.** Missouri (for use with ZIP code). **3.** mode of operation. **4.** modus operandi.

Mo *Symbol, Chemistry.* molybdenum.

Mo. 1. Missouri. **2.** Monday.

mo. month. Also, **mo**

M.O. 1. mail order. **2.** manually operated. **3.** Medical Officer. **4.** method of operation. **5.** mode of operation. **6.** modus operandi. **7.** money order.

m.o. 1. mail order. **2.** modus operandi. **3.** money order.

mod 1. *Computers.* magneto-optical drive. **2.** model. **3.** modification. **4.** modulator.

modem (mō′dəm, -dem), an electronic device that makes possible the transmission of data to or from a computer via telephone or other communication lines. [*mo(dulator)-dem(odulator)*]

MODFET (mod′fet′), *Electronics.* modulation-doped field effect transistor.

ModGk Modern Greek. Also, **Mod. Gk., Mod. Gr.**

ModHeb Modern Hebrew. Also, **Mod. Heb.**

modif. modification.

mod. praesc. (in prescriptions) in the manner prescribed; as directed. [from Latin *modō praescriptō*]

Moham. Mohammedan.

M.O.I. *British.* **1.** Ministry of Information. **2.** Ministry of the Interior.

mol *Chemistry.* mole.

mol. 1. molecular. **2.** molecule.

mol. wt. molecular weight.

mom momentary.

m.o.m. middle of month.

MOMA (mō′mə), Museum of Modern Art.

Mon. 1. Monday. **2.** Monsignor.

mon. 1. monastery. **2.** monetary. **3.** monitor. **4.** monument.

mono monophonic.

Mons. Monsieur.

Mont. Montana.

MOPED (mō′ped), motor-assisted pedal cycle.

M.Opt. Master of Optometry.

MOR *Music.* middle-of-the-road.

mor. morocco.

more dict. (in prescriptions) in the manner directed. Also, **mor. dict.** [from Latin *mōre dictū*]

more sol. (in prescriptions) in the usual manner. Also, **mor. sol.** [from Latin *mōre solitō*]

morphol. morphology.

mort morse taper.

MOS *Electronics.* metal oxide semiconductor.

mos. 1. months. **2.** mosaic.

MOSFET (mos′fet′), *Electronics.* metal oxide semiconducter field-effect transistor.

MOST (mōst), *Electronics.* metal-oxide-semiconductor transistor.

mot motor.

MP 1. Military Police. **2.** Military Policeman. **3.** Mounted Police. **4.** Northern Mariana Islands (approved for postal use).

mp 1. melting point. **2.** melting pot. **3.** *Music.* mezzo piano.

M.P. 1. Member of Parliament. **2.** Metropolitan Police. **3.** Military Police. **4.** Military Policeman. **5.** Mounted Police.

m.p. 1. melting point. **2.** (in prescriptions) in the manner prescribed; as directed. [from Latin *modō praescriptō*]

M.P.A. 1. Master of Professional Accounting. **2.** Master of Public Administration. **3.** Master of Public Affairs.

MPAA Motion Picture Association of America.

MPB Missing Persons Bureau.

MPC Multimedia PC: a system conforming to specifications covering audio, video, and other multimedia components, and able to run multimedia software.

M.P.E. Master of Physical Education.

MPEG (em/peg), Motion Picture Experts Group.

MPers Middle Persian.

mpg miles per gallon. Also, **mi/gal., m.p.g., M.P.G., MPG**

mph miles per hour. Also, **mi/h., m.p.h., MPH**

M.Ph. Master of Philosophy.

M.P.H. Master of Public Health.

M.Pharm. Master of Pharmacy.

mpl maintenance parts list.

mpt male pipe thread.

MR 1. motivation research. **2.** Moral Re-Armament. Also, **M.R.**

mR *Physics.* milliroentgen; milliroentgens. Also, **mr**

Mr. (mis/tər), *plural* **Messrs.** (mes/ərz). mister: a title of respect prefixed to a man's name or position: *Mr. Lawson; Mr. President.*

MRA Moral Re-Armament.

MRBM medium-range ballistic missile. Also, **mrbm**

M.R.E. Master of Religious Education.

mrg mooring.

MRI *Medicine.* **1.** Also called **NMR.** magnetic resonance imaging. **2.** magnetic resonance imager.

mRNA *Genetics.* messenger RNA.

M.R.P. Master in Regional Planning; Master of Regional Planning.

Mrs. (mis′iz, miz′iz), *plural* **Mmes.** (mā däm′, -dam′). a title of respect prefixed to the name of a married woman: *Mrs. Jones.*

MRV *Military.* multiple reentry vehicle. Also, **M.R.V.**

MS 1. Mississippi (for use with ZIP code). **2.** motorship. **3.** multiple sclerosis.

ms millisecond; milliseconds.

MS., *plural* **MSS.** manuscript.

Ms. (miz), *plural* **Mses.** (miz′əz). a title of respect prefixed to a woman's name or position: unlike *Miss* or *Mrs.*, it does not depend upon or indicate her marital status.

ms., *plural* **mss.** manuscript.

M/S 1. *Commerce.* months after sight. **2.** motorship.

m/s meter per second; meters per second.

M.S. 1. mail steamer. **2.** Master of Science. **3.** Master in Surgery. **4.** motorship.

m.s. 1. *Grammar.* modification of the stem of. **2.** *Commerce.* months after sight.

M.S.A. Master of Science in Agriculture.

M.S.A.E. Master of Science in Aeronautical Engineering.

M.S.A.M. Master of Science in Applied Mechanics.

M.S.Arch. Master of Science in Architecture.

MSAT Minnesota Scholastic Aptitude Test.

M.S.B.A. Master of Science in Business Administration.

M.S.B.C. Master of Science in Building Construction.

M.S.Bus. Master of Science in Business.

MSC Manned Spacecraft Center.

M.Sc. Master of Science.

M.Sc.D. Doctor of Medical Science.

M.S.C.E. Master of Science in Civil Engineering.

M.S.Ch.E. Master of Science in Chemical Engineering.

M.Sc.Med. Master of Medical Science.

M.S.Cons. Master of Science in Conservation.

M.S.C.P. Master of Science in Community Planning.

mscr machine screw.

MSD 1. mean solar day. **2.** *Math.* most significant digit.

M.S.D. 1. Doctor of Medical Science. **2.** Master of Science in Dentistry.

M.S.Dent. Master of Science in Dentistry.

MS DOS (em′es′ dôs′, -dos′), *Trademark.* a microcomputer operating system. Also, **MS-DOS**

M.S.E. 1. Master of Science in Education. **2.** Master of Science in Engineering.

msec millisecond; milliseconds.

m/sec meter per second; meters per second.

M.S.Ed. Master of Science in Education.

M.S.E.E. Master of Science in Electrical Engineering.

M.S.E.M. 1. Master of Science in Engineering Mechanics. **2.** Master of Science in Engineering of Mines.

M.S.Ent. Master of Science in Entomology.

M.S.F. Master of Science in Forestry.

M.S.F.M. Master of Science in Forest Management.

M.S.For. Master of Science in Forestry.

MSG monosodium glutamate.

msg. message.

M.S.Geol.E. Master of Science in Geological Engineering.

M.S.G.M. Master of Science in Government Management.

M.S.G.Mgt. Master of Science in Game Management.

msgr messenger.

Msgr. 1. Monseigneur. 2. Monsignor.

M.Sgt. master sergeant.

MSH 1. *Biochemistry.* melanocyte-stimulating hormone; melanotropin: a hormone that causes dispersal of the black pigment melanin of melanocytes. 2. *Mineralogy.* Mohs scale.

M.S.H.A. Master of Science in Hospital Administration.

M.S.H.E. Master of Science in Home Economics. Also, **M.S.H.Ec.**

M.S.Hort. Master of Science in Horticulture.

M.S.Hyg. Master of Science in Hygiene.

MSI *Electronics.* medium-scale integration.

M.S.J. Master of Science in Journalism.

mskg masking.

msl missile.

M.S.L. 1. Master of Science in Linguistics. 2. Also, **m.s.l.** mean sea level.

msly mostly.

M.S.M. 1. Master of Sacred Music. 2. Master of Science in Music.

M.S.M.E. Master of Science in Mechanical Engineering.

M.S.Met.E. Master of Science in Metallurgical Engineering.

M.S.Mgt.E. Master of Science in Management Engineering.

M.S.N. Master of Science in Nursing.

msnry masonry.

msp *Printing.* manuscript page.

M.S.P.E. Master of Science in Physical Education.

M.S.P.H. Master of Science in Public Health.

M.S.Phar. Master of Science in Pharmacy. Also, **M.S.Pharm.**

M.S.P.H.E. Master of Science in Public Health Engineering.

M.S.P.H.Ed. Master of Science in Public Health Education.

MSS. manuscripts. Also, **MSS, Mss, mss.**

M.S.S. 1. Master of Social Science. **2.** Master of Social Service.

M.S.Sc. Master of Social Science.

M.S.S.E. Master of Science in Sanitary Engineering.

MST 1. mean solar time. **2.** Mountain Standard Time.

M.S.T. 1. Master of Science in Teaching. **2.** Also, **m.s.t.** Mountain Standard Time.

mstr moisture.

MSTS *U.S. Military.* Military Sea Transportation Service.

M.S.W. 1. Master of Social Welfare. **2.** Master of Social Work or Master in Social Work. Also, **MSW**

MT 1. mean time. **2.** mechanical translation. **3.** *Physics.* megaton; megatons. **4.** Montana (for use with ZIP code). **5.** Mountain time.

mt mount.

Mt. 1. mount: *Mt. Rainier.* **2.** Also, **mt.** mountain.

M.T. 1. metric ton. **2.** Also, **m.t.** Mountain time.

MTA Metropolitan Transit Authority.

MTBF mean time between failures.

MTBI mean time between incidents.

MTCF mean time to catastrophic failure.

mtchd matched.

mtd 1. mean temperature difference. **2.** mounted.

mtg. 1. meeting. **2.** mortgage. **3.** mounting. Also, **mtg**

mtge. mortgage.

M.Th. Master of Theology.

mthbd *Computers.* motherboard.

mthd method.

MTI *Electronics.* moving target indicator. Also, **mti**

mtn 1. motion. **2.** mountain.

MTO *Military.* (in World War II) Mediterranean Theater of Operations.

MTR mean time to restore.

mtr 1. magnetic tape recorder. **2.** meter (instrument).

Mt. Rev. Most Reverend.

mtrg metering.

MTS *Broadcasting.* multichannel television sound.

Mts. mountains. Also, **mts.**

MTTF mean time to failure.

MTTFF mean time to first failure.

MTTM mean time to maintain.

MTTR mean time to repair.

mtu magnetic tape unit.

MTV Music Television (a cable television channel).

mtx matrix.

MUF material unaccounted for.

muf 1. maximum usable frequency. **2.** muffler.

mult 1. multiple. **2.** multiplication.

multr multiplier.

mun. 1. municipal. **2.** municipality.

munic. 1. municipal. **2.** municipality.

M.U.P. Master of Urban Planning.

Mus. Muslim.

mus. 1. museum. **2.** music. **3.** musical. **4.** musician.

Mus.B. Bachelor of Music. Also, **Mus. Bac.** [from Latin *Mūsicae Baccalaureus*]

Mus.D. Doctor of Music. Also, **Mus.Doc.,** **Mus.Dr.** [from Latin *Mūsicae Doctor*]

Mus.M. Master of Music. [from Latin *Mūsicae Magister*]

mut. 1. mutilated. **2.** mutual.

muw music wire.

mux (muks), *Electronics.* **1.** multiplex. **2.** multiplexer.

MV 1. main verb. **2.** *Electricity.* megavolt; megavolts. **3.** motor vessel.

Mv *Symbol, Chemistry.* mendelevium.

mV *Electricity.* millivolt; millivolts.

mv 1. mean variation. **2.** *Electronics.* multivibrator.

m.v. 1. market value. **2.** mean variation. **3.** *Music.* mezza voce.

mvbl movable.

M.V.Ed. Master of Vocational Education.

mvg moving.

MVP Most Valuable Player. Also, **M.V.P.**

mvt movement.

MW *Electricity.* megawatt; megawatts.

mW *Electricity.* milliwatt; milliwatts.

mw medium wave.

M.W.A. Modern Woodmen of America.

MWG music wire gauge.

mwo modification work order.

mwp maximum working pressure.

M.W.T. Master of Wood Technology.

mwv maximum working voltage.

MX missile experimental: a ten-warhead U.S. intercontinental ballistic missile.

Mx *Electricity.* maxwell; maxwells.

mxd mixed.

mxg mixing.

mxr mixer.

mxt mixture.

mycol. mycology.

M.Y.O.B. mind your own business.

myth. 1. mythological. **2.** mythology.

mythol. 1. mythological. **2.** mythology.

N

N 1. *Physics.* newton; newtons. **2.** north. **3.** northern.

N *Symbol.* **1.** the 14th in order or in a series, or, when *I* is omitted, the 13th. **2.** (*sometimes lowercase*) the medieval Roman numeral for 90. **3.** *Chemistry.* nitrogen. **4.** *Biochemistry.* asparagine. **5.** *Math.* an indefinite, constant whole number, esp. the degree of a quantic or an equation, or the order of a curve. **6.** *Chess.* knight. **7.** *Printing.* en. **8.** *Chemistry.* Avogadro's number. **9.** neutron number.

n *Symbol.* **1.** *Physics.* neutron. **2.** *Optics.* index of refraction.

n- *Chemistry.* an abbreviated form of *normal*, used in the names of hydrocarbon compounds.

N. **1.** Nationalist. **2.** Navy. **3.** New. **4.** Noon. **5.** *Chemistry.* normal (strength solution). **6.** Norse. **7.** north. **8.** northern. **9.** *Finance.* note. **10.** November.

n. **1.** name. **2.** born. [from Latin *nātus*] **3.** nephew. **4.** *Commerce.* net. **5.** neuter. **6.** new. **7.** nominative. **8.** noon. **9.** *Chemistry.* normal (strength solution). **10.** north. **11.** northern. **12.** *Finance.* note. **13.** noun. **14.** number.

NA **1.** not applicable. **2.** not available.

Na *Symbol, Chemistry.* sodium. [from Latin *natrium*]

n/a **1.** no account. **2.** not applicable.

N.A. **1.** National Army. **2.** North America. **3.** not applicable. **4.** *Microscopy.* numerical aperture.

NAA National Aeronautic Association.

NAACP National Association for the Advancement of Colored People. Also, **N.A.A.C.P.**

NAB **1.** Also, **N.A.B.** National Association of Broadcasters. **2.** New American Bible.

NACA National Advisory Committee for Aeronautics. Also, **N.A.C.A.**

NAD *Biochemistry.* a coenzyme, $C_{21}H_{27}N_7O_{14}P_2$, involved in many cellular oxidation-reduction reactions. [*n(icotinamide) a(denine) d(inucleotide)*]

N.A.D. National Academy of Design.

NADH *Biochemistry.* an abbreviation for the reduced form of NAD in electron transport reactions. [NAD + *H*, for hydrogen]

NADP *Biochemistry.* a coenzyme, $C_{21}H_{28}N_7O_{17}P_3$, similar in function to NAD. [*n(icotinamide) a(denine) d(inucleotide) p(hosphate)*]

NAFTA (naf′tə), North American Free Trade Agreement. Also, **Nafta.**

Nah. *Bible.* Nahum.

NAHB National Association of Home Builders.

NAM National Association of Manufacturers. Also, **N.A.M.**

nar narrow.

narc. narcotics.

N.A.S. 1. National Academy of Sciences. **2.** naval air station. Also, **NAS**

NASA (nas′ə), National Aeronautics and Space Administration.

NASCAR (nas′kär), National Association for Stock Car Auto Racing. Also, **N.A.S.C.A.R.**

NASD National Association of Securities Dealers. Also, **N.A.S.D.**

NASDAQ (nas′dak, naz′-), National Association of Securities Dealers Automated Quotations.

nat. 1. national. **2.** native. **3.** natural. **4.** naturalist.

natl. national.

NATO (nā′tō), an organization formed in 1949, comprising the 12 nations of the Atlantic Pact together with Greece, Turkey, and the Federal Republic of Germany, for the purpose of collective defense. [*N(orth) A(tlantic) T(reaty) O(rganization)*]

naut. nautical.

nav. 1. naval. **2.** navigable. **3.** navigation.

Nav. Arch. Naval Architect.

Nav. E. Naval Engineer.

navig. navigation.

NAVSAT (nav′sat′), navigational satellite.

NB 1. New Brunswick, Canada (for use with ZIP code). **2.** Also, **N.B.** note well; take notice. [from Latin *nota bene*]

Nb *Symbol, Chemistry.* niobium.

nb *Telecommunications.* narrowband.

N.B. New Brunswick.

NBA 1. National Basketball Association. **2.** Also, **N.B.A.** National Book Award. **3.** National Boxing Association.

nba narrowband amplifier.

NBC National Broadcasting System.

NbE north by east.

NBIOS *Computers.* network basic input-output system.

nbr number.

NBS National Bureau of Standards. Also, **N.B.S.**

NbW north by west.

NC 1. National coarse (a thread measure). **2.** no change. **3.** no charge. **4.** North Carolina (for use with ZIP code). **5.** numerical control. **6.** *Military.* Nurse Corps.

nc 1. no connection. **2.** *Electricity.* normally closed (of contacts).

n/c no charge.

N.C. 1. no charge. **2.** North Carolina.

NCA 1. National Council on the Aging. **2.** National Council on the Arts.

nca nickel-copper alloy.

NCAA National Collegiate Athletic Association. Also, **N.C.A.A.**

N.C.C. National Council of Churches. Also, **NCC**

NCCJ National Conference of Christians and Jews.

ncd no can do.

N.C.O. Noncommissioned Officer.

NCTE National Council of Teachers of English.

ND North Dakota (for use with ZIP code).

Nd *Symbol, Chemistry.* neodymium.

nd *Stock Exchange.* (especially of bonds) next day (delivery).

n.d. no date.

NDAC National Defense Advisory Commission.

N.Dak. North Dakota. Also, **N.D.**

nde near-death experience.

ndf *Photography.* neutral-density filter.

ndro nondestructive readout.

NDSL National Direct Student Loan.

ndt nondestructive testing.

NE 1. Nebraska (for use with ZIP code). **2.** northeast. **3.** northeastern.

Ne *Symbol, Chemistry.* neon.

N.E. 1. naval engineer. **2.** New England. **3.** northeast. **4.** northeastern.

n.e. 1. northeast. **2.** northeastern.

N.E.A. 1. National Education Association. **2.** National Endowment for the Arts. Also, **NEA**

Neb. Nebraska.

NEbE northeast by east.

NEbN northeast by north.

Nebr. Nebraska.

NEC National Electrical Code.

nec necessary.

n.e.c. not elsewhere classified.

N.E.D. *New English Dictionary.* Also, **NED**

NEF National extra fine (a thread measure).

neg. 1. Also, **neg** negative. **2.** negatively.

NEH National Endowment for the Humanities.

Neh. *Bible.* Nehemiah.

nem. con. no one contradicting; unanimously. [from Latin *nemine contradicente*]

nem. diss. no one dissenting; unanimously. [from Latin *nemine dissentiente*]

N. Eng. Northern England.

NEP (nep), New Economic Policy. Also, **Nep, N.E.P.**

NES New England Sports Network (a cable television channel).

n.e.s. not elsewhere specified. Also, **N.E.S.**

NESC National Electrical Safety Code.

NET National Educational Television.

Neth. Netherlands.

n. et m. (in prescriptions) night and morning. [Latin *nocte et mane*]

neurol. neurology; neurological.

neut. 1. neuter. 2. neutral.

Nev. Nevada.

Newf. Newfoundland.

NF 1. National fine (a thread measure). 2. *Pharmacology.* National Formulary. 3. Newfoundland, Canada (for use with ZIP code). 4. no funds. 5. Norman French.

nf *Telecommunications.* noise figure.

n/f no funds. Also, **N/F**

N.F. 1. no funds. 2. Norman French.

NFC National Football Conference.

NFD. Newfoundland. Also, **Nfd., Nfld.**

NFL National Football League.

NFS not for sale. Also, **N.F.S.**

NG 1. *Chemistry.* nitroglycerin. 2. *Anatomy.* nasogastric.

ng nanogram; nanograms.

N.G. 1. National Guard. 2. New Guinea. 3. no good.

n.g. no good.

NGC *Astronomy.* New General Catalogue: a catalog of clusters, nebulae, and galaxies published in 1888.

NGF nerve growth factor.

NGk New Greek. Also, **N.Gk.**

NGNP nominal gross national product.

NGS National Geodetic Survey.

NGU *Pathology.* nongonococcal urethritis.

NH New Hampshire (for use with ZIP code).

nh nonhygroscopic.

NHA National Housing Agency. Also, **N.H.A.**

nha next higher assembly.

N. Heb. New Hebrides.

NHG New High German. Also, **NHG., N.H.G.**

NHI *British.* National Health Insurance.

NHL National Hockey League.

NHS 1. *British.* National Health Service. **2.** National Honor Society.

NHSC National Highway Safety Council.

NHTSA National Highway Traffic Safety Administration.

Ni *Symbol, Chemistry.* nickel.

N.I. Northern Ireland.

NIA 1. National Intelligence Authority. **2.** Newspaper Institute of America.

NIH National Institutes of Health.

NIK Nickelodeon (a cable television channel).

NIMBY (*usually* nim′bē), not in my backyard. Also, **Nimby.**

NIMH National Institute of Mental Health.

NiMH *Electricity.* nickel-metal hydride (battery).

nip nipple.

ni. pr. (in prescriptions) unless before. [from Latin *nisi prius*]

NIRA National Industrial Recovery Act. Also, **N.I.R.A.**

NIST (nist), National Institute of Standards and Technology.

NIT National Invitational Tournament.

NJ New Jersey (for use with ZIP code).

N.J. New Jersey.

NKGB in the U.S.S.R., a secret-police organization (1941–46). [from Russian *N(aródnyï) k(omissariát) g(osudárstvennoi) b(ezopásnosti)* People's Commissariat for State Security]

nkl nickel.

NKVD in the U.S.S.R., a secret-police organization (1934–46). [from Russian *N(aródnyï) K(omissariát) V(nútrennikh) D(el)* People's Commissariat of Internal Affairs]

NL 1. Also, **NL.** New Latin; Neo-Latin. **2.** night letter.

nl nonleaded (of gasoline).

N.L. 1. *Baseball.* National League. **2.** New Latin; Neo-Latin.

n.l. 1. *Printing.* new line. **2.** *Law.* it is not allowed. [from Latin *non licet*] **3.** *Law.* it is not clear or evident. [from Latin *non liquet*]

N. Lat. north latitude. Also, **N. lat.**

N.L.F. National Liberation Front.

nlnr nonlinear.

NLRB National Labor Relations Board. Also, **N.L.R.B.**

NM 1. New Mexico (for use with ZIP code). **2.** *Grammar.* noun modifier.

nm 1. nanometer; nanometers. **2.** nautical mile. **3.** nonmetallic.

N.M. New Mexico. Also, **N. Mex.**

nmag nonmagnetic.

NMI no middle initial. Also, **nmi**

nmi *Symbol.* nautical mile.

nmlz normalize.

NMN no middle name.

NMR 1. *Physics.* nuclear magnetic resonance. **2.** *Medicine.* magnetic resonance imaging.

nmr no maintenance required.

NMSQT National Merit Scholarship Qualifying Test.

NMSS National Multiple Sclerosis Society.

N.M.U. National Maritime Union. Also, **NMU**

NNE north-northeast. Also, **N.N.E.**

NNP net national product.

NNW north-northwest. Also, **N.N.W.**

No *Symbol, Chemistry.* nobelium.

no *Electricity.* (of contacts) normally open.

no. 1. north. **2.** northern. **3.** number. Also, **No.**

N/O *Banking.* registered.

NOAA National Oceanic and Atmospheric Administration.

N.O.C. *Insurance.* not otherwise classified.

n.o.i.b.n. not otherwise indexed by name.

nol. pros. *Law.* unwilling to prosecute. [from Latin *nolle prosequi*]

nom. *Grammar.* nominative.

Nom. Cap. *Finance.* nominal capital.

nomen nomenclature.

noncom. noncommissioned.

nonflm nonflammable.

non obst. *Law.* notwithstanding. [from Latin *non obstante*]

non pros. *Law.* a judgment against a plaintiff who does not appear in court. [from Latin *non prosequitur* he does not pursue]

non rep. (in prescriptions) do not repeat. [from Latin *non repetatur* it is not repeated]

non seq. *Logic.* a conclusion which does not follow from the premises. [from Latin *non sequitur* it does not follow]

nonstd nonstandard.

nonsyn nonsynchronous.

NOP not our publication. Also, **N.O.P.**

Nor. 1. Norman. **2.** North. **3.** Northern. **4.** Norway. **5.** Norwegian.

nor. 1. north. **2.** northern.

NORAD (nôrʹad), a joint U.S.-Canadian air force command. [*Nor(th American) A(ir) D(efence Command)*]

norm normal.

Norw. 1. Norway. **2.** Norwegian.

NOS *Computers.* network operating system.

nos. numbers. Also, **Nos.**

n.o.s. not otherwise specified.

NOTA none of the above.

Nov. November.

nov. novelist.

NOW (nou), **1.** National Organization for Women. **2.** *Banking.* negotiable order of withdrawal.

noz nozzle.

NP 1. National pipe (a thread measure). **2.** noun phrase. **3.** nurse-practitioner.

Np *Physics.* neper; nepers.

Np *Symbol, Chemistry.* neptunium.

N.P. 1. new paragraph. **2.** *Law.* nisi prius. **3.** no protest. **4.** notary public.

n.p. 1. net proceeds. **2.** new paragraph. **3.**

Law. nisi prius. **4.** no pagination. **5.** no place of publication. **6.** no protest. **7.** notary public.

NPK *Horticulture.* nitrogen, phosphorus, and potassium.

npl nameplate.

npn negative-positive-negative (transistor).

n.p. or d. no place or date.

NPR National Public Radio. Also, **N.P.R.**

nprn neoprene.

NPT 1. National (taper) pipe thread. **2.** Non-proliferation Treaty.

n.p.t. normal pressure and temperature. Also, **npt**

nr 1. negative resistance. **2.** nuclear reactor.

NRA 1. National Recovery Administration: a former federal agency (1933–36). **2.** National Recreation Area. **3.** National Rifle Association. Also, **N.R.A.**

NRAB National Railroad Adjustment Board.

NRC 1. National Research Council. **2.** Nuclear Regulatory Commission.

NROTC Naval Reserve Officer Training Corps. Also **N.R.O.T.C.**

NRPB National Resources Planning Board.

NRTA National Retired Teachers Association.

nrtn nonreturn.

nrvsbl nonreversible.

nrz nonreturn-to-zero.

NS 1. not sufficient (funds). **2.** Nova Scotia, Canada (for use with ZIP code). **3.** nuclear ship.

Ns *Meteorology.* nimbostratus.

ns 1. Also, **nsec** nanosecond; nanoseconds. **2.** nonserviceable.

N.S. 1. New Style. **2.** Nova Scotia.

n.s. not specified.

NSA 1. National Security Agency. **2.** National Shipping Authority. **3.** National Standards Association. **4.** National Student Association. Also, **N.S.A.**

NSC 1. National Safety Council. **2.** National Security Council.

NSF 1. National Science Foundation. **2.** not sufficient funds. Also, **N.S.F.**

N/S/F not sufficient funds.

N.S.P.C.A. National Society for the Prevention of Cruelty to Animals.

N.S.P.C.C. National Society for the Prevention of Cruelty to Children.

n.s.p.f. not specifically provided for.

NSU *Pathology.* nonspecific urethritis; nongonococcal urethritis.

N.S.W. New South Wales.

NT 1. New Testament. **2.** Northwest Territories, Canada (for use with ZIP code).

Nt *Symbol, Chemistry.* niton.

nt *Physics.* nit; nits.

N.T. 1. New Testament (of the Bible). **2.** Northern Territory. **3.** Northwest Territories.

ntc negative temperature coefficient.

NTIA National Telecommunications and Information Administration.

ntp normal temperature and pressure.

nts not to scale.

NTSB National Transportation Safety Board.

ntwk network.

nt. wt. net weight. Also, **ntwt**.

nuc nuclear.

NUCFLASH (no͞ok′flash′, nyo͞ok′-), a report of highest precedence notifying the president or deputies of an accidental or unauthorized nuclear-weapon launch or of a nuclear attack. [*nuc(lear) flash*]

NUL National Urban League. Also **N.U.L.**

Num. *Bible.* Numbers.

num. 1. number. **2.** numeral; numerals.

numis. 1. numismatic. **2.** numismatics. Also, **numism.**

N.U.T. *British.* National Union of Teachers.

N.U.W.W. *British.* National Union of Women Workers.

NV Nevada (for use with ZIP code).

N/V *Banking.* no value.

NW 1. net worth. **2.** northwest. **3.** northwestern. Also, **N.W., n.w.**

NWbW northwest by west.

NWC *Military.* National War College.

NWLB National War Labor Board.

NWS National Weather Service.

nwt nonwatertight.

n. wt. net weight.

N.W.T. Northwest Territories.

NY New York (for use with ZIP code).

N.Y. New York.

NYA National Youth Administration. Also, **N. Y.A.**

N.Y.C. New York City. Also, **NYC**

NYCSCE New York Coffee, Sugar, and Cocoa Exchange.

nyl nylon.

NYME New York Mercantile Exchange.

NYP not yet published. Also, **N.Y.P.**

NYSE New York Stock Exchange. Also, **N.Y. S.E.**

N.Z. New Zealand. Also, **N. Zeal.**

O

O **1.** Old. **2.** *Grammar.* object.

O *Symbol.* **1.** the fifteenth in order or in a series. **2.** the Arabic cipher; zero. **3.** (*sometimes lowercase*) the medieval Roman numeral for 11. **4.** *Physiology.* a major blood group, usually enabling a person whose blood is of this type to donate blood to persons of group O, A, B, or AB and to receive blood from persons of group O. **5.** *Chemistry.* oxygen. **6.** *Logic.* particular negative.

O. **1.** Ocean. **2.** (in prescriptions) a pint. [from Latin *octārius*] **3.** octavo. **4.** October. **5.** Ohio. **6.** Old. **7.** Ontario. **8.** Oregon.

o. **1.** pint. [from Latin *octārius*] **2.** *Printing.* octavo. **3.** off. **4.** old. **5.** only. **6.** order. **7.** *Baseball.* out; outs.

OA office automation.

oa overall.

o/a **1.** on account. **2.** on or about.

OAO *U. S. Aerospace.* Orbiting Astronomical Observatory.

OAP *British.* old-age pensioner.

OAPC Office of Alien Property Custodian.

OAS Organization of American States.

O.A.S.I. Old Age and Survivors Insurance.

OAU Organization of African Unity. Also, **O. A.U.**

OB **1.** Also, **ob** *Medicine.* **a.** obstetrical. **b.** obstetrician. **c.** obstetrics. **2.** off Broadway. **3.** opening of books. **4.** ordered back. **5.** outward bound.

ob. **1.** he died; she died. [from Latin *obiit*] **2.** incidentally. [from Latin *obiter*] **3.** oboe. **4.** *Meteorology.* observation.

O.B. **1.** opening of books. **2.** ordered back. Also, **O/B**

obb. *Music.* obbligato.

obdt. obedient.

O.B.E. **1.** Officer (of the Order) of the British Empire. **2.** Order of the British Empire.

OB-GYN *Medicine.* **1.** obstetrician-gynecologist. **2.** obstetrics-gynecology.

obit. obituary.

obj. 1. object. **2.** objection. **3.** objective.

objv objective.

obl. 1. oblique. **2.** oblong.

oblg 1. obligate. **2.** obligation. **3.** oblige.

obs. 1. observation. **2.** observatory. **3.** obsolete. Also, **Obs.**

obsl obsolete.

obstet. 1. obstetric. **2.** obstetrics.

obstn obstruction.

obsv observation.

OBulg. Old Bulgarian. Also, **OBulg**

obv obverse.

oc outside circumference.

Oc. ocean. Also, **oc.**

o/c overcharge.

O.C. *Philately.* original cover.

o.c. 1. *Architecture.* on center. **2.** in the work cited. [from Latin *opere citātō*]

occ. 1. occasional. **2.** occasionally. **3.** occident. **4.** occidental. **5.** occupation. **6.** occupy.

occas. 1. occasional. **2.** occasionally.

OCD Office of Civil Defense.

OCDM Office of Civil and Defense Mobilization.

ocld oil-cooled.

OCR *Computers.* **1.** optical character reader. **2.** optical character recognition.

OCS 1. *Military.* officer candidate school. **2.** Old Church Slavonic. **3.** outer continental shelf.

ocsnl occasional.

Oct. October.

oct. 1. octagon. **2.** octavo.

octl octal.

octn octane.

OD *plural* **ODs** or **OD's.** an overdose of a drug, esp. a fatal one.

OD 1. officer of the day. **2.** Old Dutch. **3.** Ordnance Department. **4.** outside diameter.

od 1. on demand. **2.** outside diameter. **3.** outside dimensions. **4.** *Banking* overdraft. **5.** *Banking* overdrawn.

OD. Old Dutch.

O.D. 1. Doctor of Optometry. **2.** (in prescriptions) the right eye. [from Latin *oculus dexter*] **3.** officer of the day. **4.** Old Dutch. **5.** (of a military uniform) olive drab. **6.** ordinary seaman. **7.** outside diameter. **8.** *Banking.* overdraft. **9.** *Banking.* overdrawn.

o.d. 1. (in prescriptions) the right eye. [from Latin *oculus dexter*] **2.** olive drab. **3.** on demand. **4.** outside diameter.

odom odometer.

odpsk oil dipstick.

ODT Office of Defense Transportation.

OE Old English. Also, **OE.**

Oe *Electricity.* oersted; oersteds.

O.E. 1. Old English. **2.** *Commerce.* omissions excepted.

o.e. *Commerce.* omissions excepted. Also, **oe**

OEC Office of Energy Conservation.

OECD Organization for Economic Cooperation and Development.

OED *Oxford English Dictionary.* Also, **O.E.D.**

OEEC Organization for European Economic Cooperation.

OEM original equipment manufacturer.

OEO Office of Economic Opportunity.

OES 1. Office of Economic Stabilization. **2.** Order of the Eastern Star.

OF Old French. Also, **OF., O.F.**

of outside face.

ofc office.

ofcl official.

ofcr officer.

ofl offline.

OFlem Old Flemish. Also, **OFlem.**

ofltr oil filter.

O.F.M. Order of Friars Minor (Franciscan). [from Latin *Ōrdō Frātrum Minōrum*]

OFr. Old French. Also, **OFr**

OFris. Old Frisian. Also, **OFris**

oft outfit.

OG officer of the guard.

O.G. 1. officer of the guard. **2.** *Architecture.* ogee. **3.** *Philately.* See **o.g.** (def. 1).

o.g. 1. Also, **O.G.** *Philately.* original gum: the gum on the back of a stamp when it is issued. **2.** *Architecture.* ogee.

OGO *U.S. Aerospace.* Orbiting Geophysical Observatory.

OGPU (og′pōō), (in the U.S.S.R.) the government's secret-police organization (1923–1934). Also, **Ogpu.** Cf. **KGB.** [from Russian *Ógpu*, for *Ob″edinënnoe gosudárstvennoe politícheskoe upravlénie* Unified State Political Directorate]

ogr *Telephones.* outgoing repeater.

ogt *Telephones.* outgoing trunk.

OH Ohio (for use with ZIP code).

OHC *Automotive.* overhead camshaft.

OHG Old High German. Also, **OHG., O.H.G.**

O.H.M.S. On His Majesty's Service; On Her Majesty's Service.

OI opportunistic infection.

OIC officer in charge.

OIcel Old Icelandic.

OIr Old Irish. Also, **OIr.**

OIt Old Italian.

OJ *Informal.* orange juice. Also, **O.J., o.j.**

OJT on-the-job training. Also, **O.J.T.**

OK Oklahoma (for use with ZIP code).

OK (ō′kā′, ō′kā′, ō′kā′), all right; permissible or acceptable; satisfactory or under control. Also, **O.K., okay** [initials of a facetious folk phonetic spelling, e.g., *oll* or *orl korrect* representing *all correct*, first attested in Boston, Massachusetts, in 1839, then used in 1840 by Democrat partisans of Martin Van Buren during his election campaign, who allegedly named their organization, the *O.K. Club*, in allusion to the initials of *Old Kinderhook*, Van Buren's nickname, derived from his birthplace *Kinderhook*, New York]

Okla. Oklahoma.

OL Old Latin. Also, **OL.**

Ol. (in prescriptions) oil. [from Latin *oleum*]

O.L. 1. Also, **o.l.** (in prescriptions) the left eye. [from Latin *oculus laevus*] **2.** Old Latin.

Old Test. Old Testament (of the Bible).

OLE *Computers.* object linking and embedding.

OLG Old Low German. Also, **O.L.G.**

OLLA Office of Lend Lease Administration.

olvl oil level.

Om. (formerly, in East Germany) ostmark.

O.M. *British.* Order of Merit.

OMA orderly marketing agreement.

OMB Office of Management and Budget. Also, **O.M.B.**

OMBE Office of Minority Business Enterprise.

omn. bih. (in prescriptions) every two hours. [from Latin *omni bihōriō*]

omn. hor. (in prescriptions) every hour. [from Latin *omni hōra*]

omn. man. (in prescriptions) every morning. Also, **omn man** [from Latin *omni māne*]

omn. noct. (in prescriptions) every night. Also, **omn noct** [from Latin *omni nocte*]

omn. quadr. hor. (in prescriptions) every quarter of an hour. Also, **omn quadr hor** [from Latin *omni quadrante hōrae*]

ON 1. Also, **ON., O.N.** Old Norse. **2.** Ontario, Canada (for use with ZIP code).

ONF Old North French.

ONFr. Old North French.

ONI Office of Naval Intelligence.

ONR Office of Naval Research.

Ont. Ontario.

O.O.D. 1. officer of the deck. **2.** officer of the day.

OOG *Computers.* object-oriented graphics.

OOP *Computers.* object-oriented programming.

OOT out of town. Also, **O.O.T.**

OP observation post. Also, **O.P.**

op (op), a style of abstract art. [from *op(tical)*]

Op. *Music.* opus.

op. 1. opera. **2.** operation. **3.** opposite. **4.** opus.

O.P. 1. observation post. **2.** *British Theater.* opposite prompt. **3.** Order of Preachers (Dominican). [from Latin *Ōrdō Praedicātōrum*] **4.** out of print. **5.** *Distilling.* overproof.

o.p. out of print.

OPA Office of Price Administration: the federal agency (1941–46) charged with regulating rents and the distribution and prices of goods during World War II.

opa opaque.

op. cit. (op′ sit′), in the work cited. [from Latin *opere citātō*]

OPEC (ō′pek), an organization founded in 1960 of nations that export large amounts of petroleum, to establish oil-exporting policies and set prices. [*O(rganization of) P(etroleum) E(xporting) C(ountries)*]

Op-Ed (op′ed′), a newspaper page devoted to signed articles of varying viewpoints. [*op(posite) ed(itorial page)*]

OPer. Old Persian.

OPers Old Persian.

ophthal. 1. ophthalmologist. **2.** ophthalmology.

OPM 1. Office of Personnel Management. **2.** operations per minute. **3.** *Slang.* other people's money.

opn operation.

opnr opener.

Opp. *Music.* opuses. [from Latin *opera*]

opp. 1. opposed. **2.** opposite.

opp hnd opposite hand.

OPr Old Provençal.

opr 1. operate. **2.** operator.

oprg operating.

oprs oil pressure.

OPruss Old Prussian.

OPS Office of Price Stabilization. Also, **O.P.S.**

opt 1. optical. 2. optimum.

optl optional.

opty opportunity.

OR 1. *Law.* on (one's own) recognizance. 2. operating room. 3. operations research. 4. Oregon (for use with ZIP code). 5. owner's risk.

or outside radius.

O.R. 1. *Military.* orderly room. 2. owner's risk.

O.R.C. Officers' Reserve Corps.

orch. orchestra.

ord. 1. Also, **ord** order. 2. ordinal. 3. ordinance. 4. ordinary. 5. ordnance.

ordn. ordnance.

Ore. Oregon.

Oreg. Oregon.

orf orifice.

org. 1. organic. 2. organization. 3. organized.

orig. 1. origin. 2. original. 3. originally.

orn orange.

ornith. 1. ornithological. 2. ornithology.

ornithol. 1. ornithological. 2. ornithology.

ORT Registered Occupational Therapist.

Orth. Orthodox.

orth. 1. orthopedic 2. orthopedics.

ORuss Old Russian.

ORV off-road vehicle.

OS 1. Old Saxon. 2. *Computers.* operating system.

Os *Symbol, Chemistry.* osmium.

O/S (of the calendar) Old Style.

o/s 1. (of the calendar) Old Style. 2. out of stock. 3. *Banking.* outstanding.

O.S. 1. (in prescriptions) the left eye. [from Latin *oculus sinister*] 2. Old Saxon. 3. Old School. 4. old series. 5. (of the calendar) Old Style. 6. ordinary seaman.

o.s. 1. (in prescriptions) the left eye. [from Latin *oculus sinister*] **2.** ordinary seaman.

O.S.A. Order of St. Augustine.

O.S.B. Order of St. Benedict.

osc oscillator.

OSD Office of the Secretary of Defense.

O.S.D. Order of St. Dominic.

O.S.F. Order of St. Francis.

OSFCW Office of Solid Fuels Coordinator for War.

OSHA (ō′shə, osh′ə), the division of the Department of Labor that sets and enforces occupational health and safety rules. [*O(ccupational) S(afety and) H(ealth) A(dministration)*]

osl oil seal.

osmv *Electronics.* one-shot multivibrator.

OSO *U.S. Aerospace.* Orbiting Solar Observatory.

OSP died without issue. [from Latin *obiit sine prōle*]

OSp Old Spanish.

OSRD Office of Scientific Research and Development.

OSS Office of Strategic Services: a U.S. government intelligence agency during World War II. Also, **O.S.S.**

OT 1. occupational therapist. **2.** occupational therapy. **3.** *Bible.* Old Testament. **4.** overnight telegram. **5.** overtime.

O.T. Old Testament (of the Bible).

o.t. overtime.

OTA Office of Technology Assessment.

OTB offtrack betting.

OTC 1. Also, **O.T.C.** Officers' Training Corps. **2.** over-the-counter.

OTS Officers' Training School. Also, **O.T.S.**

OU (in prescriptions) **1.** both eyes. [from Latin *oculi uterque*] **2.** each eye. [from Latin *oculus uterque*]

out 1. outlet. **2.** output.

outbd outboard.

outg outgoing.

ov over.

ovbd overboard.

ovh oval head.

ovhd overhead.

ovhl overhaul.

OV language (ō′vē′), *Linguistics.* a type of language that has direct objects preceding the verb. [*O(bject)-V(erb)*]

ovld overload.

ovp oval point.

ovrd override.

ovsz oversize.

ovtr overtravel.

ovv overvoltage.

OW Old Welsh.

OWI 1. Office of War Information: the U.S federal agency (1942–45) charged with disseminating information about World War II. **2.** operating (a motor vehicle) while intoxicated.

Ox. Oxford. [from Latin *Oxonia*]

oxd oxidized.

Oxon. 1. Oxford. [from Latin *Oxonia*] **2.** of Oxford. [from Latin *Oxoniēnsis*]

oz. ounce; ounces. [abbreviation of Italian *onza*]

oz. av. ounce avoirdupois.

ozs. ounces.

oz. t. ounce troy.

P

P 1. (as a rating of student performance) passing. **2.** *Chess.* pawn. **3.** *Electronics.* plate. **4.** poor. **5.** *Grammar.* predicate. **6.** Protestant.

P *Symbol.* **1.** the 16th in order or in a series, or, when *I* is omitted, the 15th. **2.** (*sometimes lowercase*) the medieval Roman numeral for 400. **3.** *Genetics.* parental. **4.** *Chemistry.* phosphorus. **5.** *Physics.* **a.** power. **b.** pressure. **c.** proton. **d.** space inversion. **e.** poise. **6.** *Biochemistry.* proline.

p 1. penny; pence. **2.** *Music.* softly. [from Italian *piano*]

P- *Military.* (in designations of aircraft) pursuit: *P-38.*

p- *Chemistry.* designating the 1, 4 position on the benzene ring. [from Greek *para-* beside, by, beyond]

P. 1. pastor. **2.** father. [from Latin *Pater*] **3.** peseta. **4.** peso. **5.** post. **6.** president. **7.** pressure. **8.** priest. **9.** prince. **10.** progressive.

p. 1. page. **2.** part. **3.** participle. **4.** past. **5.** father. [from Latin *pater*] **6.** *Chess.* pawn. **7.** penny; pence. **8.** per. **9.** *Grammar.* person. **10.** peseta. **11.** peso. **12.** *Music.* softly. [from Italian *piano*] **13.** pint. **14.** pipe. **15.** *Baseball.* pitcher. **16.** pole. **17.** population. **18.** after. [from Latin *post*] **19.** president. **20.** pressure. **21.** purl.

PA 1. paying agent. **2.** Pennsylvania (for use with ZIP code). **3.** physician's assistant. **4.** press agent. **5.** public-address system.

Pa *Physics.* pascal; pascals.

Pa *Symbol, Chemistry.* protactinium.

Pa. Pennsylvania.

P.A. 1. Also, **PA** Parents' Association. **2.** *Insurance.* particular average. **3.** passenger agent. **4.** *Military.* post adjutant. **5.** power of attorney. **6.** press agent. **7.** public-address system. **8.** publicity agent. **9.** purchasing agent.

p.a. 1. participial adjective. **2.** per annum. **3.** press agent.

p.-a. public-address system.

PABA (pä′bə), *Chemistry, Biochemistry.* a crystalline solid, $C_7H_7NO_2$, used especially in pharmaceuticals. [*p(ara-)a(mino)b(enzoic) a(cid)*]

PABX *Telephones.* an automatically operated PBX. Also, **pabx** [*p(rivate) a(utomatic) b(ranch) ex(change)*]

PAC (pak), political action committee.

Pac. Pacific.

P.A.C. political action committee.

pacm pulse amplitude code modulation.

PaD Pennsylvania Dutch; Pennsylvania German.

p. ae. (in prescriptions) equal parts. [from Latin *partēs aequālēs*]

PaG Pennsylvania German.

Pak. Pakistan.

PAL (pal), a special air service offered by the U.S. Postal Service for sending parcels. [*P(arcel) A(ir) L(ift)*]

PAL Police Athletic League. Also, **P.A.L.**

Pal. Palestine.

pal. 1. paleography. **2.** paleontology.

paleog. paleography.

paleon. paleontology.

paleontol. paleontology.

PAM 1. *Aerospace.* payload assist module. **2.** Also, **pam** *Telecommunications.* pulse amplitude modulation.

pam. pamphlet.

pamfm pulse amplitude modulation frequency modulation.

Pan (pan), an international distress signal used by shore stations to inform a ship, aircraft, etc., of something vital to its safety or that of one of its passengers. Also, **pan.**

pan panoramic.

Pan. Panama.

P. and L. profit and loss. Also, **P. & L.,** **p. and l.**

par precision-approach radar.

par. 1. paragraph. **2.** parallel. **3.** parenthesis. **4.** parish.

para paragraph.

Para. Paraguay.

par. aff. (in prescriptions) to the part affected. [from Latin *pars affecta*]

paren parenthesis.

Parl. 1. Parliament. **2.** Parliamentary. Also, **parl.**

parl. proc. parliamentary procedure.

parsec (pär′sek′), *Astronomy.* parallax second.

part. 1. participial. **2.** participle. **3.** particular.

part. adj. participial adjective.

part. aeq. (in prescriptions) equal parts. [from Latin *partes aequales*]

part. vic. (in prescriptions) in divided doses. [from Latin *partibus vicibus*]

pas public address system.

pass. 1. passage. **2.** passenger. **3.** here and there throughout. [from Latin *passim*] **4.** passive.

PAT 1. *Football.* point after touchdown; points after touchdown. **2.** *Banking.* preauthorized automatic transfer.

pat. 1. patent. **2.** patented.

patd. patented.

path. 1. pathological. **2.** pathology.

pathol. 1. Also, **pathol** pathological. **2.** pathology.

Pat. Off. Patent Office.

pat. pend. patent pending. Also, **patpend**

P.A.U. Pan American Union.

PAX *Telephones.* private automatic exchange.

PAYE 1. pay as you enter. **2.** pay as you earn.

PB power brakes.

Pb *Symbol, Chemistry.* lead. [from Latin *plumbum*]

pb pushbutton.

P.B. 1. British Pharmacopoeia. [from Latin *Pharmacopoeia Britannica*] **2.** Prayer Book.

p.b. *Baseball.* passed ball; passed balls.

PBA 1. Professional Bowlers Association. **2.** Public Buildings Administration.

P.B.A. Patrolmen's Benevolent Association.

PBB *Chemistry.* any of the highly toxic and possibly carcinogenic aromatic compounds consisting of two benzene rings in which bromine takes the place of two or more hydrogen atoms. [*p(oly)b(rominated) b(iphenyl)*]

pbd pressboard.

PBK Phi Beta Kappa.

pblg publishing.

pblr publisher.

PBS Public Broadcasting Service.

PBX a manually or automatically operated telephone facility that handles communications within an office, office building, or organization. [*P(rivate) B(ranch) Ex(change)*]

PC 1. Peace Corps. **2.** personal computer. **3.** politically correct. **4.** printed circuit. **5.** professional corporation.

pc 1. *Astronomy.* parsec. **2.** parts catalog. **3.** *Physics, Chemistry.* picocurie; picocuries.

pc. 1. piece. **2.** prices.

P/C 1. petty cash. **2.** price current. Also, **p/c**

P.C. 1. Past Commander. **2.** *British.* Police Constable. **3.** politically correct. **4.** Post Commander. **5.** *British.* Prince Consort. **6.** *British.* Privy Council. **7.** professional corporation.

p.c. 1. percent. **2.** petty cash. **3.** postal card. **4.** (in prescriptions) after eating; after meals. [from Latin *post cibōs*] **5.** price current. **6.** printed circuit.

PCB a family of highly toxic chemical compounds consisting of two benzene rings in which chlorine takes the place of two or more hydrogen atoms. [*p(oly)c(chlorinated) b(iphenyl)*]

pcb *Electronics.* printed-circuit board.

pcf pounds per cubic foot.

pchs purchase.

pchsg purchasing.

pcht parchment.

PCI *Computers.* peripheral component interconnect.

pci pounds per cubic inch.

PCL *Computers.* Printer Control Language.

pcl pencil.

PCM 1. *Computers.* plug-compatible manufacturer. **2.** Also, **pcm** *Telecommunications.* pulse code modulation.

PCMCIA Personal Computer Memory Card International Association.

pcmd pulse code modulation digital.

pcmfm pulse code modulation frequency modulation.

PCNB *Chemistry.* a crystalline compound, $C_6Cl_5NO_2$, used as a herbicide and insecticide. [*p(enta)c(hloro)n(itro)b(enzene)*]

PCP 1. *Slang.* phencyclidine; an anaesthetic drug. [perhaps *p(hen)c(yclidine)* + *(peace) p(ill)*, an earlier designation] **2.** *Pathology.* pneumocystis pneumonia.

pct. percent. Also, **pct**

pctm pulse count modulation.

PCV *Automotive.* positive crankcase ventilation.

pcv pollution-control valve.

Pd *Symbol, Chemistry.* palladium.

pd pitch diameter.

pd. paid.

P.D. 1. per diem. **2.** Police Department. **3.** *Insurance.* property damage.

p.d. 1. per diem. **2.** potential difference.

PDA *Computers.* personal digital assistant.

PDB *Chemistry.* a crystalline solid, $C_6H_4Cl_2$, used especially as a moth repellent. [*p(ara-)d(ichloro)b(enzene)*]

Pd.B. Bachelor of Pedagogy.

Pd.D. Doctor of Pedagogy.

pdl 1. *Computers.* page description language. **2.** poundal.

pdm pulse duration modulation.

Pd.M. Master of Pedagogy.

pdmfm pulse duration modulation frequency modulation.

P.D.Q. *Informal.* immediately; at once. Also, **PDQ** [*p(retty) d(amn) q(uick)*]

PDR Physicians' Desk Reference.

pdr powder.

PDT Pacific daylight time. Also, **P.D.T.**

PE Prince Edward Island, Canada (for use with ZIP code).

pe probable error.

p/e price-earnings ratio. Also, **P/E, PE, P-E, p-e**

P.E. 1. Petroleum Engineer. **2.** physical education. **3.** Presiding Elder. **4.** printer's error. **5.** *Statistics.* probable error. **6.** Professional Engineer. **7.** Protestant Episcopal.

p.e. printer's error.

pec photoelectric cell.

ped. 1. pedal. **2.** pedestal. **3.** pedestrian.

Ped.D. Doctor of Pedagogy.

P.E.Dir. Director of Physical Education.

P.E.F. *Insurance.* personal effects floater.

P.E.I. Prince Edward Island.

pelec photoelectric.

pem *Computers.* preemptive multitasking.

pen penetration.

Pen. peninsula. Also, **pen.**

P.E.N. International Association of Poets, Playwrights, Editors, Essayists, and Novelists.

Penn. Pennsylvania. Also, **Penna.**

Pent. Pentecost.

Per. 1. Persia. **2.** Persian.

per. 1. percentile. **2.** period. **3.** person.

per an. per annum.

perc percussion.

perf. 1. perfect. **2.** perforated. **3.** performance.

perf. part. perfect participle.

perh. perhaps.

perm 1. permanent. **2.** permission.

permb permeability.

perp. perpendicular.

per pro. *Law.* by one acting as an agent; by proxy. Also, **per proc.** [from Latin *per procurationem*]

Pers Persian.

Pers. 1. Persia. **2.** Persian.

pers. 1. person. **2.** personal. **3.** personnel.

persp perspective.

PERT (pûrt), a management method of controlling and analyzing a system or program. [*P(rogram) E(valuation and) R(eview) T(echnique)*]

pert. pertaining.

PET (pet), *Medicine.* positron emission tomography.

Pet. *Bible.* Peter.

pet. petroleum.

Pet.E. Petroleum Engineer.

PETN *Chemistry, Pharmacology.* a crystalline, explosive solid, $C_5H_8N_4O_{12}$. [*p(enta)e(rythritol) t(etra)n(itrate)*]

petro petroleum.

petrog. petrography.

petrol. petrology.

pF *Electricity.* picofarad; picofarads.

pf power factor.

pf. 1. perfect. **2.** (in Germany) pfennig. **3.** *Music.* pianoforte; piano. **4.** *Finance.* (of stock) preferred. **5.** proof.

p.f. *Music.* louder. [from Italian *piu forte*]

Pfc. *Military.* private first class. Also, **PFC**

PFD personal flotation device.

pfd. preferred. Also, **pfd**

pfg. (in Germany) pfennig.

PFM *Telecommunications.* pulse frequency modulation. Also, **P.F.M.**

PG *Informal.* pregnant.

PG parental guidance: a rating assigned to a motion picture by the Motion Picture Association of America. [*p(arental) g(uidance) advised*]

pg 1. picogram; picograms. **2.** pulse generator.

Pg. 1. Portugal. **2.** Also, **Pg** Portuguese.

pg. page.

P.G. 1. Past Grand. **2.** paying guest. **3.** Postgraduate. **4.** Also, **p.g.** *Informal.* pregnant.

PGA 1. Also, **P.G.A.** Professional Golfers' Association. **2.** *Biochemistry.* folic acid [*p(teroyl) + g(lutamic) a(cid)*].

pga *Computers.* pin-grid array.

pgmt pigment.

Ph *Chemistry.* phenyl.

pH *Chemistry.* the symbol for the logarithm of the reciprocal of hydrogen ion concentration in gram atoms per liter, used to express the acidity or alkalinity of a solution.

ph *Optics.* phot; phots.

ph. 1. phase. **2.** phone.

P.H. Public Health.

PHA Public Housing Administration.

Phar. 1. pharmaceutical. **2.** pharmacology. **3.** pharmacopoeia. **4.** pharmacy. Also, **phar.**

Phar.B. Bachelor of Pharmacy.

Phar.D. Doctor of Pharmacy.

pharm. 1. pharmaceutical. **2.** pharmacology. **3.** pharmacopoeia. **4.** pharmacy.

Pharm.D. Doctor of Pharmacy.

Pharm.M. Master of Pharmacy.

Ph.B. Bachelor of Philosophy. [from Latin *Philosophiae Baccalaureus*]

Ph. C. Pharmaceutical Chemist.

Ph.D. Doctor of Philosophy. [from Latin *Philosophiae Doctor*]

Phe *Biochemistry.* phenylalanine.

P.H.E. Public Health Engineer.

phen phenolic.

Ph. G. Graduate in Pharmacy.

phh phillips head.

Phil. 1. *Bible.* Philemon. **2.** Philip. **3.** *Bible.* Philippians. **4.** Philippine.

phil. 1. philosophical. **2.** philosophy.

Phila. Philadelphia.

Philem. *Bible.* Philemon.

Phil. I. Philippine Islands.

philol. 1. philological. **2.** philology.

philos. 1. philosopher. **2.** philosophical. **3.** philosophy.

Ph.L. Licentiate in Philosophy.

phm 1. phantom. **2.** phase modulation.

Ph.M. Master of Philosophy.

phofl photoflash.

phon. phonetics.

phonet. phonetics.

phono phonograph.

phonol. phonology.

phos phosphate.

phot. 1. photograph. **2.** photographer. **3.** photographic. **4.** photography.

photog. 1. photographer. **2.** photographic. **3.** photography.

photom. photometry.

phr. phrase.

phren. 1. phrenological. **2.** phrenology.

phrenol. 1. phrenological. **2.** phrenology.

phrm pharmacy.

phrmcol pharmacological.

PHS Public Health Service. Also, **P.H.S.**

phsk phase-shift keying.

phys. 1. physical. **2.** physician. **3.** physics. **4.** physiological. **5.** physiology.

phys. chem. physical chemistry.

phys ed (fiz′ ed′), *Informal.* physical education. Also, **phys. ed.**

phys. geog. physical geography.

physiol. 1. physiological. **2.** physiologist. **3.** physiology.

PI 1. *Law.* personal injury. **2.** politically incorrect. **3.** principal investigator. **4.** private investigator. **5.** programmed instruction.

Pi. (in Turkey and other countries) piaster. Also, **pi.**

P.I. 1. Philippine Islands. **2.** Also, **p.i.** private investigator.

p.i. politically incorrect.

pias. (in Turkey and other countries) piaster.

PID *Pathology.* pelvic inflammatory disease.

PIE Proto-Indo-European.

PIK payment in kind. Also, **p.i.k.**

pil. (in prescriptions) pill. [from Latin *pilula*]

PIM personal information manager.

pim pulse-interval modulation.

PIN (pin), *Computers.* a number assigned to an individual, used to establish identity in order to gain access to a computer system. [*p(ersonal) i(dentification) n(umber)*]

pin positive-intrinsic-negative transistor.

PINS (pinz), a person of less than 16 years of age placed under the jurisdiction of a juvenile court. [*P(erson) I(n) N(eed of) S(upervision)*]

PIO *U.S. Military.* **1.** public information office. **2.** public information officer.

PIRG Public Interest Research Group.

piv peak inverse voltage.

pizz. *Music.* pizzicato.

p.j.'s (pē′jāz′), *Informal.* pajamas. Also, **P.J.'s**

pjtr projector.

PK 1. personal knowledge **2.** psychokinesis.

pk. 1. pack. **2.** park. **3.** Also, **pk** peak. **4.** peck; pecks.

pkg. package.

pkt. 1. packet. **2.** pocket.

PKU *Pathology.* phenylketonuria.

pkwy. parkway.

PL Public Law.

pl 1. parts list. **2.** place. **3.** plain. **4.** plug. **5.** private line.

pl. 1. Also, **Pl.** place. **2.** plate. **3.** plural.

P/L profit and loss.

P.L. Poet Laureate.

PLA People's Liberation Army.

PLAM price-level adjusted mortgage.
plat. 1. plateau. 2. platinum. 3. platoon.
PLC *British.* public limited company.
plc power-line carrier.
pld payload.
plf pounds per linear foot.
plf. plaintiff. Also, **plff.**
plk *Machinery.* pillowblock.
pll 1. pallet. 2. *Electronics.* phase-locked loop.
plmg plumbing.
plmr plumber.
pln plane.
plnm plenum.
plnr planar.
plnt planet.
plnty planetary.
PLO Palestine Liberation Organization.
plo phase-locked oscillator.
PL/1 *Computers.* programming language one.
plq plaque.
PLR Public Lending Right.
plr 1. pillar. 2. pliers. 3. puller.
plrs *Navigation.* pelorus.
plrt polarity.
pls. 1. please. 2. pulse.
PLSS portable life support system.
plstc plastic.
plt 1. pilot. 2. plant.
pltf platform.
pltg 1. planting. 2. plating.
PLU price lookup.
plu. plural.
plupf. pluperfect. Also, **plup., pluperf.**
plur. 1. plural. 2. plurality.
plywd plywood.
Plz. plaza.
plzd polarized.
PM preventive maintenance.
Pm *Symbol, Chemistry.* promethium.
pm 1. permanent magnet. 2. *Computers.* pri-

mary memory. **3.** *Electronics.* pulse modulation.

pm. premium.

P.M. 1. Past Master. **2.** Paymaster. **3.** p.m. **4.** Police Magistrate. **5.** Postmaster. **6.** postmortem. **7.** Prime Minister. **8.** Provost Marshal.

p.m. after noon. [from Latin *post meridiem*]

pmflt pamphlet.

P.M.G. 1. Paymaster General. **2.** Postmaster General. **3.** Provost Marshal General.

pmk. postmark.

P.M.L. *Insurance.* probable maximum loss.

PMLA Publications of the Modern Language Association of America. Also, **P.M.L.A.**

PMS 1. *Printing.* Pantone matching system. **2.** premenstrual syndrome.

PMT premenstrual tension.

pmt. payment.

PN 1. please note. **2.** promissory note. **3.** psychoneurotic.

pn 1. part number. **2.** please note. **3.** promissory note.

P/N promissory note. Also, **p.n.**

pneum. 1. Also, **pneu** pneumatic. **2.** pneumatics.

pnh pan head.

pnl panel.

pnld paneled.

pnlg paneling.

pnnt pennant.

pnp positive-negative-positive transistor.

pnt paint.

pntgn pentagon.

pnxt. he or she painted it. [from Latin *pinxit*]

PO purchase order.

Po *Symbol, Chemistry.* polonium.

po. *Baseball.* put-out; put-outs.

p/o part of.

P.O. 1. parole officer. **2.** petty officer. **3.** postal (money) order. **4.** post office.

p.o. (in prescriptions) by mouth. [from Latin *per ōs*]

POA primary optical area.

POB post-office box. Also, **P.O.B.**

POC port of call.

pocul. (in prescriptions) a cup. [from Latin *pōculum*]

POD port of debarkation.

p.o.'d (pē'ōd'), *Slang.* angry or annoyed. [*p(issed) o(ff)*]

P.O.D. **1.** pay on delivery. **2.** Post Office Department.

POE **1.** port of embarkation. **2.** port of entry. Also, **P.O.E.**

poet. **1.** poetic; poetical. **2.** poetry.

POGO (pō'gō), Polar Orbiting Geophysical Observatory.

POL petroleum, oil, and lubricants.

Pol. **1.** Poland. **2.** Also, **Pol** Polish.

pol. **1.** political. **2.** politics.

polit. econ. political economy.

pol. sci. political science.

polstr polystyrene.

polthn polyethylene.

poly. polytechnic.

POP proof-of-purchase.

pop. **1.** popular. **2.** popularly. **3.** population.

P.O.P. **1.** printout paper. **2.** point-of-purchase.

p.o.p. point-of-purchase.

p.o.r. pay on return.

Port. **1.** Portugal. **2.** Portuguese.

pos. **1.** position. **2.** positive. **3.** possession. **4.** possessive.

P.O.S. point-of-sale; point-of-sales. Also, **POS**

posn position.

poss. **1.** possession. **2.** possessive. **3.** possible. **4.** possibly.

POSSLQ (pos'əl kyōō'), either of two persons, one of each sex, who share living quarters but are not related by blood, marriage, or adoption: a categorization used by the U.S.

Census Bureau. [*p(erson of the) o(pposite) s(ex) s(haring) l(iving) q(uarters)*]

postop (pōst′op′), postoperative. Also, **post-op.**

pot. *Electricity.* **1.** potential. **2.** potentiometer.

POTS (pots), *Telecommunications.* plain old telephone service.

POV *Motion Pictures.* point of view: used especially in describing a method of shooting a scene or film.

POW prisoner of war. Also, **P.O.W.**

PP 1. parcel post. **2.** prepositional phrase.

pp *Radio.* push-pull.

pp. 1. pages. **2.** past participle. **3.** *Music.* pianissimo. **4.** privately printed.

p-p peak-to-peak.

P.P. 1. parcel post. **2.** parish priest. **3.** past participle. **4.** postpaid. **5.** prepaid.

p.p. 1. parcel post. **2.** past participle. **3.** per person. **4.** postpaid.

PPA *Pharmacology.* a substance, $C_9H_{13}NO$, used as an appetite suppressant. [*p(henyl)p(ropanol)a(mine)*]

PPB 1. Also, **P.P.B.** *Publishing.* paper, printing, and binding. **2.** provisioning parts breakdown.

ppb *Publishing.* **1.** paper, printing, and binding. **2.** parts per billion. Also, **p.p.b.**

ppd. 1. postpaid. **2.** prepaid.

p.p.d.o. per person, double occupancy.

PPE *British.* philosophy, politics, and economics.

P.P.F. *Insurance.* personal property floater.

PPH paid personal holidays. Also, **P.P.H.**

pph. pamphlet.

PPI *Pharmacology.* **1.** patient package insert. **2.** Also, **ppi** *Electronics.* plan position indicator. **3.** producer price index.

ppl. participle.

ppll programmable phase-locked loop.

PPLO *Pathology.* pleuropneumonialike organism.

PPM 1. *Computers.* pages per minute. 2. Also, **ppm** *Telecommunications.* pulse position modulation.

ppm 1. *Computers.* pages per minute: a measure of the speed of a page printer. 2. parts per million. 3. pulse per minute.

p.p.m. parts per million. Also, **P.P.M., ppm, PPM**

PPO preferred-provider organization.

ppp 1. peak pulse power. 2. *Music.* pianississimo; double pianissimo.

ppr. 1. paper. 2. Also, **p.pr.** present participle.

pps pulse per second.

P.P.S. a second or additional postscript. Also, **p.p.s.** [from Latin *post postscriptum*]

ppt. *Chemistry.* precipitate. Also, **ppt**

ppv *Television.* pay-per-view. Also, **p.p.v., PPV, P.P.V.**

PQ Quebec, Canada (for use with ZIP code).

p.q. previous question.

PR 1. payroll. 2. percentile rank. 3. public relations. 4. *Slang (often disparaging and offensive).* Puerto Rican. 5. Puerto Rico (for use with ZIP code).

Pr Provençal.

Pr *Symbol, Chemistry.* praseodymium.

Pr. 1. (of stock) preferred. 2. Priest. 3. Prince. 4. Provençal.

pr. 1. pair; pairs. 2. paper. 3. power. 4. preference. 5. (of stock) preferred. 6. present. 7. price. 8. priest. 9. *Computers.* printer. 10. printing. 11. pronoun.

P.R. 1. parliamentary report. 2. Roman people. [from Latin *populus Rōmānus*] 3. press release. 4. prize ring. 5. proportional representation. 6. public relations. 7. Puerto Rico.

p.r. public relations.

PRA Public Roads Administration.

prand. (in prescriptions) dinner. [from Latin *prandium*]

prblc parabolic.

PRC 1. Also, **P.R.C.** People's Republic of China. 2. Postal Rate Commission.

prcht parachute.
prcs process.
prcsr processor.
prcst precast.
prdn production.
prdr producer.
P.R.E. Petroleum Refining Engineer.
prec. 1. preceded. **2.** preceding.
precdg preceding.
precp precipitation.
pred. predicate.
pref. 1. preface. **2.** prefaced. **3.** prefatory. **4.** preference. **5.** preferred. **6.** prefix. **7.** prefixed. Also, **pref**
prefab prefabricated.
prelim. preliminary.
prem. premium.
pre·op (prē′op′), preoperative; preoperatively. Also, **pre′-op′.**
prep. 1. preparation. **2.** preparatory. **3.** prepare. **4.** preposition.
Pres. 1. Presbyterian. **2.** President.
pres. 1. present. **2.** presidency. **3.** president.
Presb. Presbyterian.
Presbyt. Presbyterian.
prescr prescription.
pres. part. present participle.
press pressure.
pret. *Grammar.* preterit.
prev. 1. previous. **2.** previously.
PRF 1. Puerto Rican female. **2.** Also, **prf** *Telecommunications.* pulse repetition frequency.
prf. proof. Also, **prf**
prfm performance.
prfrd *Printing.* proofread.
prfrdg *Printing.* proofreading.
prfrdr proofreader.
prft press fit.
prfx prefix.
prgm program.
prgmg *Computers.* programming.
prgmr *Computers.* programmer.

pri primary.

prin. 1. principal. 2. principally. 3. principle.

print. printing.

priv 1. private. 2. *Grammar.* privative.

priv. pr. privately printed.

prl parallel.

PRM Puerto Rican male.

prm pulse rate modulation.

prm. premium.

prmtr parameter.

prn pseudorandom noise.

p.r.n. (in prescriptions) as the occasion arises; as needed. [from Latin *prō rē nāta*]

prntg printing.

PRO public relations officer. Also, **P.R.O.**

Pro *Biochemistry.* proline.

prob. 1. probable. 2. probably. 3. problem.

prob cse probable cause.

proc. 1. procedure. 2. proceedings. 3. process. 4. proclamation. 5. proctor.

Prod. *Computers.* Prodigy.

prod. 1. produce. 2. produced. 3. producer. 4. product. 5. production.

Prof. Professor.

Prof. Eng. Professional Engineer.

Prog. Progressive.

prog. 1. progress. 2. progressive.

proj project.

PROM (prom), *Computers.* a memory chip whose contents can be programmed by a user or manufacturer. Also, **prom** [*p(rogrammable) r(ead)-o(nly) m(emory)*]

prom. promontory.

pron. 1. *Grammar.* pronominal. 2. pronoun. 3. pronounced. 4. pronunciation.

prop. 1. properly. 2. property. 3. proposition. 4. proprietary. 5. proprietor.

propr. proprietor.

pros. 1. *Theater.* proscenium. 2. prosody.

Pros. Atty. prosecuting attorney.

prot protective.

Prot. Protestant.

pro tem. for the time being. [from Latin *pro tempore*]

Prov. 1. Provençal. 2. Provence. 3. *Bible.* Proverbs. 4. Province. 5. Provost.

prov. 1. province. 2. provincial. 3. provisional. 4. provost.

prox. the next month. [from Latin *proximo*]

prp. 1. present participle. 2. purpose.

prphl peripheral.

prpsl proposal.

prs. pairs.

prsrz pressurize.

PRT personal rapid transit.

prt print.

prtg printing.

prtl partial.

prtr printer.

Prus. 1. Prussia. 2. Prussian. Also, **Pruss., Pruss**

prv peak reverse voltage.

prvw preview.

prx prefix.

PS 1. *Linguistics.* phrase structure. 2. power steering.

ps picosecond; picoseconds.

Ps. *Bible.* Psalm; Psalms. Also, **Psa.**

ps. 1. pieces. 2. pseudonym.

P.S. 1. passenger steamer. 2. permanent secretary. 3. postscript. 4. Privy Seal. 5. *Theater.* prompt side. 6. Public School.

p.s. postscript.

PSA 1. *Medicine.* prostatic specific antigen. 2. public service announcement.

Psa. *Bible.* Psalms.

p's and q's manners; behavior; conduct. [perhaps from some children's difficulty in distinguishing the two letters]

PSAT Preliminary Scholastic Aptitude Test.

PSB *Printing.* prepress service bureau.

PSC Public Service Commission.

PSD prevention of significant deterioration:

used as a standard of measurement by the U.S. Environmental Protection Agency.

PSE Pidgin Sign English.

psec picosecond; picoseconds. Also, **ps**

pseud. 1. pseudonym. 2. pseudonymous.

psf pounds per square foot. Also, **p.s.f.**

PSG 1. platoon sergeant. 2. *Medicine.* polysomnogram.

psgr passenger.

psi pounds per square inch. Also, **p.s.i.**

psia pounds per square inch, absolute.

psid pounds per square inch, differential.

psig pounds per square inch, gauge.

psiv passive.

psm prism.

psnl personal.

PSRO Professional Standards Review Organization. Also, **P.S.R.O.**

P.SS. postscripts. Also, **p.ss.** [from Latin *postscripta*]

PST Pacific Standard Time. Also, **P.S.T., p.s.t.**

pst paste.

pstl pistol.

pstn piston.

psvt *Metallurgy.* passivate.

psvtn preservation.

psych. 1. psychological. 2. psychologist. 3. psychology.

psychoanal. psychoanalysis.

psychol. 1. psychological. 2. psychologist. 3. psychology.

Pt *Symbol, Chemistry.* platinum.

pt 1. patient. 2. pint; pints.

Pt. 1. point. 2. port.

pt. 1. part. 2. payment. 3. pint; pints. 4. point. 5. port. 6. *Grammar.* preterit.

P/T part-time. Also, **p/t**

P.T. 1. Also, **PT** Pacific time. 2. Also, **PT** part-time. 3. physical therapy. 4. physical training. 5. postal telegraph. 6. post town. 7. pupil teacher.

p.t. 1. Pacific time. 2. past tense. 3. post

town. **4.** for the time being [from Latin *pro tempore*].

PTA 1. Also, **P.T.A.** Parent-Teacher Association. **2.** Philadelphia Transportation Authority.

Pta. peseta.

PTC *Biochemistry.* phenylthiocarbamide.

ptc positive temperature coefficient.

ptd painted.

ptfe polytetrafluoroethylene.

ptg. printing.

ptl patrol.

ptly partly.

PTM *Telecommunications.* pulse time modulation. Also, **ptm**

ptn 1. partition. **2.** pattern.

PTO 1. Parent-Teacher Organization. **2.** Patent and Trademark Office. **3.** *Machinery.* power takeoff.

P.T.O. 1. Parent-Teacher Organization. **2.** Also, **p.t.o.** please turn over (a page or leaf).

pts. points.

PTSD posttraumatic stress disorder.

PTT Post, Telegraph, and Telephone (the government-operated system, as in France or Turkey).

ptt push-to-talk.

PTV public television.

Pty *Australian.* proprietary.

pty party.

Pu *Symbol, Chemistry.* plutonium.

pu 1. Also, **p/u** pick up. **2.** power unit. **3.** purple.

pub. 1. public. **2.** publication. **3.** published. **4.** publisher. **5.** publishing.

publ. 1. public. **2.** publication. **3.** publicity. **4.** published. **5.** publisher.

pubn publication.

PUC Public Utilities Commission. Also, **P.U.C.**

P.U.D. pickup and delivery.

pul pulley.

pulsar (pul′sär), pulsating star.

pulv. (in prescriptions) powder. [from Latin *pulvis*]

punc. punctuation.

PUVA (pōō′və), *Medicine.* a therapy for psoriasis combining the drug psoralen and ultraviolet light. [*p*(*soralen*) + *UV-A* ultraviolet light of a wavelength between 320 and 400 nanometers]

pv 1. *Finance.* par value. **2.** plan view.

PVA polyvinyl acetate.

PVC polyvinyl chloride. Also, **pvc**

pvnt prevent.

pvntv preventive.

pvt. private.

PW Palau (approved for postal use).

pw 1. plain washer. **2.** pulse width.

PWA 1. person with AIDS. **2.** Also, **P.W.A.** Public Works Administration.

P wave a longitudinal earthquake wave that is usually the first to be recorded by a seismograph. [*p*(*rimary*) *wave*]

pwb printed-wiring board.

P.W.D. Public Works Department. Also, **PWD**

pwm pulse-width modulation.

pwr power.

pwt pennyweight. Also, **pwt.**

pwtr pewter.

PX post exchange.

P.X. please exchange.

pxt. he or she painted it. [from Latin *pinxit*]

pymt. payment.

PYO pick your own.

pyr pyramid.

Q

Q 1. quarterly. **2.** *Cards, Chess.* queen.

Q *Symbol.* **1.** the 17th in order or in a series, or, when *I* is omitted, the 16th. **2.** (*sometimes lowercase*) the medieval Roman numeral for 500. **3.** *Biochemistry.* glutamine. **4.** *Physics.* heat. **5.** *Thermodynamics.* a unit of heat energy, equal to 10^{18} British thermal units (1.055×10^{21} joules). **6.** *Electronics.* the ratio of the reactance to the resistance of an electric circuit or component. **7.** *Biblical Criticism.* the symbol for material common to the Gospels of Matthew and Luke that was not derived from the Gospel of Mark.

Q. 1. quarto. **2.** Quebec. **3.** Queen. **4.** question. **5.** (in Guatemala) quetzal; quetzals.

q. 1. farthing. [from Latin *quadrāns*] **2.** quart; quarts. **3.** query. **4.** question. **5.** quintal. **6.** *Bookbinding.* quire.

QA quality assurance.

Q and A (kyōō′ ən ā′, ənd), *Informal.* an exchange of questions and answers. Also, **Q&A**

QB 1. *Football.* quarterback. **2.** *Chess.* queen's bishop.

Q.B. *British Law.* Queen's Bench.

q.b. *Football.* quarterback.

QBP *Chess.* queen's bishop's pawn.

Q.C. 1. quality control. **2.** Quartermaster Corps. **3.** Queen's Counsel. Also, **QC**

QCD *Physics.* quantum chromodynamics.

q.d. (in prescriptions) every day. [from Latin *quāque diē*]

qdisc quick disconnect.

qdrnt quadrant.

qdrtr quadrature.

q.e. which is. [from Latin *quod est*]

QED *Physics.* quantum electrodynamics.

Q.E.D. which was to be shown or demonstrated (used especially in mathematical proofs). [from Latin *quod erat dēmōnstrandum*]

Q.E.F. which was to be done. [from Latin *quod erat faciendum*]

Q.F. quick-firing.

Q fever *Pathology.* an acute, influenzalike disease caused by rickettsia. [abbreviation of *query*]

q.h. (in prescriptions) each hour; every hour. [from Latin *quāque hōrā*]

q.i.d. (in prescriptions) four times a day. [from Latin *quater in diē*]

QKt *Chess.* queen's knight.

QKtP *Chess.* queen's knight's pawn.

ql. quintal.

q.l. (in prescriptions) as much as is desired. [from Latin *quantum libet*]

QLI quality-of-life index. Also, **qli**

qlty. quality.

QM 1. Also, **Q.M.** Quartermaster. **2.** *Physics.* quantum mechanics.

q.m. (in prescriptions) every morning. [from Latin *quoque matutino*]

QMC *Military.* Quartermaster Corps. Also, **Q. M.C.**

QMG Quartermaster-General. Also, **Q.M.G., Q. M.Gen.**

QN *Chess.* queen's knight.

q.n. (in prescriptions) every night. [from Latin *quoque nocte*]

QNP *Chess.* queen's knight's pawn.

QP *Chess.* queen's pawn.

q.p. (in prescriptions) as much as you please. Also, **q. pl.** [from Latin *quantum placet*]

Qq. *Bookbinding.* quartos.

qq. questions.

qq. v. (in formal writing) which (words, things, etc.) see. [from Latin *quae vidē*]

QR *Chess.* queen's rook.

qr. 1. farthing. [from Latin *quadrāns*] **2.** quarter. **3.** *Bookbinding.* quire.

QRP *Chess.* queen's rook's pawn.

qry quarry.

q.s. 1. (in prescriptions) as much as is sufficient; enough. [from Latin *quantum sufficit*] **2.** quarter section.

QSO *Astronomy.* quasi-stellar object.

QSS *Astronomy.* quasi-stellar radio source.

qstn question.

qt. 1. quantity. **2.** *plural* **qt., qts.** quart.

q.t. *Informal.* quiet. Also, **Q.T.**

qto. *Bookbinding.* quarto.

qtr. 1. quarter. **2.** quarterly.

qty quantity.

qu. 1. quart. **2.** quarter. **3.** quarterly. **4.** queen. **5.** query. **6.** question.

quad quadrilateral.

quad. 1. quadrant. **2.** quadratic.

quadr quadruple.

qual. 1. qualification. qualify. **2.** qualitative; quality.

quant. quantitative.

quar. 1. quarter. **2.** quarterly.

quart. 1. quarter. **2.** quarterly.

quasar (kwā′zär), *Astronomy.* quasi-stellar radio source.

quat. (in prescriptions) four. [from Latin *quattuor*]

Que. Quebec.

ques. question.

quin quintuple.

quinq. (in prescriptions) five. [from Latin *quinque*]

quint. (in prescriptions) fifth. [from Latin *quintus*]

quor. (in prescriptions) of which. [from Latin *quōrum*]

quot. 1. quotation. **2.** quotient. Also, **quot**

quotid. (in prescriptions) daily. [from Latin *quotidiē*]

q.v. 1. (in prescriptions) as much as you wish. [from Latin *quantum vis*] **2.** *plural* **qq.v.** (in formal writing) which see. [from Latin *quod vidē*]

QWERTY (kwûr′tē, kwer′-), of or pertaining to a keyboard having the keys in traditional typewriter arrangement, with the letters *q, w, e, r, t,* and *y* being the first six of the top row of alphabetic characters, starting from the left side.

R

R 1. *Chemistry.* radical. 2. *Math.* ratio. 3. regular: suit or coat size. 4. *Electricity.* resistance. 5. restricted: a rating assigned to a motion picture by the Motion Picture Association of America indicating that children under the age of 17 will not be admitted unless accompanied by an adult. 6. *Theater.* stage right. 7. *Physics.* roentgen. 8. *Chess.* rook.

R *Symbol.* 1. the 18th in order or in a series, or, when *I* is omitted, the 17th. 2. (*sometimes lowercase*) the medieval Roman numeral for 80. 3. *Biochemistry.* arginine. 4. *Physics.* universal gas constant. 5. registered trademark: written as superscript ⓡ following a name registered with the U.S. Patent and Trademark Office.

r 1. radius. 2. *Commerce.* registered. 3. *Electricity.* resistance. 4. *Physics.* roentgen. 5. royal. 6. (in Russia) ruble. 7. *Baseball.* run; runs. 8. (in India, Pakistan, and other countries) rupee.

r *Ecology.* the theoretical intrinsic rate of increase of a population; Malthusian parameter.

R. 1. rabbi. 2. radical. 3. radius. 4. railroad. 5. railway. 6. (in South Africa) rand; rands. 7. Réaumur (temperature). 8. Also, **R** (in prescriptions) take. [from Latin *recipe*] 9. rector. 10. redactor. 11. queen. [from Latin *regina*] 12. Republican. 13. response. 14. king. [from Latin *rex*] 15. river. 16. road. 17. royal. 18. (in Russia) ruble. 19. (in India, Pakistan, and other countries) rupee. 20. *Theater.* stage right.

r. 1. rabbi. 2. railroad. 3. railway. 4. range. 5. rare. 6. *Commerce.* received. 7. recipe. 8. replacing. 9. residence. 10. right. 11. rises. 12. river. 13. road. 14. rod. 15. royal. 16. rubber. 17. (in Russia) ruble. 18. *Baseball.*

run; runs. **19.** (in India, Pakistan, and other countries) rupee.

RA regular army.

Ra *Symbol, Chemistry.* radium.

R.A. 1. rear admiral. **2.** regular army. **3.** *Astronomy.* right ascension. **4.** royal academician. **5.** Royal Academy.

R.A.A.F. Royal Australian Air Force.

rab rabbet.

rad 1. *Math.* radian; radians. **2.** radiation absorbed dose. **3.** radio. **4.** radius.

rad. 1. *Math.* radical. **2.** Also, **rd** *Chemistry.* radium. **3.** radius. **4.** radix.

radar (rā′där), radio detection and ranging.

RADINT radar intelligence.

RAdm rear admiral. Also, **RADM**

radn radiation.

rad opr radio operator.

RAF Royal Air Force. Also, **R.A.F.**

rall. *Music.* rallentando.

RAM (ram), volatile computer memory available for creating, loading, or running programs and for the temporary storage and manipulation of data. [*r(andom)-a(ccess) m(emory)*]

RAM reverse annuity mortgage.

R.A.M. Royal Academy of Music.

R&B rhythm-and-blues. Also, **r&b, R and B**

R&D research and development. Also, **R and D**

R&E research and engineering.

R. & I. 1. king and emperor. [from Latin *Rēx et Imperātor*] **2.** queen and empress. [from Latin *Rēgina et Imperātrix*]

R and R 1. rest and recreation. **2.** rest and recuperation. **3.** rest and rehabilitation. **4.** rock-′n′-roll. Also, **R&R**

raser (rā′zər), radio-frequency amplification by stimulated emission of radiation.

RATO (rā′tō), *Aeronautics.* rocket-assisted takeoff.

RB 1. *Sports.* right back. **2.** *Football.* right full-back. **3.** *Football.* running back.

Rb *Symbol, Chemistry.* rubidium.

RBC red blood cell.

R.B.I. *Baseball.* run batted in; runs batted in. Also, **RBI, rbi, r.b.i.**

rbr rubber.

RC resistance-capacitance.

rc remote control.

R.C. 1. Red Cross. **2.** Reserve Corps. **3.** Roman Catholic. Also, **RC**

R.C.A.F. Royal Canadian Air Force. Also, **RCAF**

RCB 1. Retail Credit Bureau. **2.** *Football.* right cornerback.

RCC Rape Crisis Center.

R.C.Ch. Roman Catholic Church.

rcd. received.

rcdr recorder.

rcht ratchet.

rcl recall.

rclm reclaim.

R.C.M.P. Royal Canadian Mounted Police. Also, **RCMP**

rcn recreation.

R.C.N. Royal Canadian Navy. Also, **RCN**

rcndt recondition.

R.C.P. Royal College of Physicians.

rcpt. 1. receipt. **2.** receptacle.

rcptn reception.

R.C.S. Royal College of Surgeons.

Rct 1. receipt. **2.** *Military.* recruit. Also, **rct**

RCTL resistor-capacitor-transistor logic.

rcv receive.

rcvd received.

rcvg receiving.

rcvr receiver.

RD 1. Registered Dietician. **2.** rural delivery.

Rd *Symbol, Chemistry.* (formerly) radium.

rd 1. read. **2.** rod; rods.

Rd. Road.

rd. 1. rendered. **2.** road. **3.** rod; rods. **4.** round.

R/D *Banking.* refer to drawer.

R.D. 1. registered dietitian. **2.** Rural Delivery.

RDA 1. (not in technical use) recommended daily allowance. Compare **U.S. RDA. 2.** recommended dietary allowance. Also, **R.D.A.**

RdAc *Symbol, Chemistry.* radioactinium.

RD&D research, development, and demonstration.

RD&E research, development, and engineering.

rdc reduce.

rdcr reducer.

RDD *Marketing.* random digit dialing.

RDF 1. Also, **rdf** radio direction finder. **2.** rapid deployment force.

rdg 1. reading. **2.** rounding.

rdh round head.

rdl radial.

rdm recording demand meter.

rdout readout.

rdr 1. radar. **2.** reader.

RDS *Pathology.* respiratory distress syndrome.

rdsd roadside.

RDT&E research, development, testing, and engineering.

rdtr radiator.

RDX a white, crystalline explosive, $C_3H_6N_6O_6$. [*R(esearch) D(epartment) (E)x(plosive),* referring to such a department in Woolwich, England]

Re *Symbol, Chemistry.* rhenium.

Re. (in India, Pakistan, and other countries) rupee. Also, **re.**

R/E real estate. Also, **RE**

R.E. 1. real estate. **2.** Reformed Episcopal. **3.** *Football.* right end. **4.** Right Excellent.

r.e. *Football.* right end.

REA Rural Electrification Administration. Also, **R.E.A.**

Rear Adm. Rear Admiral.

reasm reassemble.

reassy reassembly.

Réaum. Réaumur (temperature).

reb. *Basketball.* rebounds.

rec. 1. receipt. **2.** (in prescriptions) fresh. [from Latin *recēns*] **3.** recipe. **4.** record. **5.** recorder. **6.** recording. **7.** recreation.

recalc recalculate.

recd. received. Also, **rec'd.**

recip. 1. reciprocal. **2.** reciprocity.

recirc recirculate.

recit. *Music.* recitative.

recl reclose.

recm recommend.

recog recognition.

recon reconnaissance.

recpt receipt.

Rec. Sec. Recording Secretary. Also, **rec. sec.**

rect. 1. receipt. **2.** rectangle. **3.** rectangular. **4.** (in prescriptions) rectified. [from Latin *rēctificātus*] **5.** rectifier. **6.** rector. **7.** rectory.

redupl. reduplication.

ref. 1. referee. **2.** reference. **3.** referred. **4.** refining. **5.** reformation. **6.** reformed. **7.** *Music.* refrain. **8.** refund. **9.** refunding.

Ref. Ch. Reformed Church.

ref des reference designation.

refl. 1. reflection. **2.** reflective. **3.** reflex. **4.** reflexive.

Ref. Pres. Reformed Presbyterian.

refr 1. refrigerate. **2.** refrigerator.

Ref. Sp. reformed spelling.

refs. req. references required.

Reg. 1. regiment. **2.** queen [from Latin *rēgina*].

reg. 1. regent. **2.** regiment. **3.** region. **4.** register. **5.** registered. **6.** registrar. **7.** registry. **8.** regular. **9.** regularly. **10.** regulation. **11.** regulator.

regd. registered.

regen regenerate.

regr. registrar.

regt. 1. regent. **2.** regiment.

reinf reinforce.

REIT (rēt), real-estate investment trust.

rej reject.

rel. 1. relating. **2.** relative. **3.** relatively. **4.** released. **5.** religion. **6.** religious.

relig. religion.

rel. pron. relative pronoun.

REM (rem), rapid eye movement.

rem (rem), *Nucleonics.* the quantity of ionizing radiation whose biological effect is equal to that produced by one roentgen of x-rays. [r(oentgen) e(quivalent in) m(an)]

rem remainder.

remitt. remittance.

rep (rep), *Physics.* a unit proposed but not adopted as a supplement to roentgen for expressing dosage of ionizing radiation. [r(oentgen) e(quivalent) p(hysical)]

Rep. 1. Representative. **2.** Republic. **3.** Republican.

rep. 1. repair. **2.** repeat. **3.** (in prescriptions) let it be repeated. [from Latin *repetātur*] **4.** report. **5.** reported. **6.** reporter.

repl. 1. replace. **2.** replacement.

repr. 1. represented. **2.** representing. **3.** reprint. **4.** reprinted.

repro 1. reproduce. **2.** reproduction.

rept. report.

Repub. 1. Republic. **2.** Republican.

req. 1. Also, **req** request. **2.** require. **3.** Also, **reqd** required. **4.** requisition.

reqn requisition.

reqt requirement.

RES *Immunology.* reticuloendothelial system.

res 1. resistance. **2.** resistor. **3.** resume.

res. 1. research. **2.** reserve. **3.** residence. **4.** resident; residents. **5.** residue. **6.** resigned. **7.** resolution.

resc rescind.

resid residual.

resln resolution.

resn resonant.

resp. 1. respective. **2.** respectively. **3.** respelled; respelling. **4.** respondent.

Res. Phys. Resident Physician.

restr. restaurant. **2.** restorer.

ret. 1. retain. **2.** retired. **3.** return. **4.** returned.

retd. 1. retained. **2.** retired. **3.** returned.

retn retain.

retr retract.

retro 1. retroactive. **2.** retrograde.

Rev. *Bible.* **1.** Revelation; Revelations. **2.** Reverend.

rev. 1. revenue. **2.** reverse. **3.** review. **4.** reviewed. **5.** revise; revised. **6.** revision. **7.** revolution. **8.** revolving.

Rev. Stat. Revised Statutes.

Rev. Ver. Revised Version (of the Bible).

rew rewind.

RF 1. radiofrequency. **2.** *Baseball.* right field; right fielder.

rf *Baseball.* right field; right fielder.

R.F. Reserve Force.

r.f. 1. range finder. **2.** rapid-fire. **3.** reducing flame. **4.** *Baseball.* right field; right fielder.

R.F.A. Royal Field Artillery.

r.f.b. *Sports.* right fullback. Also, **R.F.B.**

RFC Reconstruction Finance Corporation.

rfc radio-frequency choke.

R.F.D. rural free delivery. Also, **RFD**

RFE Radio Free Europe. Also, **R.F.E.**

rfgt refrigerant.

RFI radio frequency interference.

RFLP (rif′lip′), restriction fragment length polymorphism: a fragment of DNA used to trace family relationships. Also called **riflip.**

rflx reflex.

RFQ *Commerce.* request for quotation.

r.g. *Football.* right guard.

RGB *Television.* red-green-blue.

rgd rigid.

rglr regular.

rglt regulate.

rgltd regulated.

rgltr regulator.

RGNP real gross national product.

rgtr register.

RH *Meteorology.* relative humidity. Also, **rh**

Rh 1. *Physiology.* Rh factor. **2.** *Metallurgy.* Rockwell hardness.

Rh *Symbol, Chemistry.* rhodium.

R.H. Royal Highness.

r.h. right hand. right-handed.

r.h.b. *Football.* right halfback. Also, **RHB, R.H.B.**

rhd railhead.

rheo rheostat.

RHIP rank has its privileges.

Rhn *Metallurgy.* Rockwell hardness number.

Rho. Rhodesia. Also, **Rhod.**

rhomb 1. rhombic. **2.** rhomboid.

RI Rhode Island (for use with ZIP code).

R.I. 1. Queen and Empress. [from Latin *Rēgina et Imperātrix*] **2.** King and Emperor. [from Latin *Rēx et Imperātor*] **3.** Rhode Island.

R.I.B.A. Royal Institute of British Architects.

RICO (rē′kō), Racketeer Influenced and Corrupt Organizations Act.

RIF (rif), **1.** *Military.* a reduction in the personnel of an armed service or unit. **2.** a reduction in the number of persons employed, especially for budgetary reasons. [*R(eduction) I(n) F(orce)*]

R.I.I.A. Royal Institute of International Affairs.

RIP *Computers.* raster image processor.

R.I.P. 1. may he or she rest in peace. [from Latin *requiēscat in pāce*] **2.** may they rest in peace. [from Latin *requiēscant in pāce*] Also, **RIP**

RISC (risk), *Computers.* reduced instruction set computer.

rit. *Music.* ritardando. Also, **ritard.**

riv. river.

RJ *Military.* road junction.

rkt rocket.

RL resistance-inductance.

RLB *Football.* right linebacker.

RLC resistance, inductance, capacitance.

rlct *Electricity.* reluctance.

rld rolled.

R.L.D. retail liquor dealer.

rlf relief.

RLL *Computers.* run-length limited.

R.L.O. returned letter office.

rloc relocate.

rlr roller.

rlse release.

rlt relate.

rltn relation.

rltv relative.

rlv relieve.

rlxn relaxation.

rly relay.

RM (in Germany) reichsmark.

rm range marks.

rm. 1. ream. **2.** room.

r.m. (in Germany) reichsmark.

R.M.A. *British.* **1.** Royal Marine Artillery. **2.** Royal Military Academy.

R.M.C. *British.* Royal Military College.

rmd remedy.

rmdr remainder.

rms *Math.* root mean square. Also, **r.m.s.**

R.M.S. 1. Railway Mail Service. **2.** *British.* Royal Mail Service. **3.** *British.* Royal Mail Steamship.

rmt remote.

rmv remove.

rmvbl removable.

Rn *Symbol, Chemistry.* radon.

rn 1. radio navigation. **2.** rain.

R.N. 1. registered nurse. **2.** *British.* Royal Navy.

RNA *Genetics.* ribonucleic acid.

R.N.A.S. *British.* Royal Naval Air Service.

RNase (är′en′ās, -āz), *Biochemistry.* ribonuclease. Also, **RNAase** (är′en′ā′ās, -āz).

RNC Republican National Committee.

rnd. round.

rndm random.

rng range.

rnge range.

rngg ringing.

rngr *Telephones.* ringer.

rnl renewal.

RNP *Biochemistry.* a nucleoprotein containing RNA. [*r(ibo)n(ucleo)p(rotein)*]

R.N.R. *British.* Royal Naval Reserve.

rnwbl renewable.

R.N.W.M.P. *Canadian.* Royal Northwest Mounted Police.

rnwy runway.

rny rainy.

RO. (in Oman) rial omani.

ro. **1.** *Bookbinding.* recto. **2.** roan. **3.** rood.

R.O. **1.** Receiving Office. **2.** Receiving Officer. **3.** Regimental Order. **4.** *British.* Royal Observatory.

ROA *Accounting.* return on assets.

ROE *Accounting.* return on equity.

R.O.G. *Commerce.* receipt of goods. Also, **ROG, r.o.g.**

ROI return on investment. Also, **R.O.I.**

ROK Republic of Korea.

ROM (rom), computer memory in which program instructions, operating procedures, or other data are permanently stored. [*r(ead)-o(nly) m(emory)*]

Rom. **1.** Roman. **2.** Romance. **3.** Romania. **4.** Romanian. **5.** Romanic. **6.** *Bible.* Romans. Also, **Rom** (for defs. 2, 5).

rom. *Printing.* roman.

Rom. Cath. Roman Catholic.

Rom. Cath. Ch. Roman Catholic Church.

RONA *Accounting.* return on net assets.

R.O.P. run-of-paper: a designation specifying

that the position of a newspaper or magazine advertisement is to be determined by the publisher.

R.O.R. *Law.* released on own recognizance.

ROS *Computers.* read only storage.

ROT rule of thumb.

rot. 1. rotating. 2. rotation.

R.O.T.C. (är′ō tē sē′, rot′sē), Reserve Officers Training Corps. Also, **ROTC**

rotr rotator.

Roum. 1. Roumania. 2. Roumanian.

ROW right of way.

RP 1. *Linguistics.* Received Pronunciation. 2. repurchase agreement. 3. *Pathology.* retinitis pigmentosa.

Rp. (in Indonesia) rupiah; rupiahs.

R.P. 1. Reformed Presbyterian. 2. Regius Professor.

RPG role-playing game.

rpg *Basketball.* rebounds per game.

rplr repeller.

rplsn repulsion.

rplt repellent.

rpm revolutions per minute. Also, **r/min., r.p.m.**

R.P.O. Railway Post Office. Also, **RPO**

RPQ request for price quotation.

rpr repair.

rprt report.

rps revolutions per second. Also, **r.p.s., r/s**

rpt. 1. repeat. 2. report.

rptn repetition.

rptr repeater.

RPV *Military.* remotely piloted vehicle.

rpvntv rust preventive.

R.Q. *Physiology.* respiratory quotient.

R.R. 1. railroad. 2. Right Reverend. 3. rural route.

RRM renegotiable-rate mortgage.

rRNA *Biochemistry.* ribosomal RNA.

R.R.R. return receipt requested (used in registered mail). Also, **RRR**

RRT rail rapid transit.

R.R.T. registered respiratory therapist.

Rs. 1. (in Portugal) reis. **2.** (in India, Pakistan, and other countries) rupees.

R.S. 1. Recording Secretary. **2.** Reformed Spelling. **3.** Revised Statutes. **4.** Royal Society.

r.s. right side.

RSA Republic of South Africa.

rsc rescue.

rsch research.

RSE Received Standard English.

RSFSR Russian Soviet Federated Socialist Republic. Also, **R.S.F.S.R.**

rslvr resolver.

rspd respond.

rsps response.

rspsb responsible.

rspv 1. respective. **2.** responsive.

rsrc resource.

rss root sum square.

rst restore.

rstg roasting.

rstr 1. *Electronics.* raster. **2.** restrain. **3.** restrict.

RSV Revised Standard Version (of the Bible).

rsv reserve.

RSVP (used on invitations) please reply. Also, **R.S.V.P., rsvp, r.s.v.p.** [from French *r(épondez) s('il) v(ous) p(laît)*]

rsvr reservoir.

RSWC right side up with care.

RT radiotelephone.

rt. 1. rate. **2.** right.

r.t. *Football.* right tackle.

rtcl reticle.

rte. route. Also, **Rte.**

RTF *Genetics.* resistance transfer factor; R factor.

rtf *Computers.* rich-text format.

rtg rating.

Rt. Hon. Right Honorable.

RTL resistor-transistor logic.

rtn return.

rtng retaining.

rtnr retainer.

rtr rotor.

rtrv retrieve.

rtry rotary.

Rts. *Finance.* rights.

rtty radio teletypewriter.

rtw ready-to-wear.

rtz return-to-zero.

Ru *Symbol, Chemistry.* ruthenium.

Rum. 1. Rumania. **2.** Also, **Rum** Rumanian.

Rus. 1. Russia. **2.** Russian.

Russ. 1. Russia. **2.** Russian. Also, **Russ**

RV 1. recreational vehicle. **2.** Revised Version (of the Bible).

rv rear view.

rvam reactive volt-ampere meter.

rvlg revolving.

rvlv revolve.

rvm reactive voltmeter.

RVN Republic of Vietnam.

rvrb reverberation.

rvs 1. reverse. **2.** revise.

rvsbl reversible.

rvs cur reverse current.

rvsn revision.

RVSVP (used on invitations) please reply quickly. Also, **R.V.S.V.P., rvsvp, r.v.s.v.p.** [from French *r(épondez) v(ite) s(íl) v(ous) p(laît)*]

rvw review.

R/W right of way.

r/w read/write. Also, **r-w**

R.W. 1. Right Worshipful. **2.** Right Worthy.

Rwy. Railway.

Rx 1. prescription. **2.** (in prescriptions) take. [from Latin, representing an abbreviation of *recipe*] **3.** (in India, Pakistan, and other countries) tens of rupees.

Ry. Railway.

S

S 1. *Baseball.* sacrifice. **2.** satisfactory. **3.** Saxon. **4.** sentence. **5.** short. **6.** *Electricity.* siemens. **7.** signature. **8.** single. **9.** small. **10.** soft. **11.** *Music.* soprano. **12.** South. **13.** Southern. **14.** state (highway). **15.** stimulus. **16.** *Grammar.* subject.

S *Symbol.* **1.** the 19th in order or in a series, or, when *I* is omitted, the 18th. **2.** (*sometimes lowercase*) the medieval Roman numeral for 7 or 70. **3.** second. **4.** *Biochemistry.* serine. **5.** *Thermodynamics.* entropy. **6.** *Physics.* strangeness. **7.** *Chemistry.* sulfur.

s 1. satisfactory. **2.** signature. **3.** small. **4.** soft. **5.** *Music.* soprano. **6.** south. **7.** stere.

s *Symbol.* second.

S. 1. Sabbath. **2.** Saint. **3.** Saturday. **4.** Saxon. **5.** (in Austria) schilling; schillings. **6.** School. **7.** Sea. **8.** Senate. **9.** September. **10.** *British.* shilling; shillings. **11.** (in prescriptions) **a.** mark; write; label. [from Latin *signa*] **b.** let it be written. [from Latin *signētur*] **12.** Signor: an Italian form of address for a man. **13.** Small. **14.** Socialist. **15.** Society. **16.** Fellow. [from Latin *socius*] **17.** (in Peru) sol. **18.** South. **19.** Southern. **20.** (in Ecuador) sucre; sucres. **21.** Sunday.

s. 1. saint. **2.** school. **3.** second. **4.** section. **5.** see. **6.** series. **7.** *British.* shilling; shillings. **8.** sign. **9.** signed. **10.** silver. **11.** singular. **12.** sire. **13.** small. **14.** society. **15.** son. **16.** south. **17.** southern. **18.** species. **19.** statute. **20.** steamer. **21.** stem. **22.** stem of. **23.** substantive.

Sa *Symbol, Chemistry.* (formerly) samarium.

Sa. Saturday.

S/A *Banking.* survivorship agreement.

S.A. 1. Salvation Army. **2.** seaman apprentice. **3.** South Africa. **4.** South America. **5.** South Australia. **6.** corporation [from French *société anonyme* or Spanish *sociedad anónima*].

s.a. 1. semiannual. **2.** sex appeal. **3.** without year or date. [from Latin *sine annō*] **4.** subject to approval.

S.A.A. Speech Association of America.

Sab. Sabbath.

SAC (sak), Strategic Air Command. Also, **S.A.C.**

SAD seasonal affective disorder.

SADD Students Against Drunk Drivers.

S.A.E. 1. self-addressed envelope. **2.** Society of Automotive Engineers. **3.** stamped addressed envelope. Also, **SAE; s.a.e.** (for defs. 1, 3).

SAF single Asian female.

saf safety.

S. Afr. 1. South Africa. **2.** South African.

S. Afr. D. South African Dutch. Also, **SAfrD**

SAG (sag), Screen Actors Guild.

sal. hist. salary history.

SALT (sôlt), Strategic Arms Limitations Treaty.

Salv. Salvador.

SAM, (sam), **1.** shared-appreciation mortgage. **2.** single Asian male. **3.** surface-to-air missile. **4.** Space Available Mail: a special air service for sending parcels to overseas members of the armed forces.

Sam. *Bible.* Samuel.

S. Am. 1. South America. **2.** South American.

S. Amer. 1. South America. **2.** South American.

Saml. Samuel.

san sanitary.

sand. sandwich.

S.&F. *Insurance.* stock and fixtures.

S and H shipping and handling (charges). Also, **S&H**

S&L *Banking.* savings and loan association. Also, **S and L**

S and M sadomasochism; sadism and masochism. Also, **S&M, s&m**

S.&M. *Insurance.* stock and machinery.

S&P Standard & Poor's.

s. & s.c. (of paper) sized and supercalendered.

SANE (sān), a private nationwide organization in the U.S. that opposes nuclear testing and advocates international peace. [official shortening of its by-name *Committee for a Sane Nuclear Policy*]

Sans. Sanskrit.

Sansk. Sanskrit.

Sar. Sardinia.

S.A.R. 1. South African Republic. **2.** Sons of the American Revolution.

SASE self-addressed stamped envelope. Also, **sase, S.A.S.E., s.a.s.e.**

Sask. Saskatchewan.

SAT *Trademark.* Scholastic Aptitude Test.

Sat. 1. Saturday. **2.** Saturn.

sat. 1. satellite. **2.** saturate. **3.** saturated.

SATB *Music.* soprano, alto, tenor, bass.

satcom communications satellite.

Sax. 1. Saxon. **2.** Saxony.

Sb *Symbol, Chemistry.* antimony. [from Latin *stibium*]

sb 1. service bulletin. **2.** sideband. **3.** *Optics.* stilb. **4.** stove bolt.

sb. *Grammar.* substantive.

S.B. 1. Bachelor of Science. [from Latin *Scientiae Baccalaureus*] **2.** South Britain (England and Wales).

s.b. *Baseball.* stolen base; stolen bases.

SBA Small Business Administration. Also, **S.B.A.**

SbE south by east.

SBF single black female.

SBIC Small Business Investment Company.

SBLI Savings Bank Life Insurance.

SBM single black male.

SBN *Publishing.* Standard Book Number.

sbstr *Electronics.* substrate.

SbW south by west.

SC 1. security council. **2.** signal corps. **3.** South Carolina (for use with ZIP code). **4.**

SportsChannel New England (a cable television channel). **5.** supreme court.

Sc *Symbol, Chemistry.* scandium.

sc solar cell.

Sc. 1. Scotch. **2.** Scotland. **3.** Scots. **4.** Scottish.

sc. 1. scale. **2.** scene. **3.** science. **4.** scientific. **5.** namely. [from Latin *scilicet*, contraction of *scire licet* it is permitted to know] **6.** screw. **7.** scruple. **8.** he or she carved, engraved, or sculpted it. [from Latin *sculpsit*]

S.C. 1. Sanitary Corps. **2.** Security Council (of the U.N.). **3.** Signal Corps. **4.** South Carolina. **5.** Staff Corps. **6.** Supreme Court.

s.c. *Printing.* **1.** small capitals. **2.** supercalendered.

Scan. Scandinavia.

Scand Scandinavian.

Scand. 1. Scandinavia. **2.** Scandinavian.

s. caps. *Printing.* small capitals.

scav scavenge.

Sc.B. Bachelor of Science. [from Latin *Scientiae Baccalaureus*]

Sc.B.C. Bachelor of Science in Chemistry.

Sc.B.E. Bachelor of Science in Engineering.

scd specification control drawing.

Sc.D. Doctor of Science. [from Latin *Scientiae Doctor*]

Sc.D.Hyg. Doctor of Science in Hygiene.

Sc.D.Med. Doctor of Medical Science.

scdr screwdriver.

sce source.

SCF single Christian female.

scf standard cubic foot.

scfh standard cubic feet per hour

scfm standard cubic feet per minute.

sch socket head.

Sch. (in Austria) schilling; schillings.

sch. 1. schedule. **2.** school. **3.** schooner.

SCHDM schematic diagram.

sched. schedule.

schem schematic.

Sch.Mus.B. Bachelor of School Music.

sci. 1. science. **2.** scientific.

SCID *Pathology.* severe combined immune deficiency.

sci-fi (sī′fī′), science fiction.

scil. to wit; namely. [from Latin *scilicet*]

SCLC Southern Christian Leadership Conference. Also, **S.C.L.C.**

sclr scaler.

SCM single Christian male.

Sc.M. Master of Science. [from Latin *Scientiae Magister*]

scn specification change notice.

scng scanning.

scnr scanner.

S. Con. Res. Senate concurrent resolution.

SCORE (skôr), Service Corps of Retired Executives.

Scot 1. Scots. **2.** Scottish.

Scot. 1. Scotch. **2.** Scotland. **3.** Scottish.

ScotGael Scots Gaelic.

SCOTUS Supreme Court of the United States. Also, **SCUS**

SCR *Electronics.* semiconductor controlled rectifier.

scr. 1. screw. **2.** scruple.

Script. 1. Scriptural. **2.** Scripture.

scrn screen.

SCS Soil Conservation Service.

SCSI (skuz′ē), a standard for computer interface ports. [*s(mall) c(omputer) s(ystem) i(nterface)*]

sctd scattered.

sctrd scattered.

scty security.

SCU Special Care Unit.

scuba (skōō′bə), self-contained underwater breathing apparatus.

sculp. 1. sculptor. **2.** sculptural. **3.** sculpture. Also, **sculpt.**

SD 1. sea-damaged. **2.** South Dakota (for use with ZIP code). **3.** *Statistics.* standard deviation. **4.** the intelligence and counterespionage service of the Nazi SS [from German *S(icherheits)d(ienst)*].

sd side.

sd. sound.

S/D **1.** school district. **2.** *Commerce.* sight draft.

S.D. **1.** doctor of science. [from Latin *Scientiae Doctor*] **2.** sea-damaged. **3.** senior deacon. **4.** South Dakota. **5.** special delivery. **6.** *Statistics.* standard deviation.

s.d. **1.** without fixing a day for further action or meeting. [from Latin *sine die*] **2.** *Statistics.* standard deviation.

S.D.A. Seventh Day Adventists.

S. Dak. South Dakota.

sdg siding.

SDI Strategic Defense Initiative.

sdl saddle.

sdn sedan.

S. Doc. Senate document.

SDR *Banking.* special drawing rights. Also, **S.D.R.**

sdr sender.

SDS Students for a Democratic Society.

SE **1.** southeast. **2.** southeastern. **3.** *Football.* split end. **4.** Standard English. Also, **S.E.**

Se *Symbol, Chemistry.* selenium.

se special equipment.

SEATO (sē′tō), Southeast Asia Treaty Organization (1954–1977).

SEbE southeast by east.

SEbS southeast by south.

SEC Securities and Exchange Commission. Also, **S.E.C.**

sec **1.** *Trigonometry.* secant. **2.** second. **3.** section.

sec^{-1} *Symbol, Trigonometry.* arc secant.

sec. **1.** second. **2.** secondary. **3.** secretary. **4.** section. **5.** sector. **6.** according to [from Latin *secundum*].

sech *Math.* hyperbolic secant.

sec. leg. according to law. [from Latin *secundum lēgem*]

secs. 1. seconds. **2.** sections.

sect. 1. section. **2.** sector.

secy secretary. Also, **sec'y**

SEE Signing Essential English.

seg segment.

seismol. 1. seismological. **2.** seismology.

SEIU Service Employees International Union.

sel. 1. select. **2.** selected. **3.** selection; selections. **4.** selectivity. **5.** selector.

selsyn self-synchronous.

SEM 1. *Optics.* scanning electron microscope. **2.** shared equity mortgage.

Sem. 1. Seminary. **2.** Semitic. Also, **Sem**

sem. 1. semicolon. **2.** seminar. **3.** seminary.

semicnd semiconductor.

semih. (in prescriptions) half an hour. [from Latin *sēmihōra*]

sen. 1. senate. **2.** senator. **3.** senior. Also, **sen**

sens 1. sensitive. **2.** sensitivity.

SEP simplified employee pension.

Sep. 1. September. **2.** *Bible.* Septuagint.

sep. 1. *Botany.* sepal. **2.** separable. **3.** separate. **4.** separated. **5.** separation.

Sept. 1. September. **2.** *Bible.* Septuagint.

seq 1. sequence. **2.** sequential.

seq. 1. sequel. **2.** the following (one). [from Latin *sequēns*] **3.** that which follows. [from Latin *sequitur*]

seqq. the following (ones). [from Latin *sequentia*]

Ser *Biochemistry.* serine.

ser. 1. serial. **2.** series. **3.** sermon.

Serb. 1. Serbia. **2.** Serbian.

serno serial number.

serr serrate.

serv. service.

SES socioeconomic status.

sess. session.

setg setting.

SETI search for extraterrestrial intelligence.

setlg settling.

sew sewer.

SF 1. *Baseball.* sacrifice fly. 2. science fiction. 3. single female. 4. *Finance.* sinking fund.

sf 1. science fiction. 2. *Music.* sforzando.

s-f science fiction.

S.F. 1. San Francisco. 2. senior fellow.

Sfc *Military.* sergeant first class.

sfm surface feet per minute.

SFr. (in Switzerland) franc; francs. Also, **Sfr.**

sft shaft.

sftw software.

sfx suffix.

sfz *Music.* sforzando.

SG 1. senior grade. 2. Secretary General. 3. Solicitor General. 4. Surgeon General.

sg *Grammar.* singular. Also, **sg.**

s.g. specific gravity.

sgd. signed.

sgl single.

SGML *Computers.* Standard Generalized Markup Language.

SGO Surgeon General's Office.

Sgt. Sergeant.

Sgt. Maj. Sergeant Major.

sh 1. sheet. 2. shower. 3. shunt.

s/h 1. shipping/handling. 2. shorthand.

SHA *Navigation.* sidereal hour angle.

Shak. Shakespeare.

Shaks. Shakespeare.

SHAPE (shāp), Supreme Headquarters Allied Powers, Europe. Also, **Shape.**

shcr shipping container.

SHF 1. single Hispanic female. 2. Also, **shf** superhigh frequency.

shl shellac.

shld shield.

shldr shoulder.

shltr shelter.

SHM single Hispanic male.

S.H.M. *Physics.* simple harmonic motion. Also, **s.h.m.**

SHO Showtime (a cable channel).

shp shaft horsepower. Also, **SHP, S.H.P., s.hp., s.h.p.**

shpng shipping.

shpt. shipment.

sht. sheet.

shtc short time constant.

shtdn shutdown.

shtg. shortage.

shthg sheathing.

shv sheave.

shwr shower.

SI International System of Units. [from French *S(ystème) I(nternationale d'unités)*]

Si *Symbol, Chemistry.* silicon.

S.I. Staten Island.

SIC Standard Industrial Classification: a system used by the federal government to classify business activities.

Sic. 1. Sicilian. 2. Sicily.

SIDS (sidz), sudden infant death syndrome.

SIG special-interest group.

Sig. 1. (in prescriptions) write; mark; label: indicating directions to be written on a package or label for the use of the patient. [from Latin *signā*] 2. let it be written. [from Latin *signētur*] 3. Signore; Signori: the Italian form of address for a man.

sig. 1. signal. 2. signature. 3. signore; signori: an Italian form of address for a man.

sil silence.

sils silver solder.

sim. 1. similar. 2. simile. 3. simulator.

simlt simultaneous.

SIMM (sim), *Computers.* single inline memory module.

sing. singular.

sinh *Math.* hyperbolic sine.

SINS (sinz), *Navigation.* a gyroscopic device indicating the exact speed and position of a vessel. [*s(hip's) i(nertial) n(avigation) s(ystem)*]

SIOP (sī′op), (formerly) the secret U.S. contingency plan for waging a nuclear war with the Soviet Union. [*s(ingle) i(ntegrated) o(perations) p(lan)*]

SIP (sip), **1.** *Computers.* single inline package. **2.** supplemental income plan.

sit situation.

SI units International System of Units.

S.J. Society of Jesus.

S.J.D. Doctor of Juridical Science. [from Latin *Scientiae Jūridicae Doctor*]

SJF single Jewish female.

SJM single Jewish male.

S.J. Res. Senate joint resolution.

SK Saskatchewan, Canada (for use with ZIP code).

sk. 1. sack. **2.** sink. **3.** sketch.

sklt skylight.

sks seeks.

Skt Sanskrit. Also, **Skt., Skr., Skrt.**

skt 1. skirt. **2.** socket.

sktd skirted.

SL source language.

sl sliding.

s.l. 1. Also, **sl.** salvage loss. **2.** *Bibliography.* without place (of publication). [from Latin *sine locō*]

SLA Special Libraries Association.

S. Lat. south latitude.

Slav Slavic. Also, **Slav.**

slbl soluble.

SLBM 1. sea-launched ballistic missile. **2.** submarine-launched ballistic missile. Also, **S.L.B.M.**

slc slice.

SLCM sea-launched cruise missile. Also, **S.L.C.M.**

sld *Electricity.* single-line diagram.

sld. 1. sailed. **2.** Also, **sld** sealed.

sldr solder.

SLE *Pathology.* systemic lupus erythematosus.

slfcl self-closing.

slfcln self-cleaning.

slfcntd self-contained.

slfprop self-propelled.

slftpg self-tapping.

SLIC (Federal) Savings and Loan Insurance Corporation. Also, **S.L.I.C.**

SLMA Student Loan Marketing Association.

slp slope.

S.L.P. Socialist Labor Party.

SLR *Photography.* single-lens reflex camera.

sls sales.

slt sleet.

sltd slotted.

slv sleeve.

slvg 1. salvage. **2.** sleeving.

slvt solvent.

SM 1. service mark. **2.** single male.

Sm *Symbol, Chemistry.* samarium.

sm some.

sm. small.

S-M 1. Also, **S and M.** sadomasochism. **2.** sadomasochistic. Also, **s-m, S/M, s/m**

S.M. 1. Master of Science. [from Latin *Scientiae Magister*] **2.** sergeant major. **3.** State Militia.

SMA Surplus Marketing Administration.

s-mail (es′māl′), snail mail.

smat see me about this.

S.M.B. Bachelor of Sacred Music.

sm. c. small capital; small capitals. Also, **sm. cap.** or **sm. caps**

SMD *Pathology.* senile macular degeneration.

S.M.D. Doctor of Sacred Music.

smk smoke.

sml small.

smls seamless.

S.M.M. Master of Sacred Music.

S.M.O.M. Sovereign and Military Order of Malta.

SMPTE Society of Motion Picture and Television Engineers.

SMS Synchronous Meteorological Satellite.

SMSA Standard Metropolitan Statistical Area.

smy summary.

SN 1. Secretary of the Navy. **2.** serial number.

Sn *Symbol, Chemistry.* tin. [from Latin *stannum*]

sna·fu (sna fōō′, snaf′ōō), situation normal, all fouled up.

SNCC (snik), a U.S. civil-rights organization formed by students and active especially during the 1960s. [*S(tudent) N(onviolent) C(oordinating) C(ommittee)*]

snd sound.

SNG synthetic natural gas.

snkl snorkel.

snl standard nomenclature list.

sno 1. snow. **2.** stock number.

snr 1. signal-to-noise ratio. **2.** sonar.

sns sense.

snsr sensor.

sntr *Metallurgy.* sintered.

sntzd sensitized.

sny sunny.

SO *Baseball.* strikeout; strikeouts.

so *Electricity.* slow operate (a relay type).

So. 1. South. **2.** Southern.

s/o shipping order.

S.O. 1. Signal Officer. **2.** Special Order. **3.** Standing Order.

s.o. 1. seller's option. **2.** shipping order.

S.O.B. 1. (*sometimes lowercase*) *Slang.* son of a bitch. **2.** Senate Office Building. Also, **SOB**

Soc. 1. socialist. **2.** (*often lowercase*) society. **3.** sociology.

socd source control drawing.

sociol. 1. sociological. **2.** sociology.

socn source control number.

SOF sound on a film.

S. of Sol. *Bible.* Song of Solomon.

sol 1. solenoid. **2.** solid.

Sol. 1. Solicitor. **2.** Song of Solomon.

sol. 1. soluble. **2.** solution.

S.O.L. *Slang.* **1.** strictly out (of) luck. **2.** *Vulgar.* shit out (of) luck. Also, **SOL**

soln solution.

som start of message.

sonar (sō′när), sound navigation ranging.

SOP Standard Operating Procedure; Standing Operating Procedure. Also, **S.O.P.**

sop. soprano.

SOS **1.** the letters represented by the radio telegraphic signal (••• – – – •••) used as an internationally recognized call for help. **2.** *Slang.* creamed chipped beef on toast. [*s(hit) o(n a) s(hingle)*]

s.o.s. (in prescriptions) if necessary. [from Latin *si opus sit*]

SOV language *Linguistics.* a type of language that has basic subject-object-verb order.

Sov. Un. Soviet Union.

SP **1.** Shore Patrol. **2.** Specialist. **3.** Submarine Patrol.

sp **1.** spare. **2.** special-purpose. **3.** speed

Sp. **1.** Spain. **2.** Spaniard. **3.** Also, **Sp** Spanish.

sp. **1.** space. **2.** special. **3.** species. **4.** specific. **5.** specimen. **6.** spelling. **7.** spirit.

S.P. **1.** Shore Patrol. **2.** Socialist party. **3.** Submarine Patrol.

s.p. without issue; childless. [from Latin *sine prōle*]

Sp. Am. **1.** Spanish America. **2.** Spanish American.

Span. **1.** Spaniard. **2.** Spanish.

SPAR (spär), (during World War II) a woman enlisted in the women's reserve of the U.S. Coast Guard. Also, **Spar.** [from Latin *S(emper) par(ātus)* "Always ready" the Coast Guard motto]

SpAr Spanish Arabic.

spat silicon precision alloy transistor.

S.P.C.A. Society for the Prevention of Cruelty to Animals.

S.P.C.C. Society for the Prevention of Cruelty to Children.

spchg supercharge.

spcl special.

spcr spacer.

SPDA single-premium deferred annuity.

sp. del. special delivery.

spdl spindle.

spdom speedometer.

spdt sw single-pole double-throw switch.

spec. 1. special. 2. specially. 3. specifically. 4. specification. 5. specimen.

specif. 1. specific. 2. specifically.

SPECT (spekt), *Medicine.* single photon emission computed tomography.

Sp.Ed. Specialist in Education.

SPF sun protection factor.

spg spring.

sp. gr. specific gravity. Also, **spg.**

spher spherical.

sp.ht. *Physics.* specific heat.

spkl sprinkler.

spkr speaker.

spkt sprocket.

splc splice.

splt spotlight.

spltr splitter.

sply supply.

spmkt supermarket.

spnr spanner.

spp. species.

sp/ph split/phase.

sppl spark plug.

S.P.Q.R. the Senate and People of Rome. Also, **SPQR** [from Latin *Senātus Populusque Rōmānus*]

spr spring.

S.P.R. Society for Psychical Research.

sprdr spreader.

SPRF single Puerto Rican female.

sprl spiral.

SPRM single Puerto Rican male.

sprt support.

spst sw single-pole single-throw switch.

spt. seaport.

spvn supervision.

Sq. 1. Squadron. **2.** Square (of a city or town).

sq. 1. sequence. **2.** the following; the following one. [from Latin *sequēns*] **3.** squadron. **4.** square.

sqdn squadron.

sq. ft. square foot; square feet.

sq. in. square inch; square inches.

sq. km square kilometer; square kilometers.

SQL *Computers.* structured query language.

sq. m square meter; square meters.

sq. mi. square mile; square miles.

sq. mm square millimeter; square millimeters.

sqq. the following; the following ones. [from Latin *sequentia*]

sq. r. square rod; square rods.

sq. rt. square root.

SQUID (skwid), *Medicine.* superconducting quantum interference device.

sq. yd. square yard; square yards.

SR *Postal Service.* star route.

Sr *Symbol, Chemistry.* strontium.

sr 1. selenium rectifier. **2.** shift register. **3.** *Electricity.* slow release (a relay type). **4.** *Geometry.* steradian.

Sr. 1. Senhor: a Portuguese form of address for a man. **2.** Senior. **3.** Señor: a Spanish form of address for a man. **4.** Sir. **5.** *Ecclesiastical.* Sister [from L *Soror*].

S-R stimulus-response.

S.R. Sons of the Revolution.

s.r. semantic reaction.

Sra. 1. Senhora: a Portuguese form of address for a woman. **2.** Señora: a Spanish form of address for a woman.

SRAM short-range attack missile.

SRB solid rocket booster.

SRBM short-range ballistic missile.

srch search.

S. Rept. Senate report.

S. Res. Senate resolution.

srng syringe.

SRO 1. single-room occupancy. **2.** standing room only. Also, **S.R.O.**

SRS air bag. [*s(upplemental) r(estraint) s(ystem)*]

Srta. 1. Senhorita: a Portuguese form of address for a girl or unmarried woman. **2.** Señorita: a Spanish form of address for a girl or unmarried woman.

srvln surveillance.

SS 1. an elite military unit of the Nazi party. [from German *S(chutz)s(taffel)*] **2.** *Baseball.* shortstop. **3.** social security. **4.** steamship. **5.** *Football.* strong safety. **6.** supersonic.

ss 1. same size. **2.** (in prescriptions) a half. Also, **ss.** [from Latin *sēmis*] **3.** single-shot.

SS. 1. Saints. [from Latin *sāncti*] **2.** See **SS** (def. 1). **3.** See **ss.** (def. 1).

ss. 1. to wit; namely (used especially on legal documents, to verify the place of action). [from Latin *scilicet*] **2.** sections. **3.** *Baseball.* shortstop.

S.S. 1. See **SS** (def. 1). **2.** (in prescriptions) in the strict sense. [from Latin *sēnsū strictō*] **3.** steamship. **4.** Sunday School.

SSA 1. Social Security Act. **2.** Social Security Administration.

SSAE stamped self-addressed envelope.

SSB 1. Selective Service Board. **2.** Social Security Board.

ssb single sideband.

SSBN the U.S. Navy designation for the fleet ballistic missile submarine. [*S(trategic) S(ubmarine) B(allistic) N(uclear)*]

SSC *Banking.* small-saver certificate.

S.Sc.D. Doctor of Social Science.

sscr setscrew.

SS.D. Most Holy Lord: a title of the pope. [from Latin *Sānctissimus Dominus*]

S.S.D. Doctor of Sacred Scripture. [from Latin *Sacrae Scriptūrae Doctor*]

ssdd *Computers.* single-side, double-density.

SSE south-southeast. Also, **S.S.E., s.s.e.**

sse solid-state electronics.

ssf saybolt second furol.

ssfm single-sideband frequency modulation.

sshd *Computers.* single-side, high-density.

SSI 1. *Electronics.* small-scale integration: the technology for concentrating semiconductor devices in a single integrated circuit. **2.** Supplemental Security Income.

S sleep slow-wave sleep.

SSM surface-to-surface missile.

ssm 1. single-sideband modulation. **2.** solid-state materials.

SSN Social Security number.

SSPE *Pathology.* subacute sclerosing panencephalitis.

SSR Soviet Socialist Republic. Also, **S.S.R.**

ssr solid-state relay.

SSS Selective Service System.

sssd *Computers.* single-side, single-density.

SST supersonic transport.

ssu saybolt second universal.

SSW south-southwest. Also, **S.S.W., s.s.w.**

ST *Real Estate.* septic tank.

St *Physics.* stoke.

st 1. sawtooth. **2.** stere.

St., 1. Saint. **2.** statute; statutes. **3.** Strait. **4.** Street.

st. 1. stanza. **2.** state. **3.** statute; statutes. **4.** *Printing.* let it stand. [from Latin *stet*] **5.** stitch. **6.** *British.* stone (weight). **7.** strait. **8.** street.

s.t. short ton.

Sta. 1. Saint. [from Italian or Spanish *Santa*] **2.** Station.

sta. 1. station. **2.** stationary.

stab. 1. stabilization. **2.** stabilizer. **3.** stable.

stacc. *Music.* with disconnected notes. [from Italian *staccato*]

START (stärt), Strategic Arms Reduction Talks.

stat (stat), *Medicine.* immediately. [from Latin *statim*]

stat. 1. (in prescriptions) immediately. [from Latin *statim*] 2. statuary. 3. statue. 4. status. 5. statute.

S.T.B. 1. Bachelor of Sacred Theology. [from Latin *Sacrae Theologiae Baccalaureus*] 2. Bachelor of Theology. [from Latin *Scientiae Theologicae Baccalaureus*]

stbd. starboard.

stbln stabilization.

stby standby.

STC Society for Technical Communication.

stc sensitivity time control.

stch stitch.

STD sexually transmitted disease.

std. standard. Also, **std**

S.T.D. Doctor of Sacred Theology. [from Latin *Sacrae Theologiae Doctor*]

stdy steady.

stdzn standardization.

Ste. (referring to a woman) Saint. [from French *Sainte*]

sten stencil.

steno. 1. stenographer. 2. stenographic. 3. stenography. Also, **stenog.**

ster. sterling.

stereo. stereotype.

St. Ex. Stock Exchange.

stg. 1. stage. 2. sterling.

stge. storage.

stif stiffener.

stk. stock.

stl 1. steel. 2. studio-transmitter link.

S.T.L. Licentiate in Sacred Theology.

STM scanning tunneling microscope.

stm 1. steam. 2. storm.

S.T.M. Master of Sacred Theology.

stmt statement.

stmy stormy.

stng sustaining.

STOL (es**/**tôl**/**), a convertiplane that can become airborne after a short takeoff run and has forward speeds comparable to those of conventional aircraft. [*s(hort) t(ake)o(ff and) l(anding)*]

stor storage.

STP 1. standard temperature and pressure. 2. *Slang.* a potent long-acting hallucinogen. [def. 2 probably after *STP*, trademark of a motor-oil additive]

stp stamp.

stpd stripped.

stpg stepping.

stpr *Telephones.* stepper.

str 1. straight. 2. strength.

str. 1. steamer. 2. strait. 3. *Music.* string; strings.

strat strategic.

stratig. stratigraphy.

strato stratosphere.

strg 1. steering. 2. strong.

strk stroke.

strl structural.

strln streamline.

strm 1. storeroom. 2. stream.

strn strainer.

sttg starting.

sttr stator.

stud. student.

STV subscription television; pay television.

stv satellite television.

Su. Sunday.

SUB supplemental unemployment benefits.

sub. 1. submissive. 2. subordinated. 3. subscription. 4. substitute. 5. suburb. 6. suburban. 7. subway.

subassy subassembly.

subch. subchapter.

subj. 1. subject. 2. subjective. 3. subjectively. 4. subjunctive.

submin subminiature.

subq subsequent.

subsc subscription.

subst. 1. *Grammar.* substantive. **2.** substantively. **3.** substitute.

substa substation.

subtr subtract.

suc 1. succeeding. **2.** successor.

suct suction.

suf sufficient.

suf. suffix. Also, **suff.**

Suff. 1. Suffolk. **2.** *Ecclesiastical.* suffragan.

suff. 1. sufficient. **2.** suffix.

Suffr. *Ecclesiastical.* suffragan.

SUM surface-to-underwater missile.

Sun. Sunday. Also, **Sund.**

sup. 1. superior. **2.** superlative. **3.** supine. **4.** supplement. **5.** supplementary. **6.** supply. **7.** above. [from Latin *supra*]

super. 1. superintendent. **2.** superior.

superl. superlative.

supp. 1. supplement. **2.** supplementary. Also, **suppl.**

Supp. Rev. Stat. Supplement to the Revised Statutes.

supr. 1. superior. **2.** suppress. **3.** supreme.

supra cit. cited above. [from Latin *supra citato*]

supsd supersede.

Supt. superintendent. Also, **supt.**

supv supervise.

supvr. supervisor.

surf surface.

surg. 1. surgeon. **2.** surgery. **3.** surgical.

surv. 1. survey. **2.** surveying. **3.** surveyor.

survey. surveying.

susp suspend.

Sv *Physics.* sievert; sieverts.

S.V. Holy Virgin. [from Latin *Sāncta Virgō*]

s.v. 1. under the word (or heading). [from Latin *sub verbo*] **2.** under the word. [from Latin *sub voce*]

SV 40 *Microbiology.* simian virus 40. Also, **SV-40, SV40**

svc. service. Also, **svce.**

SVGA *Computers.* super video graphics adapter.

svgs. savings.

SVO language *Linguistics.* a type of language that has basic subject-verb-object word order.

svr (of weather) severe.

S.V.R. (in prescriptions) rectified spirit of wine (alcohol). [from Latin *spiritus vini rēctificātus*]

SVS still-camera video system.

SW 1. shipper's weight. **2.** southwest. **3.** southwestern.

sw 1. short wave. **2.** single weight. **3.** switch.

Sw. 1. Sweden. **2.** Swedish. Also, **Swed**

S/W *Computers.* software.

S.W. 1. South Wales. **2.** southwest. **3.** southwestern.

S.W.A. South West Africa.

Swab. 1. Swabia. **2.** Swabian.

S.W.A.K. sealed with a kiss. Also, **SWAK** (swak).

SWAT (swot), a special section of some law enforcement agencies trained and equipped to deal with especially dangerous or violent situations. Also, **S.W.A.T.** [*S(pecial) W(eapons) a(nd) T(actics)*]

Swazil. Swaziland.

swbd switchboard.

SWbS southwest by south.

SWbW southwest by west.

SWC Southwest Conference.

Swed. 1. Sweden. **2.** Swedish.

SWF single white female.

swg sewage.

S.W.G. standard wire gauge.

swgr switchgear.

Swit. Switzerland.

Switz. Switzerland.

SWM single white male.

SWP Socialist Workers Party.

swp sweep.

swr *Electronics.* standing-wave ratio.

Swtz. Switzerland.

swvl swivel.

sxs *Telephones.* step-by-step: switching system.

syll. 1. syllable. 2. syllabus.

sym. 1. symbol. 2. *Chemistry.* symmetrical. 3. symphony. 4. symptom.

symm symmetrical.

symp symposium.

syn. 1. synonym. 2. synonymous. 3. synonymy. 4. synthetic.

sync 1. synchronize. 2. synchronous.

synd. 1. syndicate. 2. syndicated.

synop. synopsis.

synth synthetic.

synthzr synthesizer.

syr *Pharmacology.* syrup.

Syr. 1. Syria. 2. Syriac. 3. Syrian.

SYSOP (sis′op′), systems operator.

syst. system. Also, **sys**

sz. size.

T

T 1. tablespoon; tablespoonful. **2.** tera-; one trillion of a base unit. **3.** *Electricity.* tesla; teslas. **4.** *Physics.* temperature. **5.** time. **6.** (*sometimes lowercase*) T-shirt.

T *Symbol.* **1.** the 20th in order or in a series, or, when *I* is omitted, the 19th. **2.** (*sometimes lowercase*) the medieval Roman numeral for 160. **3.** surface tension. **4.** *Biochemistry.* **a.** threonine. **b.** thymine. **5.** *Photography.* T number. **6.** *Physics.* **a.** tau lepton. **b.** time reversal. **7.** the launching time of a rocket or missile.

T₁ *Biochemistry.* triiodothyronine.

T₂ *Biochemistry.* thyroxine.

t *Statistics.* **1.** a random variable having Student's t distribution. **2.** the statistic employed in Student's t-test.

T- *U.S. Military.* (in designations of aircraft) trainer: *T-11.*

t- *Chemistry.* tertiary.

T. 1. tablespoon; tablespoonful. **2.** Territory. **3.** Thursday. **4.** Township. **5.** Tuesday.

t. 1. *Football.* tackle. **2.** taken from. **3.** *Commerce.* tare. **4.** teaspoon; teaspoonful. **5.** temperature. **6.** in the time of. [from Latin *tempore*] **7.** *Music.* tenor. **8.** *Grammar.* tense. **9.** territory. **10.** time. **11.** tome. **12.** ton. **13.** town. **14.** township. **15.** transit. **16.** *Grammar.* transitive. **17.** troy.

TA 1. transactional analysis. **2.** transit authority.

Ta *Symbol, Chemistry.* tantalum.

t-a *Immunology.* toxin-antitoxin.

tab 1. tabular. **2.** tabulate.

tab. 1. tables. **2.** (in prescriptions) tablet. [from Latin *tabella*]

tac tactical.

TACAN (tə kan′), tactical air navigation.

tach tachometer.

T/Agt transfer agent. Also, **T. Agt.**

tal. (in prescriptions) such; like this. [from Latin *tālis*]

TAN (tan), tax-anticipation note.

tan *Trigonometry.* tangent.

tan [1] *Trigonometry.* arc tangent.

T&A 1. *Slang.* tits and ass. **2.** tonsillectomy and adenoidectomy. Also, **T and A**

t&a tonsils and adenoids.

T&E travel and entertainment. Also, **T and E**

Tang. Tanganyika.

tanh *Math.* hyperbolic tangent.

TAP Trans-Alaska Pipeline.

TAR (tär), terrain-avoidance radar.

tas true airspeed.

Tasm. Tasmania.

TAT *Psychology.* Thematic Apperception Test.

taut. *Logic.* tautological; tautology.

TB 1. technical bulletin. **2.** *Baseball.* **a.** times at bat. **b.** total bases. **3.** *Boxing.* total bouts. **4.** treasury bill. **5.** tubercle bacillus. **6.** tuberculosis. Also **T.B.**

Tb 1. tubercle bacillus. **2.** tuberculosis.

Tb *Symbol, Chemistry.* terbium.

tb terminal board.

T/B title block.

t.b. 1. tablespoon. **2.** tablespoonful. **3.** *Bookkeeping.* trial balance. **4.** tubercle bacillus. **5.** tuberculosis.

T.B.A. to be announced. Also, **TBA, t.b.a.**

TBD to be determined.

TBI *Automotive.* throttle-body injection.

T-bill (tē′bil′), a U.S. Treasury bill.

tblr tumbler.

tblsht troubleshoot.

T.B.O. *Theater.* total blackout.

T-bond (tē′bond′), a U.S. Treasury bond.

TBS 1. *Nautical.* talk between ships: a radiotelephone for short-range communication between vessels. **2.** Turner Broadcasting System (a cable television channel).

tbs. tablespoon; tablespoonful.

TC 1. Teachers College. **2.** technical circular.

3. Trusteeship Council (of the United Nations).

Tc *Symbol, Chemistry.* technetium.

tc 1. thermocouple. **2.** time constant.

TCA *Chemistry.* trichloroacetic acid.

TCB taking care of business.

TCBM transcontinental ballistic missile.

TCDD *Pharmacology.* dioxin.

TCE *Chemistry.* trichloroethylene.

tchr. teacher.

tci terrain-clearance indicator.

TCL transistor-coupled logic.

TCP/IP *Computers.* Transfer Control Protocol/Internet Protocol.

TCS traffic control station.

TCTO time-compliance technical order.

TD 1. technical directive. **2.** *Football.* touchdown; touchdowns. **3.** trust deed.

td time delay.

T/D *Banking.* time deposit.

T.D. 1. Traffic Director. **2.** Treasury Department.

tdc 1. *Electricity.* time-delay closing (of contacts). **2.** top dead center.

TDD telecommunications device for the deaf.

tdg twist drill gauge.

TDI temporary disability insurance.

TDL tunnel-diode logic.

TDM *Telecommunications.* time-division multiplex. Also, **tdm**

tdm tandem.

TDN totally digestible nutrients. Also, **t.d.n.**

tdo *Electricity.* time-delay opening (of contacts).

TDOS tape disk operating system.

TDRS Tracking and Data Relay Satellite.

t.d.s. (in prescriptions) to be taken three times a day. [from Latin *ter die sumendum*]

TDTL tunnel-diode transistor logic.

TDY temporary duty.

TE *Football.* tight end.

Te *Symbol, Chemistry.* tellurium.

te thermoelectric.

T/E table of equipment.

tech. 1. technic. **2.** technical. **3.** technology.

technol. technology.

tech. sgt. technical sergeant.

TEE Trans-Europe Express. Also, **T-E-E**

TEFL teaching English as a foreign language.

TEL *Chemistry.* tetraethyl lead.

tel. 1. telegram. **2.** telegraph. **3.** telephone.

telecom telecommunications.

teleg. 1. telegram. **2.** telegraph. **3.** telegraphy.

teleph. telephony.

telesat (tel′ə sat′), telecommunications satellite.

temp. 1. temperature. **2.** temporary. **3.** in the time of [from Latin *tempore*].

ten. 1. tenor. **2.** *Music.* tenuto.

Tenn. Tennessee.

TENS (tenz), *Medicine.* a self-operated portable device used to treat chronic pain by sending electrical impulses through electrodes placed over the painful area. [*t(ranscutaneous) e(lectrical) n(erve) s(timulator)*]

TEPP *Chemistry.* tetraethyl pyrophosphate.

ter tertiary.

term. 1. terminal. **2.** termination.

terr. 1. Also, **Ter** terrace. **2.** territorial. **3.** territory.

terz terrazzo.

TESL teaching English as a second language.

TESOL (tē′sôl, tes′əl), **1.** teaching English to speakers of other languages. **2.** Teachers of English to Speakers of Other Languages.

Test. Testament.

test. 1. testator. **2.** testimony.

tetfleyne tetrafluoroethylene.

Teut. 1. Teuton. **2.** Teutonic.

TeV *Physics.* trillion electron-volts. Also, **Tev, tev.**

Tex. 1. Texan. **2.** Texas.

t/f true/false.

TFE *Chemistry.* tetrafluoroethylene; Teflon.

TFN till further notice.

tfr. transfer.

TFT thin-film transistor.

TFX *Military.* (in designations of aircraft) tactical fighter experimental.

TG 1. transformational-generative (grammar). **2.** transformational grammar.

tg *Trigonometry.* tangent.

t.g. *Biology.* type genus.

TGG transformational-generative grammar.

TGIF *Informal.* thank God it's Friday. Also, **T.G.I.F.**

tgl toggle.

tgn *Trigonometry.* tangent.

tgt target.

TGV a high-speed French passenger train. [from French *t(rain à) g(rande) v(itesse)* high-speed train]

Th. Thursday.

T.H. Territory of Hawaii.

Th 227 *Symbol, Chemistry.* radioactinium. Also, **Th-227**

Thai. Thailand.

Th.B. Bachelor of Theology. [from Latin *Theologicae Baccalaureus*]

THC *Pharmacology.* a compound, $C_{21}H_{30}O_2$, the active component in cannabis preparations. [*t(etra)h(ydro)c(annabinol)*]

thd 1. thread. **2.** total harmonic distortion.

Th.D. Doctor of Theology. [from Latin *Theologicae Doctor*]

theat. 1. theater. **2.** theatrical.

theol. 1. theologian. **2.** theological. **3.** theology.

theor. 1. theorem. **2.** theoretical.

theos. 1. theosophical. **2.** theosophy.

therm. thermometer.

thermodynam. thermodynamics.

Thes. *Bible.* Thessalonians. Also, **Thess.**

T.H.I. temperature-humidity index. Also, **thi**

thkf *Electronics.* thick film.

thkns thickness.

thm *Physics.* therm.

Th.M. Master of Theology.

thml thermal.

thmom thermometer.

thms *Electronics.* thermistor.

thnf *Electronics.* thin film.

thnr thinner.

Thr *Biochemistry.* threonine.

thr threshold.

3b *Baseball.* **1.** third base. **2.** triple (3-base hit).

thrmo thermostat.

throt throttle.

thrt throat.

thstm thunderstorm.

Thu. Thursday.

Thurs. Thursday.'

thwr thrower.

thyr *Electronics.* thyristor.

THz terahertz.

Ti *Symbol, Chemistry.* titanium.

TIA *Medicine.* transient ischemic attack.

TIAA Teachers Insurance and Annuity Association of America.

t.i.d. (in prescriptions) three times a day. [from Latin *ter in die*]

tif telephone interference factor.

Tim. *Bible.* Timothy.

TIN (tin), taxpayer identification number.

tinct. *Pharmacology.* tincture.

tip. truly important person.

TIROS (tī/rōs), television and infrared observation satellite.

Tit. *Bible.* Titus.

tit. title.

TKO *Boxing.* technical knockout. Also, **T.K.O.**

tkt. ticket.

TL 1. target language. **2.** trade-last. **3.** truckload.

Tl *Symbol, Chemistry.* thallium.

TL. (in Turkey) lira; liras.

T/L time loan.

T.L. 1. Also, **t.l.** trade-last. **2.** *Publishing.* trade list.

TLC tender loving care. Also, **T.L.C., t.l.c.**

tlg telegraph.

tlld total load.

tlmy telemetry.

t.l.o. *Insurance.* total loss only.

TLR *Photography.* twin-lens reflex camera.

tlscp telescope.

TM 1. technical manual. **2.** trademark. **3.** Transcendental Meditation.

Tm *Symbol, Chemistry.* thulium.

t.m. true mean.

tmbr timber.

TMC The Movie Channel (a cable television channel).

tmd timed.

TMF The Menninger Foundation.

tmfl time of flight.

tmg timing.

TMI Three Mile Island.

TMJ *Anatomy.* temporomandibular joint.

TML 1. *Chemistry.* tetramethyllead. **2.** three-mile limit.

TMO telegraph money order.

tmpl template.

TMV tobacco mosaic virus.

TN 1. technical note. **2.** Tennessee (for use with ZIP code).

Tn *Symbol, Chemistry.* thoron.

tn. 1. ton. **2.** tone. **3.** town. **4.** train.

TNB *Chemistry.* trinitrobenzene, especially the 1,3,5- isomer.

TNF *Biochemistry.* tumor necrosis factor.

tng 1. tongue. **2.** training.

tnk trunk.

tnl tunnel.

TNN The Nashville Network (a cable television channel).

tnpk. turnpike.

tnsl tensile.

tnsn tension.

TNT **1.** *Chemistry.* a crystalline solid, $C_7H_5N_3O_6$, a high explosive. Also, **tnt, T.N.T.** [*t(ri)n(itro)t(oluene)*] **2.** Turner Network Television (a cable television channel).

tntv tentative.

TO technical order.

T/O table of organization.

T.O. telegraph office. Also, **TO**

t.o. **1.** turnover. **2.** turn over.

TOA time of arrival.

Tob. *Bible.* Tobit.

TOEFL (tō'fəl), Test of English as a Foreign Language.

TOFC trailer-on-flatcar.

tol tolerance.

tonn. tonnage.

TOP temporarily out of print.

topog. **1.** topographical. **2.** topography.

torentl torrential.

torndo tornado.

TOS tape operating system.

tot. total.

TOW (tō), a U.S. Army antitank missile, steered to its target by two thin wires connected to a computerized launcher. [*t(ube-launched,) o(ptically-guided,) w(ire-tracked missile)*]

tox. toxicology.

tp. **1.** telephone. **2.** test point. **3.** township. **4.** troop.

t.p. **1.** title page. **2.** *Surveying.* turning point.

TPA *Biochemistry.* tissue plasminogen activator.

TPC The Peace Corps.

tpd **1.** tapped. **2.** tons per day.

tpg tapping.

tph tons per hour.

tpi **1.** teeth per inch. **2.** turns per inch.

tpk. turnpike. Also, **Tpk**

tpl triple.

tpm tons per minute.

TPN *Medicine.* total parenteral nutrition.

TPR *Medicine.* temperature, pulse, respiration.

tpr 1. taper. **2.** teleprinter.

tptg tuned-plate tuned-grid.

t quark *Physics.* top quark.

TR technical report.

tr. 1. *Commerce.* tare. **2.** tincture. **3.** trace. **4.** train. **5.** transaction. **6.** *Grammar.* transitive. **7.** translated. **8.** translation. **9.** translator. **10.** transpose. **11.** transposition. **12.** treasurer. **13.** *Music.* trill. **14.** troop. **15.** trust. **16.** trustee.

T.R. 1. in the time of the king. [from Latin *tempore rēgis*] **2.** Theodore Roosevelt. **3.** tons registered. **4.** trust receipt.

TRA Thoroughbred Racing Association.

TRACON (trā′kon), terminal radar approach control.

trad. tradition; traditional.

traj trajectory.

tranfd. transferred.

trans. 1. transaction; transactions. **2.** transfer. **3.** transferred. **4.** transformer. **5.** transit. **6.** *Grammar.* transitive. **7.** translated. **8.** translation. **9.** translator. **10.** transparent. **11.** transportation. **12.** transpose. **13.** transverse.

transa transaction.

transl. 1. translated. **2.** translation. **3.** translator.

transp transparent.

trav. 1. traveler. **2.** travels.

trb treble.

trd tread.

treas. 1. treasurer. **2.** treasury. Also, **Treas.**

treasr. treasurer.

TRF *Biochemistry.* thyrotropin-releasing factor.

trf 1. transfer. **2.** tuned radio frequency.

trfc traffic.

TRH *Biochemistry.* thyrotropin-releasing hormone.

trh truss head.

trib. tributary.

trid. (in prescriptions) three days. [from Latin *triduum*]

trig. 1. trigger. 2. trigonometric. 3. trigonometrical. 4. trigonometry.

trip. 1. triple. 2. triplicate.

trit. *Pharmacology.* triturate.

trk 1. track. 2. truck.

trkg tracking.

Trl. (used in addresses) trail.

trlg trailing.

trlr trailer.

trly trolley.

TRM trademark.

trm training manual.

trmr trimmer.

trn train.

tRNA *Genetics.* transfer RNA.

trnbkl turnbuckle.

trnd turned.

trngl triangle.

trnr trainer.

trnspn transportation.

trntbl turntable.

TRO *Law.* temporary restraining order.

troch. (in prescriptions) troche; tablet or lozenge.

trop. 1. tropic. 2. tropical.

tropo troposphere.

Trp *Biochemistry.* tryptophan.

trp *Military.* troop.

trq torque.

trsbr transcriber.

trscb transcribe.

trtd treated.

trtmt treatment.

trun trunnion.

trx triplex.

TS 1. tool shed. 2. top secret. 3. Also, **t.s.**

Slang (vulgar). tough shit. **4.** transsexual. Also, **T.S.**

T.Sgt. technical sergeant.

TSH *Biochemistry.* thyroid-stimulating hormone.

tsi tons per square inch.

TSO time-sharing option.

TSP *Chemistry.* sodium phosphate.

tsp. 1. teaspoon. **2.** teaspoonful.

TSR a computer program with any of several ancillary functions, usually held resident in RAM for instant activation while one is using another program. [*t(erminate and) s(tay) r(esident)*]

TSS *Pathology.* toxic shock syndrome.

tsteq test equipment.

tstg testing.

tstr tester.

tstrz transistorize.

TSWG Television and Screen Writers' Guild.

TT Trust Territories.

TTL transistor-transistor logic.

ttl total.

TTL meter *Photography.* through-the-lens meter.

TTS teletypesetter.

TTY teletypewriter.

Tu *Chemistry.* (formerly) thulium.

Tu. Tuesday.

T.U. 1. thermal unit. **2.** toxic unit. **3.** Trade Union. **4.** Training Unit.

t.u. trade union.

Tue. Tuesday.

tun tuning.

Tun. Tunisia.

tung tungsten.

tur turret.

turb turbine.

turbo alt turbine alternator.

turbo gen turbine generator.

Turk. 1. Turkey. **2.** Also, **Turk** Turkish.

TV 1. Also, **tv** television. **2.** transvestite.

TVA 1. tax on value added: a sales tax imposed by member nations of the Common Market on imports from other countries. **2.** Tennessee Valley Authority.

tvi television interference.

tvl travel.

tvlg traveling.

tvlr traveler.

tvm transistor voltmeter.

TVP *Trademark.* a brand of textured soy protein.

tw typewriter.

T.W.I.M.C. to whom it may concern.

2b *Baseball.* **1.** double (2-base hit). **2.** second base.

2WD two-wheel drive.

twp. township. Also, **Twp.**

twr tower.

twt traveling-wave tube.

TWU Transport Workers Union of America.

TWX (*often* twiks), a teletypewriter service operating in the United States and Canada. [*t(eletype)w(riter) (e)x(change service)*]

twy taxiway.

TX Texas (for use with ZIP code).

txtl textile.

Ty. Territory.

typ. 1. typical. **2.** typographer. **3.** typographic; typographical. **4.** typography.

typo. 1. typographer. **2.** typographic; typographical. **3.** typographical error. **4.** typography.

typog. 1. typographer. **2.** typographic; typographical. **3.** typography.

typstg typesetting.

typw. 1. typewriter. **2.** typewritten.

tyvm thank you very much.

U

U *Symbol.* **1.** the 21st in order or in a series, or, when *I* is omitted, the 20th. **2.** *Chemistry.* uranium. **3.** *Biochemistry.* uracil. **4.** *Thermodynamics.* internal energy. **5.** *British.* a designation for motion pictures determined as being acceptable for viewing by all age groups. **6.** kosher certification.

u (unified) atomic mass unit.

U. 1. uncle. **2.** and. [from German *und*] **3.** uniform. **4.** union. **5.** unit. **6.** united. **7.** university. **8.** unsatisfactory. **9.** upper.

u. 1. and. [from German *und*] **2.** uniform. **3.** unit. **4.** unsatisfactory. **5.** upper.

U.A.E. United Arab Emirates. Also, **UAE**

UAM underwater-to-air missile.

u. & l.c. *Printing.* upper and lowercase.

U.A.R. United Arab Republic.

UART (yoo′ärt), *Computers.* universal asynchronous receiver-transmitter.

UAW United Automobile Workers. Also, **U.A.W.**

U.B. United Brethren.

ubl unbleached.

U.C. 1. Upper Canada. **2.** under construction. **3.** undercover.

u.c. 1. *Music.* una corda: with the soft pedal depressed. **2.** *Printing.* upper case.

ucc Universal copyright convention.

UCR Uniform Crime Report.

U.C.V. United Confederate Veterans.

U/D under deed.

u.d. (in prescriptions) as directed. [from Latin *ut dictum*]

UDAG (yoo′dag), a federal program providing funds to local governments or private investors for urban redevelopment projects. [*U(rban) D(evelopment) A(ction) G(rant)*]

UDC Universal Decimal Classification.

U.D.C. United Daughters of the Confederacy.

udtd updated.

U.F.C. United Free Church (of Scotland).

UFD user file directory.

UFO (yōō′ef′ō′ *or, sometimes,* yōō′fō′), unidentified flying object.

UFT United Federation of Teachers. Also, **U.F.T.**

UFW United Farm Workers of America.

ugnd underground.

UHF ultrahigh frequency. Also, **uhf**

UHT ultrahigh temperature.

UI unemployment insurance.

u.i. as below. [from Latin *ut infra*]

UIT unit investment trust.

UJT unijunction transistor.

U.K. United Kingdom.

UL Underwriters' Laboratories (used especially on labels for electrical appliances approved by this safety-testing organization).

ULCC a supertanker with a deadweight capacity of over 250,000 tons. [*u(ltra) l(arge) c(rude) c(arrier)*]

ulf ultralow frequency.

ULMS underwater long-range missile system.

ULSI *Computers.* ultra large-scale integration.

ult. 1. Also, **ult** ultimate. **2.** ultimately. **3.** Also, **ulto.** the last month. [from Latin *ultimo*]

umbc umbilical cord.

Umbr. Umbrian.

UMT universal military training.

umus unbleached muslin.

UMW United Mine Workers.

UN 1. unified. **2.** Also, **U.N.** United Nations.

un union.

unan. unanimous.

unauth unauthorized.

UNC 1. Unified coarse (a thread measure). **2.** Also, **U.N.C.** United Nations Command.

unc. *Numismatics.* uncirculated.

UNCF United Negro College Fund.

UNCIO United Nations Conference on International Organization.

unclas unclassified.

uncond unconditional.

und under.

undc undercurrent.

undef undefined.

undetm undetermined.

undf underfrequency.

undld underload.

undv undervoltage.

UNEF 1. Unified extra-fine (a thread measure). 2. United Nations Emergency Force.

UNESCO (yōō nes′kō), United Nations Educational, Scientific, and Cultural Organization.

UNF Unified fine (a thread measure).

unfin unfinished.

ung. (in prescriptions) ointment. [from Latin *unguentum*]

ungt. (in prescriptions) ointment. [from Latin *unguentum*]

Unh *Symbol, Chemistry, Physics.* unnilhexium.

UNICEF (yōō′nə sef′), United Nations Children's Fund. [*U(nited) N(ations) I(nternational) C(hildren's) E(mergency) F(und)* (an earlier official name)]

unif uniform.

unifet unipolar field-effect transistor.

Unit. Unitarian.

Univ. 1. Universalist. 2. University.

univ. 1. universal. 2. universally. 3. university.

UNIVAC (yōō′ni vak′), Universal Automatic Computer.

unk unknown.

unl unloading.

unlim unlimited.

unlkg unlocking.

unmkd unmarked.

unmtd unmounted.

Unp *Symbol, Chemistry, Physics.* unnilpentium.

Unq *Symbol, Chemistry, Physics.* unnilquadium.

unrgltd unregulated.

UNRRA (un′rə), United Nations Relief and Rehabilitation Administration. Also, **U.N.R.R.A.**

UNRWA United Nations Relief and Works Agency.

uns unserviceable.

UNSC United Nations Security Council.

unstpd. unstamped.

untrtd untreated.

u/o used on.

up. 1. underproof (alcohol). 2. Also, **upr** upper.

U.P. Upper Peninsula (of Michigan).

UPC Universal Product Code.

updt update.

UPI United Press International. Also, **U.P.I.**

uprt upright.

UPS 1. *Computers.* uninterruptible power supply. 2. *Trademark.* United Parcel Service.

UPSW Union of Postal Service Workers.

UPU Universal Postal Union.

U.P.W.A. United Packinghouse Workers of America.

upwd upward.

UR unsatisfactory report.

ur urinal.

Ur. Uruguay.

URE Undergraduate Record Examination.

urol. 1. urological. 2. urologist. 3. urology.

Uru. Uruguay.

US 1. *Psychology.* unconditioned stimulus. 2. *Photography.* Uniform Systems: lens-stop marking. 3. United States. 4. United States highway (used with a number): *US 66.*

U.S. 1. Uncle Sam. 2. United Service. 3. United States.

u.s. 1. where mentioned above. [from Latin *ubi suprā*] 2. as above: a formula in judicial acts, directing that what precedes be reviewed. [from Latin *ut suprā*]

USA 1. United States of America. 2. United States Army. 3. USA Network (a cable television channel). **4.** United Steelworkers of America.

U.S.A. 1. Union of South Africa. **2.** United States of America. **3.** United States Army.

USAEC United States Atomic Energy Commission.

U.S.A.F. United States Air Force. Also, **USAF**

USAFI United States Armed Forces Institute.

U.S.A.F.R. United States Air Force Reserve. Also, **USAFR**

USAID United States Aid for International Development.

USAR United States Army Reserve.

usb upper sideband.

USBC United States Bureau of the Census.

USBLS United States Bureau of Labor Statistics.

USBP United States Border Patrol.

U.S.C. 1. United States Code. **2.** United States of Colombia. Also, **USC**

U.S.C.A. United States Code Annotated. Also, **USCA**

U.S.C.&G.S. United States Coast and Geodetic Survey.

USCC United States Chamber of Commerce.

USCG United States Coast Guard. Also, **U.S.C.G.**

USCRC 1. United States Citizens Radio Council. **2.** United States Civil Rights Commission.

USCS United States Civil Service.

U.S.C. Supp. United States Code Supplement.

USDA United States Department of Agriculture. Also, **U.S.D.A.**

USDE 1. United States Department of Education. **2.** United States Department of Energy.

USDHEW United States Department of Health Education and Welfare.

USDHUD United States Department of Housing and Urban Development.

USDI United States Department of the Interior.

USDJ United States Department of Justice.

USDL United States Department of Labor.

USDT United States Department of Transportation.

USECC United States Employees' Compensation Commission.

USES United States Employment Service. Also, **U.S.E.S.**

USG United States Gauge.

U.S.G.A. United States Golf Association. Also, **USGA**

USGPO United States Government Printing Office.

USGS United States Geological Survey.

USHA United States Housing Authority. Also, **U.S.H.A.**

USIA United States Information Agency. Also, **U.S.I.A.**

USIS United States Information Service. Also, **U.S.I.S.**

USITC United States International Trade Commission.

U.S.L.T.A. United States Lawn Tennis Association. Also, **USLTA**

USM 1. underwater-to-surface missile. 2. United States Mail. 3. United States Marines. 4. United States Mint. Also, **U.S.M.**

U.S.M.A. United States Military Academy. Also, **USMA**

USMC 1. United States Marine Corps. 2. United States Maritime Commission. Also, **U.S.M.C.**

USMS United States Maritime Service.

USN United States Navy. Also, **U.S.N.**

USNA 1. United States National Army. 2. United States Naval Academy. Also, **U.S.N.A.**

USNG United States National Guard. Also, **U.S.N.G.**

USNR United States Naval Reserve. Also, **U.S.N.R.**

USO United Service Organizations. Also, **U.S.O.**

USOC United States Olympic Committee.

U.S.P. United States Pharmacopeia. Also, **U.S. Pharm.**

uspd underspeed.

USPHS United States Public Health Service. Also, **U.S.P.H.S.**

USPO 1. United States Patent Office. **2.** United States Post Office. Also, **U.S.P.O.**

USPS United States Postal Service. Also, **U.S.P.S.**

USR United States Reserves. Also, **U.S.R.**

USRC United States Reserve Corps. Also, **U.S.R.C.**

U.S. RDA *Nutrition.* United States recommended daily allowance.

U.S.S. 1. United States Senate. **2.** United States Service. **3.** United States Ship. **4.** United States Steamer. **5.** United States Steamship. Also, **USS**

U.S.S.B. United States Shipping Board. Also, **USSB**

U.S.S.Ct. United States Supreme Court.

U.S.S.R. Union of Soviet Socialist Republics. Also, **USSR**

U.S.S.S. United States Steamship. Also, **USSS**

USTA United States Trademark Association.

USTC United States Tariff Commission.

USTS United States Travel Service: part of the Department of Commerce.

usu. 1. usual. **2.** usually.

U.S.V. United States Volunteers. Also, **USV**

USW ultrashort wave.

usw and so forth; etc. Also, **u.s.w.** [from German *und so weiter*]

USWAC United States Women's Army Corps.

usz undersize.

UT 1. Also, **u.t.** universal time. **2.** Utah (for use with ZIP code).

Ut. Utah.

U/T under trust.

UTC universal time coordinated.

utend. (in prescriptions) to be used. [from Latin *ūtendum*]

UTI urinary tract infection.

util 1. Also, **util.** utility. **2.** utilization.

utn utensil.

U.T.W.A. United Textile Workers of America. Also, **UTWA**

UUM underwater-to-underwater missile.

UV ultraviolet. Also, **U.V.**

UV filter *Photography.* ultraviolet filter.

UVM universal vendor marking.

U/W under will.

U/w underwriter. Also, **u/w**

u/w used with.

uwtr underwater.

ux. *Chiefly Law.* wife. [from Latin *uxor*]

V

V 1. vagabond. **2.** variable. **3.** *Math.* vector. **4.** velocity. **5.** verb. **6.** victory. **7.** *Electricity.* volt; volts. **8.** volume. **9.** vowel.

V *Symbol.* **1.** the 22nd in order or in a series, or, when *I* is omitted, the 21st. **2.** (*sometimes lowercase*) the Roman numeral for five. **3.** *Chemistry.* vanadium. **4.** *Biochemistry.* valine. **5.** *Physics.* electric potential. **6.** (especially during World War II) the symbol of Allied victory.

v 1. variable. **2.** velocity. **3.** *Crystallography.* vicinal. **4.** victory. **5.** *Electricity.* volt; volts. **6.** voltage.

V. 1. valve. **2.** Venerable. **3.** verb. **4.** verse. **5.** version. **6.** versus. **7.** very. **8.** Vicar. **9.** vice. **10.** see. [from Latin *vidē*] **11.** Village. **12.** violin. **13.** Virgin. **14.** Viscount. **15.** vision. **16.** visual acuity. **17.** *Grammar.* vocative. **18.** voice. **19.** volume.

v. 1. valve. **2.** (in personal names) van. **3.** vector. **4.** vein. **5.** ventral. **6.** verb. **7.** verse. **8.** version. **9.** *Printing.* verso. **10.** versus. **11.** very. **12.** vicar. **13.** vice. **14.** see. [from Latin *vidē*] **15.** village. **16.** violin. **17.** vision. **18.** *Grammar.* vocative. **19.** voice. **20.** volt. **21.** voltage. **22.** volume. **23.** (in personal names) von.

VA 1. Veterans Administration. **2.** Virginia (for use with ZIP code). **3.** Also, **va** *Electricity.* volt-ampere; volt-amperes.

Va. Virginia.

V.A. 1. Veterans Administration. **2.** Vicar Apostolic. **3.** Vice-Admiral. **4.** (Order of) Victoria and Albert. **5.** visual aid.

v.a. 1. verb active. **2.** *Grammar.* verbal adjective.

vac. 1. vacant. **2.** vacation. **3.** vacuum.

vacc. vaccination.

V. Adm. Vice-Admiral.

Val *Biochemistry.* valine.

val. 1. valentine. 2. valley. 3. valuation. 4. value. 5. valued.

valdtn validation.

vam voltammeter.

var. 1. variable. 2. variant. 3. variation. 4. variety. 5. variometer. 6. various.

varhm var-hour meter.

variac (vâr′ē ak′), variable-voltage transformer.

varistor (vâr′ə stər), voltage-variable resistor.

varitran (vâr′ə tran′), variable-voltage transformer.

VAT (vē′ā′tē′, vat), value-added tax.

Vat. Vatican.

v. aux. auxiliary verb.

vb. 1. verb. 2. verbal.

VBE vernacular black English.

vbtm verbatim.

VC 1. venture capital. 2. Vietcong. 3. vital capacity.

V.C. 1. venture capital. 2. Veterinary Corps. 3. Vice-Chairman. 4. Vice-Chancellor. 5. Vice-Consul. 6. Victoria Cross. 7. Vietcong.

vcl vehicle centerline.

vco voltage-controlled oscillator.

VCR videocassette recorder.

vctr vector.

VD venereal disease. Also, **V.D.**

vd void.

v.d. various dates.

V-Day (vē′dā′), a day of final military victory. [V(ictory) Day]

V.D.M. Minister of the Word of God. [from Latin *Verbi Dei Minister*]

vdr voltage-dependent resistor: varistor.

VDT *Computers.* 1. video display terminal. 2. *Chiefly British.* visual display terminal.

VDU *Computers.* visual display unit.

V-E Day (vē′ē′), May 8, 1945, the day of victory in Europe for the Allies. [V(ictory) in E(urope) Day]

veg. vegetable.

veh vehicle.

vel. *Printing.* **1.** vellum. **2.** velocity.

Ven. 1. Venerable. **2.** Venice.

Venez. Venezuela.

vent. 1. ventilate. **2.** ventilation. **3.** ventilator. **4.** venture.

ver. 1. verse; verses. **2.** version.

verif verification.

vers. *Trigonometry.* versed sine.

verst versatile.

vert. 1. vertebra. **2.** vertebrate. **3.** vertical.

vet. 1. veteran. **2.** veterinarian. **3.** veterinary.

vet. med. veterinary medicine.

vet. sci. veterinary science.

VF 1. *Botany.* a designation applied to various plant varieties, indicating resistance to verticillium wilt and fusarium wilt. **2.** *Numismatics.* very fine. **3.** *Television.* video frequency. **4.** visual field. **5.** voice frequency.

vf 1. variable frequency. **2.** voice frequency.

vfc voice-frequency carrier.

VFD volunteer fire department.

vfo variable-frequency oscillator.

VFR visual flight rules.

V.F.W. Veterans of Foreign Wars of the United States. Also, **VFW**

VG very good.

V.G. Vicar-General.

v.g. for example. [from Latin *verbi gratia*]

VGA *Computers.* video graphics adapter.

VHF very high frequency. Also, **vhf, V.H.F.**

VHS *Trademark.* Video Home System: a format for recording and playing VCR tape, incompatible with other formats.

VI Virgin Islands (for use with ZIP code).

Vi *Symbol, Chemistry.* virginium.

vi variable interval.

V.I. 1. Vancouver Island. **2.** Virgin Islands.

v.i. 1. intransitive verb. **2.** see below. [from Latin *vidē infrā*]

Via. viaduct (in addresses).

vib vibration.

Vic. **1.** Vicar. **2.** Vicarage. **3.** Victoria.

vic. vicinity.

vice pres. vice president. Also, **Vice Pres.**

Vict. **1.** Victoria. **2.** Victorian.

vid. **1.** see. [from Latin *vide*] **2.** Also, **vid** video.

vidf video frequency.

vil. village.

v. imp. verb impersonal.

VIN vehicle identification number.

vin. (in prescriptions) wine. [from Latin *vīnum*]

VIP (vē′ī′pē′), *Informal.* very important person. Also, **V.I.P.**

Virg. Virginia.

v. irr. irregular verb.

Vis. **1.** Viscount. **2.** Viscountess. **3.** vista (in addresses).

vis. **1.** visibility. **2.** visual.

visc viscosity

Visc. **1.** Viscount. **2.** Viscountess.

Visct. **1.** Viscount. **2.** Viscountess.

VISTA (vis′tə), a national program in the U.S., sponsored by ACTION, for sending volunteers into poor areas to teach various job skills. [*V(olunteers) i(n) S(ervice) t(o) A(merica)*]

vitr vitreous.

viz. (used to introduce examples, etc.) namely. [from Latin *videlicet*]

VJ (vē′jā′), *Informal.* **1.** Also, **V.J.** video jockey. **2.** a video journalist.

V-J Day (vē′jā′), August 15, 1945, the day Japan accepted the Allied surrender terms. [*V(ictory over) J(apan) Day*]

VL Vulgar Latin.

v.l. variant reading. [from Latin *varia lectio*]

VLA *Astronomy.* Very Large Array.

vla very low altitude.

VLBI *Astronomy.* very long baseline interferometry.

VLCC a supertanker with a deadweight capacity of up to 250,000 tons. [V(ery) L(arge) C(rude) C(arrier)]

VLDL *Biochemistry.* very-low-density lipoprotein.

VLF very low frequency. Also, **vlf**

vlmtrc volumetric.

vlr very long range.

VLSI *Electronics.* very large scale integration: the technology for concentrating many thousands of semiconductor devices on a single integrated circuit.

vm velocity modulation.

V.M.D. Doctor of Veterinary Medicine. [from Latin *Veterinäriae Medicinae Doctor*]

v.n. verb neuter.

vo. *Printing.* verso.

V.O. very old (used especially to indicate the age of whiskey or brandy, usually 6 to 8 years old).

VOA 1. Also, **V.O.A.** Voice of America. **2.** Volunteers of America.

voc. *Grammar.* vocative.

vocab. vocabulary.

voc. ed. vocational education.

vodat (vō′dat), voice-operated device for automatic transmission.

vogad (vō′gad), voice-operated gain-adjusting device.

vol. 1. volcano. **2.** volume. **3.** volunteer.

VO language *Linguistics.* a type of language that has direct objects following the verb. [V(erb)-O(bject)]

vom volt-ohm-milliammeter.

VOR *Navigation.* omnirange. [v(ery) high frequency) o(mni) r(ange)]

vordme vhf omnirange distance-measuring equipment.

vou. voucher.

VOX (voks), a device in certain types of telecommunications equipment, that converts an incoming voice or sound signal into an electrical signal. [acronym from *voice-*

operated keying, altered to conform to Latin *vōx* voice]

vox pop. the voice of the people. [from Latin *vox populi*]

VP 1. verb phrase. **2.** Also, **vp, v-p** vice president.

vp vapor pressure.

V.P. Vice President. Also, **V. Pres.**

v.p. passive verb. [from Latin *verbum passivum*]

vprs voltage-regulated power supply.

vprz vaporize.

VR 1. virtual reality. **2.** voltage regulator.

vr 1. variable response. **2.** voltage regulator.

V.R. Queen Victoria. [from Latin *Victōria Rēgīna*]

v.r. reflexive verb. [from Latin *verbum reflexivum*]

V region *Immunology.* variable region.

V. Rev. Very Reverend.

vrfy verify.

vris *Electricity.* varistor.

VRM variable-rate mortgage.

vs. 1. verse. **2.** versus.

V.S. Veterinary Surgeon.

v.s. see above. [from Latin *vide supra*]

vsb vestigial sideband.

vsbl visible.

vsd variable-speed drive.

vsm vestigial-sideband.

V. S. O. (of brandy) very superior old.

VSO language *Linguistics.* a type of language that has basic verb-subject-object word order.

V.S.O.P. very superior old pale (used especially to indicate a type of aged brandy).

VSR very special reserve (a classification of fortified wines).

vss. versions.

vstbl vestibule.

vstm valve stem.

V/STOL (vē′stôl′), *Aeronautics.* vertical and short takeoff and landing.

VSWR *Electronics.* voltage standing-wave ratio. Also, **vswr**.

VT Vermont (for use with ZIP code).

Vt. Vermont.

v.t. transitive verb. [from Latin *verbum trānsitivum*]

V.T.C. 1. Volunteer Training Corps. **2.** voting trust certificate.

Vte. Vicomte.

Vtesse. Vicomtesse.

VT fuze a variable time fuze.

vtm voltage-tunable magnetron.

VTO *Aeronautics.* vertical takeoff.

VTOL (vē′tôl′), *Aeronautics.* a convertiplane capable of taking off and landing vertically, having forward speeds comparable to those of conventional aircraft. [*v(ertical) t(ake)o(ff and) l(anding)*]

VTR *Television.* videotape recorder.

vtvm vacuum-tube voltmeter.

vu *Audio.* volume unit. Also, **VU**.

Vul. Vulgate (bible).

vulc vulcanize.

Vulg. Vulgate (bible).

vulg. 1. vulgar. **2.** vulgarly.

VU meter a meter used with sound-reproducing or recording equipment that indicates average sound levels.

vv. 1. verses. **2.** violins.

v.v. vice versa.

V. V. O. (of brandy) very, very old.

V. V. S. (of brandy) very very superior.

V.W. Very Worshipful.

W

W **1.** watt; watts. **2.** west. **3.** western. **4.** white. **5.** wide. **6.** widowed. **7.** width. **8.** withdrawn; withdrew. **9.** withheld.

W *Symbol.* **1.** the 23rd in order or in a series, or, when *I* is omitted, the 22nd. **2.** *Chemistry.* tungsten. [from German *Wolfram*] **3.** *Biochemistry.* tryptophan.

w **1.** *Baseball.* walk. **2.** watt; watts. **3.** withdrawn; withdrew. **4.** withheld.

W. **1.** Wales. **2.** warden. **3.** warehouse. **4.** Washington. **5.** watt; watts. **6.** Wednesday. **7.** weight. **8.** Welsh. **9.** west. **10.** western. **11.** width. **12.** *Physics.* work.

w. **1.** warden. **2.** warehouse. **3.** water. **4.** watt; watts. **5.** week; weeks. **6.** weight. **7.** west. **8.** western. **9.** wide. **10.** width. **11.** wife. **12.** with. **13.** won. **14.** *Physics.* work. **15.** wrong.

w/ with.

WA **1.** Washington (for use with ZIP code). **2.** *Banking.* withholding agent.

W.A. **1.** West Africa. **2.** Western Australia. **3.** *Marine Insurance.* with average.

WAAC (wak), **1. a.** Women's Army Auxiliary Corps: founded during World War II. **b.** a member of the Women's Army Auxiliary Corps. **2.** *British.* **a.** Women's Army Auxiliary Corps: founded in 1917. **b.** a member of the Women's Army Auxiliary Corps. Also, **W.A. A.C.**

WAAF Women's Auxiliary Air Force.

waf width across flats.

W. Afr. **1.** West Africa. **2.** West African.

WAFS Women's Auxiliary Ferrying Squadron. Also, **W.A.F.S.**

WAIS (wās for def. 1), **1.** Wechsler Adult Intelligence Scale. **2.** *Computers.* wide-area information server.

WAIS-R (wās′är′), Wechsler Adult Intelligence Scale-Revised.

Wal. **1.** Wallachian. **2.** Walloon.

WAM wraparound mortgage.

WAN (wan), wide-area network.

w. & f. (in shipping) water and feed.

WAP Women Against Pornography.

war. warrant.

warrty. warranty. Also, **warr**

Wash. Washington.

WASP (wosp), **1.** *Sometimes Disparaging and Offensive.* white Anglo-Saxon Protestant. Also, **Wasp 2.** a member of the Women's Air Force Service Pilots (in World War II).

WATS (wots), a bulk-rate long-distance telephone service. [*W(ide) A(rea) T(elecommunications) S(ervice)*]

WAVAW Women Against Violence Against Women.

Wb *Electricity.* weber; webers.

wb 1. wet bulb. **2.** workbench.

W/B waybill. Also, **W.B.**

w.b. 1. warehouse book. **2.** water ballast. **3.** waybill. **4.** westbound.

WBA World Boxing Association.

wba wideband amplifier.

wbfp *Real Estate.* wood-burning fireplace.

wbg webbing.

WbN west by north.

WbS west by south.

WC water closet.

W.C. 1. water closet. **2.** west central.

w.c. 1. water closet. **2.** without charge.

W.C.T.U. Women's Christian Temperance Union.

WD wiring diagram.

wd 1. *Stock Exchange.* when distributed. **2.** width. **3.** wind. **4.** wood. **5.** word.

wd. 1. ward. **2.** word.

W/D *Banking.* withdrawal.

w/d withdrawn.

W.D. War Department.

WDC War Damage Corporation.

wdg winding.

wdo window.

wea weather.

WEAL Women's Equity Action League.

Wed. Wednesday.

West. western. Also, **west.**

Westm. Westminster.

WF 1. wind force. **2.** withdraw failing.

wf *Printing.* wrong font. Also, **w.f.**

wfr wafer.

WFTU World Federation of Trade Unions. Also, **W.F.T.U.**

wg 1. waveguide. **2.** wing.

W.G. 1. water gauge. **2.** *Commerce.* weight guaranteed. **3.** wire gauge. Also, **w.g.**

W. Ger. 1. West Germanic. **2.** West Germany.

WGmc West Germanic. Also, **W. Gmc.**

WH *Banking.* withholding. Also, **w/h**

Wh watt-hour; watt-hours. Also, **wh, whr**

WHA World Hockey Association.

whf. wharf.

whl wheel.

WHO World Health Organization.

whr. watt-hour; watt-hours.

whse. warehouse. Also, **whs.**

whsle. wholesale.

whs. stk. warehouse stock.

wht white.

WI Wisconsin (for use with ZIP code).

wi *Stock Exchange.* when-issued. Also, **w.i.**

W.I. 1. West Indian. **2.** West Indies.

WIA *Military.* wounded in action.

wid. 1. widow. **2.** widower.

WIMP (wimp), *Physics.* any of a group of weakly interacting elementary particles characterized by relatively large masses. [*W(eakly) I(nteracting) M(assive) P(article)*]

WIP 1. work in process. **2.** work in progress. Also, **W.I.P.**

wip work in progress.

Wis. Wisconsin. Also, **Wisc.**

WISC (wisk), Wechsler Intelligence Scale for Children.

WISC-R (wisk′är′), Wechsler Intelligence Scale for Children-Revised.

Wisd. *Bible.* Wisdom of Solomon.

wk. 1. week. **2.** work.

wkg working.

wkly. weekly.

wks workshop.

wl wavelength.

WLB War Labor Board.

wlb wallboard.

wld welded.

WLF Women's Liberation Front.

w. long. west longitude.

Wm. William.

w/m *Commerce.* weight and/or measurement.

WMC War Manpower Commission.

wmgr worm gear.

wmk. watermark.

WMO World Meteorological Organization.

wmwhl wormwheel.

wnd wound.

wndr winder.

WNW west-northwest.

WO 1. wait order. **2.** War Office. **3.** Warrant Officer. Also, **W.O.**

w/o without.

w.o.b. *Commerce.* washed overboard.

w.o.c. without compensation.

WP word processing.

wp waste pipe.

wp. *Baseball.* wild pitch; wild pitches.

W.P. 1. weather permitting. **2.** wire payment. **3.** working pressure. Also, **WP, w.p.**

WPA Work Projects Administration: a former federal agency (1935–43), originally, Works Progress Administration.

WPB War Production Board. Also, **W.P.B.**

WPBL Women's Professional Basketball League.

wpg waterproofing.

WPI wholesale price index.

wpm words per minute.

wpn weapon.

WPPSI (wip′sē), Wechsler Preschool and Primary Scale of Intelligence.

wps words per second.

Wr *Medicine.* Wassermann reaction.

wr 1. washroom. **2.** wrench. **3.** writer.

w.r. 1. warehouse receipt. **2.** *Insurance.* war risk.

WRA War Relocation Authority.

WRAC *British.* Women's Royal Army Corps. Also, **W.R.A.C.**

WRAF (raf), *British.* Women's Royal Air Force. Also, **W.R.A.F.**

wrb wardrobe.

wrk work.

wrkg wrecking.

wrn warning.

wrngr wringer.

W.R.N.S. *British.* Women's Royal Naval Service.

wrnt. warrant.

wrpg warping.

W.R.S.S.R. White Russian Soviet Socialist Republic.

W-R star *Astronomy.* Wolf-Rayet star.

wrtr writer.

WS weapon system.

W.S. West Saxon.

WSA War Shipping Administration.

wshg washing.

wshld windshield.

wshr washer.

WSW west-southwest.

wt. weight.

WTA 1. Women's Tennis Association. **2.** World Tennis Association.

wtd wanted.

wtg 1. waiting. **2.** weighting.

wtr water.

wtrprf waterproof.

wtrtt watertight.

wtrz winterize.

WV West Virginia (for use with ZIP code).

W.Va. West Virginia.

wvfm waveform.

W.V.S. *British.* Women's Voluntary Service.

WW 1. World War. **2.** *Real Estate.* wall-to-wall. Also, **W/W**

ww 1. wirewound. **2.** *Stock Exchange.* with warrants (offered to the buyer of a given stock or bond).

WWI World War I.

WWII World War II.

w/wo with or without.

WWW *Computers.* World Wide Web (part of Internet).

WY Wyoming (for use with ZIP code).

Wy. Wyoming.

Wyo. Wyoming.

WYSIWYG (wiz′ē wig′), *Computers.* of, pertaining to, or noting a screen display that shows text exactly as it will appear in printed output. [*w(hat) y(ou) s(ee) i(s) w(hat) y(ou) g(et)*]

X

X 1. experimental. 2. extra. 3. extraordinary.

X *Symbol.* 1. the 24th in order or in a series, or, when *I* is omitted, the 23rd. 2. (*sometimes lowercase*) the Roman numeral for 10. 3. Christ. 4. Christian. 5. cross. 6. *Electricity.* reactance. 7. *Slang.* a ten-dollar bill. 8. (in the U.S.) a rating of the Motion Picture Association of America for movies with subject matter that is suitable for adults only. 9. (in Great Britain) a designation for a film recommended for adults only. 10. a person, thing, agency, factor, etc., of unknown identity. 11. *Chemistry.* (formerly) xenon.

x 1. *Finance.* without. [from Latin *ex*] 2. excess. 3. *Stock Exchange.* **a.** (of stock trading) ex dividend; without a previously declared dividend. **b.** (of bond trading) ex interest; without accrued interest. 4. experimental. 5. extra.

x *Symbol.* 1. an unknown quantity or a variable. 2. (used at the end of letters, telegrams, etc., to indicate a kiss.) 3. (used to indicate multiplication) times: $8 \times 8 = 64$. 4. (used between figures indicating dimensions) by: $3'' \times 4''$. 5. power of magnification: *a 50x telescope.* 6. (used as a signature by an illiterate person.) 7. cross. 8. crossed with. 9. (used to indicate a particular place or point on a map or diagram.) 10. out of; foaled by: *Flag-a-way x Merrylegs.* 11. (used to indicate choice, as on a ballot, examination, etc.) 12. (used to indicate an error or incorrect answer, as on a test.) 13. *Math.* (in Cartesian coordinates) the x-axis. 14. *Chess.* captures. 15. a person, thing, agency, factor, etc., of unknown identity.

xarm crossarm.

xbar *Telephones.* crossbar.

xbra crossbracing.

xbt *Telecommunications.* crossbar tandem.

xc *Stock Exchange.* without coupon. Also, **xcp**.

X-C cross-country.

xcl *Insurance.* excess current liabilities.

xconn *Telephones.* cross-connection.

xcvr transceiver.

xcy cross-country.

xd *Stock Exchange.* ex dividend. See **x** (def. 3a). Also, **xdiv.**

xdcr transducer.

Xe *Symbol, Chemistry.* xenon.

XF *Numismatics.* extra fine.

xfmr *Electronics.* transformer.

xfr transfer.

xhair crosshair.

xhd crosshead.

xhvy extra heavy.

x in *Stock Exchange.* ex interest. See **x** (def. 3b).

xing crossing.

XL 1. extra large. **2.** extra long.

xmsn transmission.

xmt transmit.

xmtd *Electronics.* transmitted.

xmtg *Electronics.* transmitting.

xmtr *Electronics.* transmitter.

Xn. Christian.

Xnty. Christianity.

xpl explosive.

xpndr transponder.

x pr *Stock Exchange.* without privileges.

xprt transport.

xpt *Electricity.* crosspoint.

xptn transportation.

XQ cross question. Also, **xq**.

xr *Stock Exchange.* ex rights; without rights.

xref cross reference.

XS extra small.

xsect cross section.

xstg extra strong.

xstr transistor.

Xt. Christ.

xtal *Electronics.* crystal.
xtalk *Telephones.* crosstalk.
Xtian. Christian.
xtlo crystal oscillator.
Xty. Christianity.
xvs transverse.
XX powdered sugar.
XXL extra, extra large.
XXXX confectioners' sugar.
xya *Math.* x-y axis.
xyv *Math.* x-y vector.

Y

Y (wī), *Informal.* YMCA, YWCA, YMHA, or YWHA.

Y (in Japan) yen.

Y *Symbol.* **1.** the 25th in order or in a series, or, when *I* is omitted, the 24th. **2.** (*sometimes lowercase*) the medieval Roman numeral for 150. **3.** (*sometimes lowercase*) *Electricity.* admittance. **4.** *Chemistry.* yttrium. **5.** *Biochemistry.* tyrosine.

y *Symbol, Math.* **1.** an unknown quantity. **2.** (in Cartesian coordinates) the y-axis.

y. 1. yard; yards. **2.** year; years.

YA young adult.

YAG (yag), a synthetic yttrium aluminum garnet, used for infrared lasers and as a gemstone. [*y(ttrium) a(luminum) g(arnet)*]

yap young aspiring professional.

Yb *Symbol, Chemistry.* ytterbium.

Y.B. yearbook. Also, **YB**

Y.C.L. Young Communist League.

ycw you can't win.

YD. (in the People's Democratic Republic of Yemen) dinar; dinars.

yd. yard; yards.

yd³ *Symbol.* cubic yard.

yds. yards.

yel yellow.

yeo. yeomanry.

YHA Youth Hostels Association.

YHVH *Judaism.* a transliteration of the Tetragrammaton, the four-letter name of God. Also, **YHWH, JHVH, JHWH** [from Hebrew *yhwh* God]

YIG (yig), a synthetic yttrium iron garnet, used in electronics in filters and amplifiers. [*y(ttrium) i(ron) g(arnet)*]

YMCA Young Men's Christian Association. Also, **Y.M.C.A.**

Y.M.Cath.A. Young Men's Catholic Association.

YMHA Young Men's Hebrew Association. Also, **Y.M.H.A.**

y.o. year old; years old.

y.o.b. year of birth. Also, **YOB**

Y.P.S.C.E. Young People's Society of Christian Endeavor.

yr. 1. year; years. **2.** your.

yrbk. yearbook.

yrs. 1. years. **2.** yours.

YT Yukon Territory, Canada (for use with ZIP code).

Y.T. Yukon Territory.

YTD *Accounting.* year to date.

Yugo. Yugoslavia.

yuppie (yup′ē), (*sometimes capital*) a young, ambitious, educated city dweller who has a professional career and an affluent lifestyle. Also, **yuppy.** [*y(oung) u(rban) p(rofessional) + -ie*]

YWCA Young Women's Christian Association. Also, **Y.W.C.A.**

YWHA Young Women's Hebrew Association. Also, **Y.W.H.A.**

Z

Z 1. *Astronomy.* zenith distance. 2. zone.

Z *Symbol.* 1. the 26th in order or in a series, or, when *I* is omitted, the 25th. 2. (*sometimes lowercase*) the medieval Roman numeral for 2000. 3. *Chemistry, Physics.* atomic number. 4. *Electricity.* impedance.

z zone.

z *Symbol, Math.* 1. an unknown quantity or variable. 2. (in Cartesian coordinates) the *z*-axis.

z. zero.

Z⁰ *Symbol, Physics.* Z-zero particle.

ZBB zero-base budgeting.

Zech. *Bible.* Zechariah.

ZEG zero economic growth.

Zeph. *Bible.* Zephaniah.

ZI *Military.* Zone of the Interior.

ZIF (zif), *Computers.* zero insertion force.

ZIP code (zip), *Trademark.* a system used to facilitate delivery of U.S. mail, consisting of five or nine digits. [*Z(one) I(mprovement) P(lan)*]

ZIP + 4 (zip′ plus′ fôr′, fōr′), a ZIP code of nine digits.

Zn *Symbol, Chemistry.* zinc.

zn zone.

zod. zodiac.

zof zone of fire.

zoochem. zoochemistry.

zool. 1. zoological. 2. zoologist. 3. zoology.

ZPG zero population growth.

Zr *Symbol, Chemistry.* zirconium.

ZZ zigzag approach.

zz zigzag.

Zz. ginger. Also, **zz.** [from Latin *zingiber*]